ALLOW ME TO RETORT

ALLOW ME TO RETORT

A BLACK GUY'S GUIDE TO
THE CONSTITUTION

ELIE MYSTAL

NEW YORK
LONDON

CONTENTS

ALLOW ME TO RETORT

INTRODUCTION

Our Constitution is not good. It is a document designed to create a society of enduring white male dominance, hastily edited in the margins to allow for what basic political rights white men could be convinced to share. The Constitution is an imperfect work that urgently and consistently needs to be modified and reimagined to make good on its unrealized promises of justice and equality for all.

And yet you rarely see liberals make the point that the Constitution is actually trash. Conservatives are out here acting like the Constitution was etched by divine flame upon stone tablets, when in reality it was scrawled out over a sweaty summer by people making deals with actual monsters who were trying to protect their rights to rape the humans they held in bondage.

Why would I give a fuck about the original public meaning of the words written by these men? Conservatives will tell you that the text of laws explicitly passed in response to growing political, social, or economic power of nonwhite minorities should be followed to their highest grammatical accuracy, and I'm supposed to agree the text of this bullshit is the valid starting point of the debate?

Nah. As Rory Breaker says in the movie *Lock, Stock and Two Smoking Barrels*: "If the milk turns out to be sour, I ain't the kind of pussy to drink it." The Constitution was so flawed upon its release in 1787 that it came with immediate updates. The first ten amendments, the "Bill of Rights," were demanded by some to ensure ratification of the rest of the document. All of them were written by James Madison, who didn't think they were actually necessary but did it to placate political interests. Video gamers would call the Bill of Rights a "day one patch," and they're a good indication that the developers didn't have enough time to work out all the kinks. And yet conservatives use these initial updates to justify modern bigotry against all sorts of people.

If the Constitution were really the triumph of reason over darkness, as it is often treated, it probably wouldn't have failed so miserably that a devastating civil war would break out less than one hundred years later. But that happened. And if the fixes applied to the Constitution after that war ended in 1865 were so redemptive, I imagine that my mother—born in 1950 in Mississippi—would have been allowed to go inside her ostensibly "public" library while she was growing up, which of course she was not.

The Constitution is not gospel, it's not magic, and it's not even particularly successful if you count one civil war, one massive minority uprising for justice that kind of worked against tons that have been largely rebuffed, and one failed coup led by the actual president, as "demerits." It was written by a collection of wealthy slavers, wealthy colonizers, and wealthy antislavery white men who were nonetheless willing to compromise and profit together with slavers and colonizers. *At no point* have people of color or women been given a real say in how it was written, interpreted, or amended. Even the amendments that granted equal rights to minorities and women were written by white men. They were ratified by all-white-male state legislatures. Nonwhites have, obviously, never held majority power in this country (yet); women have only held a majority of the seats in one state legislature, Nevada, and that didn't happen until 2018. Minorities or women have never held a majority in either chamber of Congress, or on the Supreme Court, and there has been only one nonwhite president of the United States in American history.

White people got so pissed off at that they replaced Barack Obama with a bigoted con man who questioned whether the Black president was even born in this country, and when their guy lost the next election, his people tried to start a coup.

And yet people still act like the Constitution is our most hallowed ground. I get it from Republicans; white supremacist governments aren't a deal breaker for them. And I'll admit that the Constitution is not without its charms. That stuff about banning cruel and unusual punishment, for instance? Fantastic. Everybody should ban it. I wish I could like that amendment twice.

Too bad we actually don't.

That's the thing about the Constitution: many of the rules, rights, prohibitions, and concepts are actually pretty decent. The problem is they've never been applied to all of the people living here. Not even for a day just to see how it would feel. They've never been anything more than a cruel tease. Most of our written principles serve only as a mocking illustration that the white people running this place know the right thing to do but simply refuse, out of spite, to do it. The Constitution is the impassive villain pouring a bottle of water into the ground in front of you as you're driven mad by thirst.

And so I have written this book. My goal is to expose what the Constitution looks like from the vantage of a person it was designed to ignore. My goal is to illustrate how the interpretation of the Constitution that conservatives want people to accept is little more than an intellectual front for continued white male hegemony. And my goal is to help people understand the key role the courts play in *interpreting* the Constitution and to arm additional people with the knowledge, information, and resolve to fight conservatives for control over the third branch of government in every election, and over every nomination.

Everybody has seen the gleaming, air-brushed face of the Constitution. I'm going to tell you what this motherfucker looks like after it has had its foot on your neck for almost 250 years. The perspective is a little different. I believe more people would try to fix it if more people saw it for what it truly is.

If this is your first time reading me, welcome. My name is Elie, and as I write this I am the justice correspondent for *The Nation* magazine. Prior to that, I was for a very long time a writer and editor at Above the Law, the most-read legal-industry news site in the country. Sometimes I appear on television and radio programs where I talk about the law and scream about Republicans. I was the legal editor of *More Perfect*, an excellent (dare I say) podcast about the Supreme Court that was produced by the same people who make *Radiolab*. I've been covering this space for over ten years now, as a journalist.

I used to be a lawyer, though not technically a "barred attorney-at-law." After I graduated from Harvard Law School in 2003, I worked as an associate attorney at Debevoise & Plimpton, one of the hundred or so most profitable law firms in the country. I passed the bar, but I never completed the rest of my bar application, mainly because I hated my job (no offense to Debevoise, which is a fantastic law firm, if you like being a corporate attorney), hated the practice of law, and wanted to get out almost as soon as I got in.

Being barred wasn't really necessary at a gigantic law firm where I was too junior ever to be the "named" attorney for any client anyway, and I felt like not being able to fall back on a law license would motivate me to get out there and figure out what I really wanted to do. Things have worked out, and I have many nights of hunting mice in my old, crappy apartment to prove that I probably would have given up trying to become a writer had I maintained a reasonable escape route back to corporate law wealth.

But I bring up my background in the law because *hatred* is a pretty big reason I've written this book. Not the healthiest emotion, I know, but for me it's clarifying. What conservatives do and try to do through the Constitution and the law is disgusting. They use the law to humiliate people, to torture people, and to murder people, and tell you they're just "following orders" from the Constitution. They frustrate legislation meant to help people, free people, or cure people, and they tell you it's because of "doctrinal interpretative framework." They use the very same legal arguments that have been used to justify slavery, segregation, and oppression for four hundred years on this continent and tell you it's the only "objective" way of interpreting the law.

Most legal stories and analysis scarcely acknowledge the dystopian, apartheid state that conservatives are trying to recapture through legal maneuvers. Most people take all the blood out of it. Most people assume the law is a function of "both sides, operating in good faith," without wrestling with what the polity would look like if conservatives actually got their way.

Part of that is because lawyers are trained to be "dispassionate" when analyzing the law, almost robotic, as if the best lawyer would present like Data from *Star Trek*, the android programmed to self-improve.

In case you haven't already guessed, I reject that form of legal analysis. A 5–4 ruling on the Supreme Court directly affects the likelihood of me getting shot to death by the police while driving to the store. It directly affects whether my kids can walk to the bus stop unmolested and unafraid of the cops driving by. I refuse to pretend to be intellectually dispassionate about such things. I refuse to act as if second-class status within my own country is one option among many. My "emotion chip" is fully operational.

The other difference one will notice about this book is that I treat the law as an *argument*. People are told that the law is an "objective" thing, almost like it's a form of physics. But it's not: the law is a collection of subjective decisions we—well, white people—have made over the years to protect people and activities they like, and to punish people and activities they don't like. The law can be *applied* objectively, though it isn't most of the time. But the notion that the law is a mathematical equation that can be fed into a supercomputer to produce "justice" is a total fallacy.

The law is not science; it's jazz. It's a series of iterations based off a few consistent beats. I make my argument for why the notes that I like, people and activities I like, should be protected and promoted, and I'm not ashamed of it. I think that if we interpret laws to protect the people and activities I like, and then apply those laws objectively to all people, everybody will come out ahead. Except racists. Who can kiss my ass, as far as I'm concerned. When I'm wrong, it's usually because I haven't fully thought through how insidious and creative racists can be.

What follows is my argument for what the Constitution is, versus what it should be and must be for us to live in a just society. I've focused almost exclusively on the Constitutional amendments. Most of the original Constitution focuses on the powers and structures of the government: there's a Congress, there's a president, it works like this, it can or cannot do that. Most of the amendments, by contrast, focus on citizens: you are a person, the government can't make you do this, it must allow you to do that.

Remember that the founders didn't even think amendments were necessary, because they thought they had so limited the federal government that it *couldn't* do most of the things people were worried about. But we now know that the government can do almost anything, and the amendments have become the place where we first look to make it stop.

Please feel free to use any of my arguments against any conservatives in your life. Free of charge (well, free of *additional* charge). Indeed, I've tried to use as little legal jargon as possible to explain why conservatives are almost always entirely full of shit (*full of shit* being a term of art derived from the Latin: *Borkium shittialis*).

Everybody knows how to fight conservative political candidates. There is a well-developed language around explaining why "tax cuts for the rich" is bad policy or how a two-thousand-mile wall is racist and stupid. But it's harder to spot the bad conservative *legal* arguments, because they're so often covered in jargon and discussed as if only an expensively educated lawyer could truly understand the nuance.

It's not true. This stuff can be complicated, but it's not *beyond the reach* of most people. It's like building a bike. A box of tires and pipes and chains and screws is intimidating, unless it comes with an instruction manual. I'm going to show how conservatives are building their white supremacist ride, and how liberals can throw a spanner in the works.

1

CANCELING TRASH PEOPLE IS NOT A CONSTITUTIONAL CRISIS

In 399 BCE, the Athenian philosopher Socrates was tried and convicted of impiety toward the Gods of Athens, and corruption of Athenian youth. Despite the fact that Socrates was already seventy years old at the time of his conviction—which is pretty old for a person living in a pre-Robitussin society—the philosopher was sentenced to death.

Socrates was known as a sophist, though he denied being one. *Sophist* was a derogatory term for a person, usually a professional philosopher, who used clever but fallacious arguments to make contrarian points. Socrates left no written works behind, but based on what we know of him from his former students (like Plato) or classical plays, I imagine Socrates to be the greatest internet troll of all time. In a society that seamlessly merged secular governing principles with unexamined religious beliefs, Socrates easily toyed with precepts the ancient Athenians believed were literally handed down by Gods who lived on a mountain. Socrates was the original "devil's advocate." He challenged people to provide logical reasoning for their deeply held beliefs, and would justify outrageous behavior (for his time) with appeals to reason while rejecting the widely shared morality of his day.

I imagine he'd have been an annoying little shit to argue with. He was a walking "whataboutism" walrus meme in a toga, exasperating people who were just trying to run a practical society without catching a lightning bolt from a fickle and horny Zeus.

Trolling the Athenian Illuminati is not what got Socrates a death sentence, however. Socrates's sophistry was mainly a front for antidemocratic, authoritarian views. He believed that only reasonable, logical, and competent people should be in charge. He believed that men of merit should be elevated into positions of power.

The problem, which is more obvious to our modern eyes than it has been in decades, is that the idea of a meritocracy is almost in direct conflict with the idea of a democracy. Democracies tend to elevate any person with enough wealth and charisma to stand out in a crowd. Democracies neither necessarily nor naturally reward merit. Nor do they punish incompetence. Democracies tend to go along with the popular will, and Socrates knew that the popular will could be easily manipulated into believing any odd thing.

Most likely, it was Socrates's message, not his methods, that got him in trouble. Socrates wasn't killed in some back alley by a rogue vigilante or religious fanatic. He was put on trial by the Athenian state, and convicted and sentenced to death by the appropriate Athenian legal courts. We don't know for sure how many people participated in Socrates's trial, but Athenian juries traditionally were comprised of 500 or more men over the age of thirty, chosen by random lots. At least 251 Athenian men sat around, thought about it, and concluded their society would be better off if a seventy-year-old social gadfly who held no political or military power was poisoned to death for transmitting ideas he didn't even bother to write down.

Socrates was canceled.

In contrast, Donald Trump was banned from Twitter. Roseanne Barr lost a television show. Andrew Sullivan gave up a column in a magazine. J.K. Rowling, I mean, she hasn't even lost anything, she's just mad that decent people don't want to buy books (books off which she's already made millions) written by an out transphobe. White people with contrarian views who find themselves on the wrong end of a Twitter ratio spend a lot of time complaining about "cancel culture." They spend a lot of time talking about their "free speech" rights. But these people have no claim to constitutional protection, because our laws and the laws of most modern societies are written to avoid tragedies like the trial of Socrates, not to protect trash people from losing endorsement contracts.

Cancel culture, as defined by conservative thinkers and hot take aficionados, involves a person (usually a famous media person or college professor) losing a job, an endorsement, or some opportunity because of something they've said. Complaints about cancel culture are inextricably tied to complaints about "political correctness." The people who think you should be able to spew racist, sexist, or homophobic slurs against others are the very same people who think that losing acting gigs or magazine columns because of their knuckle-dragging views is the greatest First Amendment issue of our time.

The thing is, a publisher firing a media person for something they say involves no First Amendment issue at all. There's no constitutional right to, say, continued employment after supporting a failed insurrection. Free speech does not protect a Fox News employee's right to a *job* any more than it protects a 7-Eleven employee who desperately needs to wear a racist hat while serving Slurpees. Free speech also does not confer a constitutional right to tenure upon professors who feel the need to say the n-word in class. These people can say whatever they want, but the Constitution does not protect their right to employment.

Constitutional protections of speech are mainly concerned with the government's attempts to silence or punish views the ruling party doesn't like. The Constitution cares about people limiting the inquiry of a free press through lawsuits or the threat of lawsuits. It cares about armed agents of the state threatening or jailing citizens who dare to protest the actions of that state.

In short, the First Amendment cares about the things Republicans do when they control the government.

Protest against the government is at the heart of why the First Amendment exists in the first place. Political speech against the government, speaking truth to power, is the speech that is given the most robust legal protection. But the people who make a living decrying cancel culture rarely lift a pen or hashtag when Republicans use the powers of the state to chill political protests. In fact, they do the opposite: those who claim to care about cancel culture treat political protest as the thing that threatens freedom of speech. They claim their freedoms are being threatened by the very thing the First Amendment is designed to protect.

They call it the "heckler's veto." Snowflake Republicans have spent much of the last decade trying to prevent people from protesting their speeches. Remember Desiree Fairooz? She was the lady who was arrested and charged for laughing during Jeff Sessions's confirmation hearing for attorney general back in 2017. She was charged with disrupting Congress and illegally protesting on Capitol Grounds. Again, this was for laughing at a ridiculous statement made by Alabama Republican senator Richard Shelby during the hearing. (Shelby said that Jeff Sessions's "extensive record of treating all Americans equally under the law is clear and well-documented." Sessions was one of the most well-documented racists available at the start of the Trump administration: he was literally on record as a Klan sympathizer and was deemed too racist to get a federal judgeship before the people of Alabama elected him senator. Fairooz's laugh was a kind response, relatively speaking, to Shelby's falsehood.)

Once confirmed, Sessions's Department of Justice hounded Fairooz for a couple of months, trying to force her into a plea where she admitted guilt, before eventually dropping the charges.

Did the cancel culture–concern club raise a ruckus over the Fairooz prosecution? No. Andrew Sullivan wrote no screeds about the dangerous precedent of the Justice Department prosecuting somebody for laughing at Congress. Did these people write about Juli Briskman, a woman who was fired after she was caught flipping off the Donald Trump motorcade while she was out for a bike ride? No. David Brooks found no spare words to defend the right of American citizens to flip the president the bird. Name me your favorite cancel culture writer or thinker, and I will show you a person who remained mute in 2020 when Attorney General William Barr ordered the gassing of peaceful protesters outside the White House so President Trump could take a photo-op with a Bible.

Not one of these people who care so much when an editor gets pushed out of the *New York Times* for soliciting fascist columns was there when Peter Thiel came for Gawker.

Gawker was an independent news website. It was a blog, back when blogging was cool. Gawker reported the news with a heavy side helping of snark, back when that was still new and interesting. It was irreverent, it was exciting, it was occasionally wrong, and often trashy.

And it was murdered by a wealthy white man.

Thiel is a billionaire venture capitalist who co-founded PayPal and founded a hedge fund and did, I don't know, whatever it is one does to make a billion dollars in a country that can't be bothered to address poverty and food insecurity.

Thiel happens to be gay. I know that because Gawker published a story "outing" him in 2007. You won't get any debate from me if you want to argue that outing people is not the best use of the freedom of the press that human civilizations took around four thousand years to codify and protect. But you also won't get any serious debate from anybody who has spent more than five minutes in a constitutional law class on whether reporting on the private sex lives of billionaires and public figures is squarely within the protection of the First Amendment.

The Gawker story angered Thiel. In response, Thiel determined to destroy Gawker. Not the reporter who outed him or the man who owned the publication, like a normal megalomaniacal billionaire. No, Thiel's thirst for vengeance would only be satisfied by destroying the entire media conglomerate itself. Gawker owned a bunch of spinoff blogs, vertices that reported on industries as varied as video games and sports. All had to suffer because the main Gawker website offended Thiel.

Thiel's plan, which I imagine he hatched in a lair carved into a volcano, was to attack Gawker through a series of retaliatory lawsuits. As I said, Thiel himself had no legitimate legal case against Gawker for the article that deeply angered him. But he figured other people might. With virtually unlimited funds, Thiel decided to fund lawsuit after lawsuit against the publication. He told the *New York Times* that he spent nearly $10 million in supporting lawsuits against Gawker, chump change when you are as wealthy as Peter Thiel.

It's important to understand that Thiel didn't think any particular lawsuit would succeed in bringing down the site. Winning the lawsuits wasn't actually the goal. The goal was to drain Gawker of funds by having to fight these lawsuits. Most media companies have insurance policies they take out to cover the expenses of fighting off the occasional defamation lawsuit. We live in a litigious society, and getting sued from time to time is just part of the cost of being in the media business in late-republic America. But these policies are expensive; they typically have significant deductibles, and the premiums go up the more times your company is sued. Even if a company is undefeated in court, it has to spend a lot of resources fighting off lawsuits.

Thiel's strategy might well have worked. It's expensive for media companies to fight lawsuits, even when their adversary is an unhinged person who accuses the company of planting subliminal messages in auto-play ads to trick readers into eating their dogs. Gawker's adversary was a billionaire with nothing but time and money on his side.

But we'll never know how much time and money Thiel was truly willing to put into legally harassing Gawker, because Thiel actually won one of the lawsuits he funded.

Thiel funded a lawsuit brought by Terry Bollea, who is much better known as Hulk Hogan. Gawker had published a sex tape of Bollea and the wife of Bollea's friend. Bollea didn't sue for defamation—again, reporting on the sex lives of public people is squarely within First Amendment protections. Instead, Bollea sued for invasion of privacy. Invasion of privacy is a simple tort, and a tort is just a claim that some action caused harm, and the victim should be paid for their trouble. Even though Gawker didn't actually make or solicit the making of the sex tape, Bollea sued Gawker for illegally capturing a private moment without Bollea's consent to be recorded.

Bollea shouldn't have won. It was Bollea's cuckolded friend who invaded Bollea's privacy and recorded the sex tape. Gawker just reported on it. But, the case got in front of a jury in the state of Florida, and, well, let's just say that if you ever find yourself trying to explain how laws work to a jury comprised of "Florida Man," you've probably already lost.

The jury found Gawker liable and awarded Bollea $140 million.

Gawker did not have that kind of bank, and the site was permanently shuttered in 2016. I imagine Gawker's servers now hang on Peter Thiel's wall, frozen in carbonite.

Gawker was canceled. Even though the death certificate reads that it was pinned by Hulk Hogan in 2016, Gawker was killed because it wrote a story a conservative man didn't like in 2007.

But there is no Bret Stephens column lashing out at this unabashed attack on the First Amendment and the freedom of an independent publication to report the news it deems relevant to its readers. There is no Bari Weiss book about the dangers of billionaires who demand a safe space in American media. There is only deafening silence from the people who squeal the loudest every time Nike pulls a shoe contract from an athlete who gets caught on a hot mic using a homophobic slur.

Understand, Peter Thiel could have spent a billion dollars constructing a space laser and melted Gawker's servers and five surrounding city blocks from orbit, and done *less* damage to free speech in America. I used to write for an independent publication, Above the Law (a legal website inspired by the same people who created Gawker). After the Hulk Hogan lawsuit, there wasn't a story I wrote about a wealthy person where I didn't at least consider the possibility that the wealthy person could sue my company into oblivion if they were too angered by my protected speech. I used to tell my boss, "I can't stop people from suing us, I can only stop them from winning." He would fire back, "If they sue us we've lost already."

In my current job, I've all but stopped writing about conservative individuals. I try to stick to conservative institutions and, occasionally, conservative politicians who would look bad and lose votes if they sued me. But even that is dangerous. Congressman Devin Nunes sued a cow on Twitter. I'm not making that up; Congressman Nunes sued parody accounts on Twitter (one labeled "Devin Nunes'

Cow" and another called "Devin Nunes' Mom") for defamation and trying to "intimidate" him and influence the 2018 midterm elections. Nunes is a public person; calling clear parody accounts making fun of him defamatory is utter Devin Nunes' Horseshit. It's funny, but I'm not the one who had to lawyer up to defend myself.

Wealthy white businesspeople suing my employer because I notice their bullcrap is now an ever-present threat to my livelihood.

The real cancel culture is the one practiced by conservatives. They are the ones leading the assault on the First Amendment and freedom of speech. It's rich people and conservative politicians using frivolous lawsuits to chill journalism and clean up their mentions. It's law enforcement using tear gas and rubber bullets to clear the streets of peaceful protesters. It's the police committing police brutality against people protesting police brutality. It's the attorney general trying to prosecute people who laugh at him. These are the First Amendment threats of our time.

I'm not worried about getting ratioed on Twitter or getting fired from my job if I write a bad column. I'm worried about the Department of Justice forcing me to drink a cup of hemlock because I wrote a good one.

2

BIGOTRY IS ILLEGAL EVEN IF YOU'VE BEEN ORDERED TO BY JESUS

The First Amendment has a lot in common with the First Avenger, Captain America. Both are mascots for an American ideal. Both are muscular reflections of how America would like to see itself. Both are shields who are supposed to protect those who cannot on their own stand up to bullies, intimidation, or oppression. If you want to shoot something, you'd better call Iron Man, who is a walking and flying embodiment of the Second Amendment. If you want to smash evil into submission, you'd better call the Incredible Hulk with the Fourteenth Amendment (I could do this all day). But if you just want to live your life with the dignity of your own thoughts and your own beliefs, Captain First Amendment is your hero.

Unfortunately, we live in an instance of the multiverse where Captain America has been captured and manipulated by the neo-Nazi group HYDRA and turned into a weapon against us. We live in a constitutional environment where the First Amendment has been infected by the religious right, who don't use it as a shield to protect their beliefs but instead use it as a sword to enforce dogmas and to humiliate members of the LGBTQ community. The First Amendment is being weaponized. It's being turned into a thing that bullies schoolchildren in homerooms and bathrooms. It's being used to strike at women who want health care, but won't protect condemned men on death row who want a spiritual advisor. It's being corrupted into a constitutional justification for bigotry and injustice.

That corruption didn't start with conservative zealots or Supreme Court justices acting as theocrats in robes. Instead, the roots of this modern First Amendment infection can be traced to "the good guys" (according to me): the Democrats.

In 1993, Democrat and then-representative Charles Schumer introduced the Religious Freedom Restoration Act (RFRA). Support in the House of Representatives was so overwhelming that it passed with a voice vote (which means that enough congresspeople literally shouted "yea" that there was no need to force the House to call each individual to vote, like winning a rap battle). Senator Ted Kennedy introduced the bill in the Senate, where it passed 97–3. President Bill Clinton signed it into law.

The RFRA was passed to reverse a Supreme Court decision. Sometimes people forget that most of the decisions made by the Court are issues of interpretation that can be directly reversed by legislation, if you have the votes. Here, the RFRA addressed a 1990 Supreme Court decision—*Employment Division v. Smith*—where the Court changed the interpretation of the free exercise clause of the First Amendment.

The free exercise clause is one of the ideas that made America unique among eighteenth-century governments. It's not complicated. Here's the text of the First Amendment (don't worry, it's ridiculously short considering its importance):

> Congress shall make no law respecting an establish-
> ment of religion, or prohibiting the free exercise there-
> of; or abridging the freedom of speech, or of the press;
> or the right of the people peaceably to assemble, and to
> petition the Government for a redress of grievances.

The "free exercise thereof" did all of the constitutional work protecting the freedom of religion, at least until the adoption of the
Fourteenth Amendment. I would argue that America has been
pretty lax when it comes to preventing the "establishment" of religion by the government. There are laws and customs throughout
our system that are inextricably tied to Christian theology: in a
fully secular nation the Monday after the Super Bowl would be a
federal holiday, but December 25 would be just "a day."

But we've done a better job of allowing people to practice their
faith—or ignore faith all together—as they see fit. We're not perfect
(don't @ me all at once, Muslim friends), but we're generally good at
allowing people to pray to whomever, however they want.

As long as the "however" doesn't disrupt the normal order of secular law and business. The Supreme Court often hears challenges
under the free exercise clause for those who feel that some generally
applicable, faith-neutral law or regulation impinges on their ability
to practice their religious beliefs. Think about a truancy law that
compels a certain kind of public education, if you are Amish, or a
draft law that compels military service, if you are Quaker.

For a long time, the Supreme Court had a test (called the "Sherbert test," from the 1963 Supreme Court case *Sherbert v. Verner*) for
balancing the interests of the state in passing neutral secular laws,
against the interests of believers who really need a tax shelter or
something. The Sherbert test called for "strict scrutiny" of laws that
impact religious freedom, which is a judge's way of saying that the
state has to have a really, really good reason for doing anything that

impacts a person's faith, and the state has to prove that there's no other way to achieve its really good reason.

But that is the test the Supreme Court overturned in 1990 in *Employment Division v. Smith*. The case involved a couple of Native Americans who were working at a drug rehabilitation clinic in Oregon. They were fired after the clinic learned that the Native Americans used peyote (a hallucinogen) during some religious ceremonies. The men then applied for unemployment benefits, but were denied for "drug use," and that's how the case became a federal issue of constitutional interpretation, instead of two guys getting fired from a private job.

A reasonable person might say: "Wait, you can be denied unemployment benefits because you get high? What kind of uptight Victorian-Jesus bullshit is that?" But, instead of changing the law so that unemployment benefits were easier to get (which I somehow doubt would have been supported by Republicans in Congress screaming "yea"), the Democrats decided to pass the RFRA, which restored the old Supreme Court strict scrutiny test for issues regarding the free exercise clause.

People like Schumer, Kennedy, and Clinton had the best of intentions. But the entire damn country would be better off if they had failed on this one.

The RFRA did a lot more than "restore" a standard of interpretation. That's because a Supreme Court test like Sherbert is something that judges and justices are more than capable of ignoring when they want a case to turn out a certain way. Lawyers call this "distinguishing": if I'm a judge and I don't like the conclusion a test leads me to, I can just create a "distinction" (often without a difference). If your test applies to a burning bush and I don't like it, I can just call the bush a "tree" and be done with you.

But only the most faithless hacks in robes would do that to a law. Most judges aren't like Brett Kavanaugh. If there is a piece of legislation saying that judges have to apply certain tests to their cases, most judges are going to dutifully apply those tests instead of getting cute with semantics.

It's easy to support the RFRA and a robust interpretation of the free exercise clause when you think about it as defending the rights of practitioners of minority religions who have requirements that put them at odds with mainstream Judeo-Christian laws and customs. But when members of the powerful majoritarian religion get ahold of it, something like the RFRA becomes a cudgel they can use to impose religious dogma upon the secular sphere. Again, Captain America is great when he's fighting for "the little guy." But when he's used as a tool of powerful special interests, he's villainous.

The failure of Clinton and '90s-era Democrats to appreciate the double-edged danger of the RFRA is what led to Hobby Lobby. Officially known as *Burwell v. Hobby Lobby Stores*, the 2014 case is the nadir of the RFRA approach to free exercise cases. In it, the owners of Hobby Lobby (I don't know what they sell because I'm never going to set foot in there) argued that providing women's health care, specifically birth control, as part of their employee health plans as mandated by the Affordable Care Act, robbed them of the free exercise of their religious beliefs. Those "beliefs" allegedly included making it difficult for their women employees to access a basic health service, while doing nothing to stop their male employees from getting "a pill" to help them sustain enough of an erection to use their penises as knitting needles (okay, I *do* know what they sell).

The Supreme Court agreed. In a 5–4 ruling written by Justice Samuel Alito, the Court found that the RFRA, initially passed to protect the rights of people being denied government services because of their religious beliefs, actually also applied to corporations eager to deny health services to women. It took only twenty years for the RFRA to go from something that defended people who

used drugs as part of religious ceremonies, to something that pre-
,vents women from accessing drugs for their own health.

Here's one of my little rules for constitutional interpretation: if
Republicans agree with me, I need to think again about how what
I'm saying can be used to hurt women, people of color, or people
who are LGBTQ. If Republicans are for it, chances are there's something about my law that can be weaponized against vulnerable communities, otherwise I wouldn't be getting conservative support.

Hobby Lobby is a giant corporation, but its approach to using
free exercise as a sword against marginalized people has now been
fully adopted by small businesses too. Conservative lawyers have
made a cottage industry out of turning free exercise into an excuse
for unwashed bigotry.

It is this evil and twisted version of the free exercise clause that
Charlie Craig and David Mullins found waiting for them when they
walked into Masterpiece Cakeshop in Lakewood, Colorado. Craig
and Mullins were Colorado residents who were married in Mas-
sachusetts in 2012, because at the time Colorado did not recognize
same-sex marriage rights. Their plan was to celebrate their nup-
tials in Colorado among family and friends. Masterpiece Cakeshop
was a Colorado business owned and operated by Jack Phillips. The
name of Phillips's store was neither ironic nor misleading. This was
not a Dollar Tree that sells no saplings or a Popeyes that sells no
spinach. Masterpiece Cakeshop sold cakes, and Craig and Mullins
visited the store, whose products were well reviewed, in search of a
cake for their celebration.

Phillips refused to make and sell them a cake, citing religious
objections to same-sex marriage. Craig and Mullins left. The next
day, Craig's mother called the store, and Phillips reiterated his religious objections and refused to sell the couple a cake.

Craig's mom always gets overlooked when people tell this story.
It's so easy for right-wingers and even some moderates to say, "Well,

just go to another bakery." It's so easy for people to overlook the humanity of those who suffer from this kind of bigotry. I was bullied a bit in middle school. One of the worst parts was driving home with my parents from some event, and they would ask, "Why didn't you play with [those boys]?" And I'd always try to mislead them by saying, "I just don't like them very much," when the obvious problem was that they didn't like me. I, for whatever reason, never wanted my parents to know that I was unliked, and I lived in near constant terror that if my parents found out the truth about those boys, my parents would call their parents and try to force us into playdates or something, compounding my shame.

It pains me to think of Craig's mom, calling this bigot baker, maybe hoping she could make him understand, hoping she could make him see the decency of her boy. And it enrages me that Phillips had the audacity to tell somebody's mother that God *required him* to deny service to her son. I wouldn't bake a cake for Jack Phillips, even if it was to celebrate his funeral.

Luckily, "Jack Phillips" is not a protected class. Protected class status is a concept that is crucial to our antidiscrimination laws but often overlooked by mainstream media reports. People make choices with how to dole out scarce resources (like college tenure or roles on Netflix specials) all the time. Many of those choices could be called "discriminatory": smart people tend to get tenure, pretty people tend to get television shows. But colleges and producers are not constantly getting slapped with discrimination lawsuits, because being stupid or asymmetrical is not a protected class. Being short or tall is not a protected class. Being an asshole is not a protected class, which is lucky because I discriminate against them all the time.

There are actually very few protected classes. You can discriminate against anybody for anything other than race, color, creed, and *maybe* gender, age, disability, and sexual orientation in certain contexts (later we will get into the weeds on this). That is, pretty much, the entire list. Some states don't even protect that much. It's almost amazing that people so consistently discriminate against those few protected classes when there is such a wealth of human difference that is not protected for us to work with.

Phillips decided to discriminate against Craig and Mullins because they were gay, and that was a point-and-click violation of the Colorado Anti-Discrimination Act (CADA). Craig and Mullins (after securing a different cake) sued Phillips under the CADA and, in a reasonable world, Phillips would have paid a fine and agreed to stop discriminating against people based on their sexual orientation.

But, against this normal operation of a normal antidiscrimination law, Phillips raised an objection under the First Amendment's free exercise clause. The so-called religious objection to same-sex marriage is always taken at face-value, and it shouldn't be. Craig and Mullins were not asking Phillips to get married to a man. They weren't attempting to pay Phillips in sexual favors. They did not want Phillips to put himself inside the cake and jump out and scream "I love gay people" at an opportune moment.

They simply wanted Phillips to accept payment for services he started an entire business to render. Phillips's claim that his religious freedom would be compromised by being forced to engage in his own business is ludicrous on its face. Refusing to do your job because the person paying you to do it has different beliefs than you is not a religious objection, it's plain and simple bigotry.

The Colorado Civil Rights Commission saw through Phillips's bullshit use of free exercise and ordered him to make restitution to Craig and Mullins. But Phillips appealed and eventually the case ended up in front of the Supreme Court.

Waiting for him there was Supreme Court justice Anthony Kennedy, then in his last year on the bench. Kennedy—once people more forgiving than I am forget that he gave up his seat on the Supreme Court so Donald Trump could replace him with his protégé, alleged attempted rapist Brett Kavanaugh*—will be remembered as one of the good guys in the LGBTQ rights movement. Despite being a conservative appointed by President Ronald Reagan, Kennedy was the tie-breaking vote and decision-author on a number of critical gay rights cases. Kennedy wrote the opinion in *Lawrence v. Texas*, which invalidated criminal laws against "sodomy." He was the author of *United States v. Windsor*, which struck down the Defense of Marriage Act (another horrible Bill Clinton triangulation-of-crap law, which progressives had to spend decades fighting). And he was the author of *Obergefell v. Hodges*, which finally recognized the right of same-sex couples to be married.

But Kennedy also wrote *Citizens United*, which essentially wrecked the ability of the government to regulate political campaign contributions from corporations on grounds of free speech. Kennedy is what I'd call a First Amendment extremist: where others see reasonable distinctions between types of speech and the level of protection each should be accorded, Kennedy thinks the Constitution is the First Amendment and a bunch of other suggestions nobody would have the right to complain about without the First Amendment.

Masterpiece Cakeshop therefore pitted two of Kennedy's pet projects against themselves: his defense of LGBTQ rights versus his vision of a First Amendment injected with Captain America's super soldier serum.

The First Amendment was never going to lose this battle on Kennedy's desk. But the way Kennedy decided to make it win solved nothing.

---

*Kavanaugh was a former clerk for Justice Kennedy.

Kennedy refused to decide whether Phillips had a constitutional right to bigotry under the free exercise clause. Instead, he ruled that the Colorado Civil Rights Commission, which punished Phillips under the CADA, was insufficiently respectful of Phillips's religious objections. That's right: Kennedy wouldn't call Phillips illegally bigoted against gay couples; instead he called the Colorado board illegally bigoted against religious people.

It was a punk move, done by a man who was sick of history having its eyes on him. Kennedy peaced out less than two months later and gave Brett Kavanaugh his job. But it was still a victory for the religious right, who get to continue pressing the argument that their exercise of religion should allow them to strike down or ignore antidiscrimination laws.

You can tell the right wingers are in it for the bigotry and not the protection of private freedoms. That's because if they actually wanted to win the argument, they'd be making an entirely different First Amendment argument. If a person like Phillips is allowed to be bigoted toward people who enter his business, it would be under the First Amendment's free speech clause, not free exercise.

As I indicated earlier, nobody is trying to make Phillips jump out of a cake and say "I love gay people." Most people intuitively understand that Phillips cannot be forced to say anything he doesn't want to say. Free speech, not free exercise, is why Phillips cannot be compelled to say something he does not believe.

Extrapolating from there, one can imagine a number of things that are *speech-like* that a person cannot be compelled to do. In a free society, you can't compel a sculptor to make a statue of a political figure they detest. You can no longer compel a painter to draw a portrait of their liege. You can't compel a scientist to make a weapons system for a warlord: and trying to do that will result in that scientist making powered armor to destroy the warlord and, eventually, aliens. Just watch the first Iron Man movie if you don't believe me.

Now, I happen to believe there's a big difference between Jack Phillips and Tony Stark. I don't think baking a cake is a speech act. I find *Cakeshop* to be the legally important word on Phillips's store, not *Masterpiece*. But I can't bake and I'm not a drooling bigot, so maybe I'm not the right guy to ask. A reasonable person can argue that Phillips has free speech protections for his *artistry*.

But the free speech argument doesn't get bigots to where they want to go. Protecting free speech doesn't allow them to fight their culture war against the LGBTQ community and women. Free speech does nothing for Kim Davis, the Kentucky clerk who refused to do her job of issuing marriage licenses because she had "religious" objections to same-sex marriage. Free speech doesn't help the co-op board who refuses to rent to a gay couple, or the employer who refuses to cover birth control as part of their employee health plan. Free speech protects people with theocratic views, but it doesn't give them the right to impose those views on things like the market economy and the health care system.

This is why free speech is relatively useless to theocrats. Conservative lawyers who fight against LGBTQ equality would rather make the wrong legal argument and risk losing than make the correct legal argument and try to win. These people are not trying to claim protection under the law; they're trying to change the laws so that they can discriminate against the LGBTQ community, not just in the wedding cake business but in all businesses across all levels of society.

If you don't believe me, just look at the legal battle Jack Phillips took on next. In 2017, Autumn Scardina went into Masterpiece Cakeshop and requested a cake to celebrate her birthday and gender transition. Phillips refused to make it, citing his "Christian beliefs" that gender is handed down by God.

I promise you that Phillips does not check the virginity of the heterosexual couples he makes cakes for, even though sex before marriage allegedly makes Jesus cry. I can't imagine how many cakes this man has made for unrepentant sinners who nonetheless had the right mix of genitalia to pass the Gospel according to Jack. But whatever. If you still think Phillips is just a man with deep religious convictions, I can't help you.

You can see how free speech is a useless argument, when his objection comes down to "I'll make cakes for girls, but not *that* girl." Scardina sued and, as of this writing, that case is still in litigation.

This is what conservative lawyers do for a living. They go out and find people like Phillips and enlist their private legal concerns for the larger culture war. Phillips is currently being defended by a group called the Alliance Defending Freedom, a nonprofit Christian legal defense group labeled as an "anti-LGBTQ hate group" by the Southern Poverty Law Center. In addition to taking cases, the group runs a nine-week seminar (called the Blackstone Legal Fellowship) where they teach people how to use the law to support evangelical causes. New Supreme Court justice Amy Coney Barrett has been an instructor at one of these seminars, to give you a sense of how integrated these people are into conservative politics and judicial interpretation. Their goal is not to protect clients with deeply held religious beliefs from persecution *by the government*. Instead, they're interested in persecuting people they don't like, while using religion to cloak their daggers.

Conservatives are, however, illustrating a fundamental truth about laws: even "good" laws can be manipulated by bad people to perform evil. The First Amendment is a fantastic idea, but that doesn't make it immune from being twisted and weaponized. We shouldn't give deference to people who simply claim to be following sacred constitutional principles or claim to have devout beliefs. Because sometimes they're lying. Sometimes they're wrong.

Sometimes they're straight-up evildoers wearing an American flag uniform.

We should defend the principles enshrined in our laws, not the random text of the laws themselves. Otherwise, any yahoo in a Captain America costume can hide their authoritarianism under constitutional-sounding platitudes.

3

EVERYTHING YOU KNOW ABOUT THE SECOND AMENDMENT IS WRONG

You cannot have a conversation with a Republican about the virtues of progressive policies in this country without running into that Republican's interpretation of the Second Amendment. The Republican might not be well educated, the Republican might not be functionally literate, but the Republican believes that the Constitution protects the right to bear arms. Our entire, intricate system of representative self-government carefully balanced with countervailing, overlapping spheres of power and protection of interests gets reduced, in the Republican mind, to the ironclad right to shoot something that pisses them off.

I've met people who cannot accurately tell me how a bill becomes a law but can quote the Second Amendment verbatim:

> A well regulated Militia, being necessary to the security of a free State, the right of the people to keep and bear Arms, shall not be infringed.

Maybe they leave out the "well regulated militia" part, depending on how closely they were paying attention to Fox News last night.

Arguing with devout ammosexuals (*ammosexual* is the scientific categorization for a person who fetishizes firearms and can't win at Scrabble) is among the most frustrating experiences available on the internet. It's almost impossible to have a rational discussion with them, because their arguments are not based on reason—they're drenched in fear. The Republican argument for inviolable gun rights always comes back to the core fear of being unarmed or disarmed at the crucial moment when a gun could be used for self-defense, no matter how unlikely it is that such a moment will occur. These people are willing to suffer the ongoing national tragedies of mass shootings, they're willing to ignore the epidemics of suicides and violence against women, they're willing to sacrifice the lives of schoolchildren, all so that they might feel a little less afraid when something goes bump in the night.

We live in the most violent industrialized nation on earth because too many dudes can't admit they still need a night-light.

When you ask these people *why* they think the Constitution protects gun rights, it won't take long for them to make the "self-defense" argument. Oh, they might take a detour through hunting. They might try to convince you that their constitutional right to sit in a tree, covered in deer piss, for five hours until a defenseless animal wanders in range of their military-grade sniper rifle *shall not be infringed*! Or they may make the "violent overthrow of the government" argument. Yeah, there are people who will argue with a straight face that their private arsenal is necessary to protect them from the most formidable military force in the history of the earth. A single Tomahawk missile has an operational range of one thousand five hundred miles and carries a thousand-pound payload of high explosives, but sure, your AR15 will totally protect you from the tyranny of the government. Buy two! The crew of the USS *Ticonderoga* is super concerned now.

In fact, the events of January 6, 2021, showed definitively how useless guns are, even to violent insurrectionists trying to overthrow the government. Some of the people who stormed the Capitol that day were armed, but you'll remember that those people didn't actually use their firearms. If they had, they likely would have been met with a hail of gunfire from Capitol police. (If the mob had been predominately Black, they would have been met with a hail of gunfire from the Capitol police anyway.) Instead of using guns, the violent mob beat cops and killed one of them using blunt objects. It turns out, you don't need guns to overthrow the government: you just need to be white and enjoy the permissiveness of people like Josh Hawley and Ted Cruz, and a little bit of better luck while trying to find the leaders you intend to kidnap or assassinate.

That's why, eventually, the ammosexuals in your life will make the self-defense argument. They'll tell you the Second Amendment is there because everybody should have the right to protect themselves.

What these people don't understand is that the right to gun ownership for self-defense is an entirely *new* constitutional argument, made up whole-cloth by the gun lobby, and only recently given the force of constitutional validity by Republicans on the Supreme Court. Self-defense is a philosophical right, but that right was not grounded in the "original" meaning of the Second Amendment; self-defense is not mentioned once in the text of the Constitution. What Republicans think is their strongest and most ancient defense of gun rights is actually a mere advertising campaign from gun manufacturers.

Our current interpretation of the Second Amendment was invented by the National Rifle Association in the 1970s. You see, in the 1960s, Republicans were all about gun control, because in the 1960s Black people thought that they should start carrying guns. The Black Panthers figured out that white people were much less likely to mess with them if the Panthers were openly carrying loaded weapons around with them. It's not as fun to shout the n-word at a Black guy who happens to be carrying a loaded rifle, I imagine. You could lose an eye trying to do something like that.

Of course, Black people being able and willing to defend themselves from racist Americans was a very serious problem for racist Americans. In a direct response to African Americans patrolling Oakland, California, and "copwatching," Republicans in California passed the Mulford Act, which banned open carry of loaded firearms in California. Who signed that law? Republican patron saint and then governor of California Ronald Reagan. The absolutist interpretation of the Second Amendment is new, but using gun rights or gun control, as necessary, to maintain racial dominance is old.

California's Mulford Act was followed by a national law, the Gun Control Act of 1968, which significantly restricted the sales of firearms across state lines. It's important to understand that neither of these laws triggered any real constitutional consternation. Both fit squarely within the interpretation of the Second Amendment that existed in this country for its first two hundred years. The government's authority to regulate firearms didn't used to be constitutionally controversial: *regulation* is already in the text of the damn Amendment.

The controlling Supreme Court case on gun rights used to be *United States v. Miller*, which was a case about the National Firearms Act of 1934. The NFA of 1934 was basically an "Al Capone Is Kind of an Asshole" law. It mandated the registration and allowed for the taxation of firearms, and attempted to create different classifications of guns in order to make certain kinds harder to get.

(It's worth pointing out here that Prohibition was repealed at the end of 1933. So, for those playing along at home, Franklin Delano Roosevelt's entirely rational response to gang violence was to liberalize drug laws and restrict gun access. And it worked! The inability of modern Republicans to figure out how to stop street violence is truly beyond me.)

The plaintiffs in *United States v. Miller* complained that the Firearms Act treated sawed-off shotguns differently from regular shotguns. The Supreme Court easily dispensed with that argument:

> The Court cannot take judicial notice that a shotgun having a barrel less than 18 inches long has today any reasonable relation to the preservation or efficiency of a well regulated militia, and therefore cannot say that the Second Amendment guarantees to the citizen the right to keep and bear such a weapon.

You see what they did there? They asked if the gun law had any impact at all on the necessity of keeping a well regulated militia. Finding the answer to be no, the Court kindly escorted 1930s-era Duke Nukem out of the courtroom.

This basic, obvious rationale is why the Mulford Act and the Gun Control Act were also constitutional. Preventing the Black Panthers from defending themselves might have been racist, but it didn't really have anything to do with militia readiness, and so it really didn't have anything to do with the Second Amendment.

America might well have kept on its racist but rational track of adjudicating gun rights, but hard-liners at the NRA really didn't like the Gun Control Act of 1968. At an NRA annual meeting in Cincinnati in 1977, Second Amendment "absolutists" took control of the NRA from previous leaders who thought the organization was really there to protect marksmen. Gun nuts call this event the

Revolt at Cincinnati. Our modern epidemic of mass shootings can, more or less, be traced to these yahoos winning control of that organization.

The ammosexuals reformed the NRA from the generally benign conglomeration of Bambi killers to the grotesque weapon of mass destruction we know it to be today. It was this new NRA that invented the radical rationalization of the Second Amendment as a right to armed self-defense. It was this new NRA that gained political supremacy in the Republican party. It was this new NRA that got Ronald Reagan, who once signed one of the most sweeping gun restrictions in the nation, to sign the Firearm Owners Protection Act of 1986, an act that rolled back many of the restrictions from the Gun Control Act.

The NRA's wholesale reimagining of the Second Amendment hasn't just lured Republican politicians, it's become part of the gospel of Republican judges. The Federalist Society and the Heritage Foundation, the two outside interest groups most responsible for telling Republican judges how to rule, have fully adopted an absolutist, blood-soaked interpretation of the Second Amendment. These groups of alleged "textualists" read "well regulated militia" clear out of the text of the Amendment. Instead, they substitute self-defense as the "original purpose" of the language.

There was an original purpose to the Second Amendment, but it wasn't to keep people safe. It was to preserve white supremacy and slavery.

The Second Amendment is in the Constitution because Patrick Henry (Virginia's governor at the time that the Constitution was being debated) and George Mason (the intellectual leader of the movement against the Constitution, the "anti-federalists") won a debate against James Madison (the guy who wrote most of the Constitution and its original ten amendments). Henry and Mason wanted the Second Amendment in there to guard against slave revolts.

Although, overall, white Southerners outnumbered their enslaved populations, that numerical advantage did not hold in every region. In parts of Virginia, for instance, enslaved Black people outnumbered whites. Predictably, whites were worried about slave revolts because, you know, holding people in bondage against their will is not all that easy to do without numerical and military superiority. The principal way of quelling slave revolts was (wait for it): armed militias of white people. Gangs of white people roving around, imposing white supremacy, is nothing new.

But the slavers worried that the new Constitution put the power of raising militias with the federal government and not with the individual states. That would mean that the federal government, dominated by Northerners, could choose to not help the South should their population of oppressed humans demand freedom.

In a May 2018 *New York Times* article, Professor Carl Bogus of Roger Williams University School of Law explained the argument like this:

> During the debate in Richmond, Mason and Henry suggested that the new Constitution gave Congress the power to subvert the slave system by disarming the militias. "Slavery is detested," Henry reminded the audience. "The majority of Congress is to the North, and the slaves are to the South."

Henry and Mason argued that because the Constitution gave the federal government the power to arm the militias, only the federal government could do so: "If they neglect or refuse to discipline or arm our militia, they will be useless: the states can do neither—this power being exclusively given to Congress." Why would the federal government "neglect" a Southern militia? Henry and Mason feared the Northerners who "detested" slavery would refuse to help the South in the event of a slave uprising.

Madison eventually gave in to the forces of slavery and included the Second Amendment, along with his larger Bill of Rights.

In 2008, Antonin Scalia wrote the majority opinion in *District of Columbia v. Heller,* the case where the Supreme Court created an individual right to own a gun for self-defense, for the first time in American history. Pay close attention to how Scalia whitewashes the nature of Henry and Mason's reasons for wanting the Second Amendment to exist in the first place, as part of Scalia's effort to sanitize the Amendment from its slavers' rationale:

> The Antifederalists feared that the Federal Government would disarm the people in order to disable this citizens' militia, enabling a politicized standing army or a select militia to rule. The response was to deny Congress power to abridge the ancient right of individuals to keep and bear arms, so that the ideal of a citizens' militia would be preserved.

The original public purpose for a citizens' militia was not some theoretical worry about standing armies or an idealized right of citizens' militias to resist federal power. Instead the original purpose was a practical concern that the antislavery North would leave the South vulnerable to slave revolts. Scalia omits that rationale. And of course he has to. Because grounding the case for "self-defense" that satisfies the NRA's permissiveness of shooting Black children walking home with Skittles, in an amendment designed to help slavers keep people in bondage, would be a little too on the nose. If Scalia told the truth about the original purpose of the Second

Amendment, people might realize that the Second Amendment is illegitimate, or that looking to the original intentions of the people who wanted it is monstrous, or both.

Now, one can argue that the Second Amendment has *evolved*, past its purely evil original intent, to encompass a right to self-defense. I'd be willing to hear such an argument, because I don't think the Constitution means only what slavers and colonizers wanted it to mean. But conservatives won't make that argument. Here we see another example where making the intellectually stronger argument doesn't take conservatives where they want to go. If they accept that the Second Amendment has evolved to protect a different right than was originally intended, then they'd have to admit that gun restrictions can also evolve to better protect our modern society.

The Founders didn't know that guns would be used in over half of the nation's suicides. We know. The Founders didn't know that guns would be used in over half of domestic partner homicides. We know. If the Second Amendment has evolved to incorporate the right to self-defense, surely it's evolved to allow us to make it harder for people to kill themselves or their spouses.

But conservatives don't want the Second Amendment to evolve, because they don't actually have a problem with the original slavers' purpose of the thing. If you gave these people a truth serum, they'd tell you that the Second Amendment is working "as intended."

Which brings us back to the ammosexual in your life, caterwauling about how they need their gun for "self-defense." Gun rights are not about self-defense. They literally never have been. Gun rights are about menacing, intimidating, and killing racial minorities, if necessary. That's why Reagan and company had no problem restricting gun rights when the Black Panthers started to use them; that's why the NRA never speaks up when a "law-abiding gun owner" who happens to be Black is executed in the streets by a cop. The

Second Amendment could be rewritten to say: "White Supremacy, being necessary to the security of a free state, the right of white people to keep and bear Arms shall not be infringed," without any appreciable difference to the laws and rights of gun ownership as currently experienced.

People think that the continued mass murder of innocent civilians will, one day, shake Republicans loose from the thrall of the NRA. That will not happen. Republicans will not make the killing stop, because they still think that near-unfettered access to guns is the only thing keeping them safe from Black people.

As I said, the entire Republican argument on guns reduces down to the desire to shoot something that pisses them off. Until you can convince Republicans that shooting Black people is not okay, we will get nowhere. That's the argument you have to be willing to have, when conservatives bring up the original purpose of the Second Amendment.

4

STOP FRISKING ME

The first four times I was stopped for driving while Black, I was living in the state of Indiana. The first time, I was legitimately speeding, in an area of town called "Speedway," go figure. The second time, I had four white girls in my car, designated-driving them home: it's the kind of mistake you make once and, if you survive, never, ever again. The fourth time, I had just dropped off my mother, who is a speech pathologist, to do a school visit in Southern Indiana. The officer was super polite when he stopped me and straight up said, "We just don't get a lot of people who look like you around here." I assured him that if he went to the school, he'd find another person who "I'm told I look like" at the school who could "corroborate" my story.

The third time was terrifying. My summer job between high school and college was working for the state Bureau of Motor Vehicles. My position involved doing advance setup for events highlighting the pace car for the Indianapolis 500. After the big race in the spring, the pace car used to spend the summer traveling around the state, parking at diners and whatnot, and people come out to take pictures with it. Indiana is weird. My job was to go to these places the night before, figure out where the car would park, and tell the owner of whatever business it was visiting the rules for engagement. It was pretty cool as far as summer jobs go for eighteen-year-olds: you're out in your car, listening to your music (CDs, back then), staying in motels, feeling adult-like and free.

Of course, I had a white partner. They weren't just going to send an eighteen-year-old Black kid to talk to small business owners in rural Indiana by himself. Come on. But mostly we drove to the locations separately. And so it was that I was alone one night, driving from Fort Wayne to Lafayette, which is about two-and-a-half hours, east to west, across Northern Indiana.

I wasn't speeding. I know I wasn't because the first state trooper started tailing me soon after I pulled out of a gas station with a pack of cigarettes (don't tell my mother) and some Slim Jims. These Indiana highways are long, straight, and empty. When a cop is following you, you know. I slowed down at first, hoping he was trying to pass me. When he reduced his speed to match my own, I knew I was being followed. I tried my best to remember Han Solo's advice and "fly casual."

I don't know how long he followed me, because it felt like *forever*, but eventually, mercifully, he got into the passing lane and drove by me. I don't know if we made eye contact as he passed, but I felt like he slowed down to get a look at me.

I could still see his taillights when the second trooper appeared. This one had his police lights on, no siren, but I knew what he wanted. I pulled over. Again, I wasn't speeding, wasn't turning, and my car was in good order. I figured I was in for some low-grade police harassment. Like I said, this wasn't the first time I'd been stopped by the police.

The trooper came up to my window, which was already rolled

down, and the first thing he says to me is "Smells funny in here." I nod, and say in my most respectful voice: "Would you like me to get my license and registration?" He responded, more aggressively this time: "I said it *smells funny* in here."

I've come to understand that my next line is what got me in trouble. I've come to be embarrassed that, despite all the effort and education poured into me by my parents, and aunts, and uncles, in this critical moment I forgot my training. I forgot "The Rules."

The thing of it is, I don't remember precisely what I said. It was something like "Well I did get it washed the other day . . . maybe you should try it." Or "I just got it washed . . . maybe I need a refund." I don't remember the specific witticism I used, but I remember my tone. It was a Sharon Stone in *Basic Instinct*–level of "What are you gonna do, charge me with smoking?"

The officer must have noticed that I wasn't a white woman. There was something about me that got his panties in a bunch.

Everything happened quickly after I gave the officer lip. He told me to unbuckle my seat belt and exit my vehicle. I did. He told me to walk toward the front of the car. I did, with my hands held high in the air. He told me to turn around. I did. Then, from my upright and stiff position, he slammed my entire head into the hood of my car. "Oh, we're going to see about that smell now, boy."

By this time his partner, who I didn't know existed, was also out of his cruiser and at my car. The initial officer told his buddy to search my car. I expressed that they would not find anything, other than my license and registration, which they had still not requested or looked at.

The trooper put me in some kind of full nelson, a hold from behind where his arms came under my arms with his hands clasped behind my neck. From that position he dragged me to the embankment on the side of the highway, put me flat on the ground, and then put his full weight on my back with his knee.

I can still taste the grass. It's different from how football field grass tastes. It's stale. I could taste that it hadn't been cared for, turns out.

I couldn't see what was going on after that, but at some point he called for backup on his cop walkie-talkie thing. Backup. With his knee in my back and his buddy tossing my car. Another police car appeared almost immediately. I have come to assume that this second car was the one that initially tailed me: he was on the scene so quickly after the bogus call for backup went out, I really think they were acting together.

But I couldn't process all of that at the time. All I knew was that they traded knees. The new cop assumed the position on my back (he was lighter), while the old cop proceeded to taunt me. "We're gonna find it, you know. Your stash. And then you're going to jail." "We'll see if your car wash defense holds up in court . . . I hope you kept a receipt." I wasn't talking anymore. I was just thinking, "I'm going to die in Indiana. I'm going to freaking die in goddamn Indiana, because of my tone of voice. My mom is going to be so disappointed with me."

Eventually, they stopped. The lighter officer got off my back and told me to stand up. By that point, the other three officers, including the one who initiated the stop, had gone back to their cars. The lighter officer led me back to my car, which was ruined. They'd taken out all my seat cushions and pulled up all my floor rugs. My smokes and Slim Jims were gone too.

The light officer let me look at it for a second before handing me back my keys. He didn't hand me a ticket. He said, with a smile, "You drive safe now." I was still trying to put my car back into a drivable state when they drove off. They never did ask for my license and registration. My wallet remained in my back pocket the whole time.

What I experienced was the vehicular version of what the lawyers call a "Terry stop." It's named after a seminal 1968 Supreme

Court case: *Terry v. Ohio.* In an 8–1 ruling, the Court found that the Fourth Amendment's protection against unreasonable searches and seizures still allows police officers to lay hands all over you, if they had reasonable suspicion to stop you in the first place. The Court also ruled that any evidence turned up against the person who is searched in this way can be used against the suspect.*

It's important to distinguish Terry stops from being arrested. You've probably heard of the case that governs your rights if you are arrested: they were explained in the 1966 Supreme Court case *Miranda v. Arizona.*

Miranda rights—the right to remain silent, the right to an attorney, the right to be served Burger King if you are a white boy who just shot up a Black church, but be choked to death if you are a Black man selling loose cigarettes and "resist" your arrest—flow from the Fifth Amendment's protections against self-incrimination and right to due process. *Terry* is the case that governs what Fourth Amendment rights you have against cops who have no cause to arrest you.

Very few Black men will ever be arrested. But almost all of us have a story about a Terry stop that nearly killed us.

The difference between how Terry stops are used today versus the case against John W. Terry is striking. A white beat cop, Martin McFadden, observed Terry, a Black man, walking back and forth in front of a Cleveland store, reportedly a dozen times. After each circuit, Terry would stop and talk with another Black man, and then a third white man, and then walk back past the store.

---

* Technically, the authority to search vehicles without a warrant flows through *Carroll v. United States,* which is a different line of Supreme Court cases that authorize warrantless searches of automobiles that would otherwise be prohibited under the Fourth Amendment. But the rationale for those cases is similar to *Terry,* which applies to warrantless searches of people who are just walking around. I'm focusing on Terry stops here because the case is more interesting and more relevant to our current laws.

Perhaps Terry was having a very deep existential crisis about
making a purchase? Lord knows there are items I've put in and then
taken out of my Amazon cart at least a dozen times. But the cop
intuited that Terry was "casing the joint." He stopped Terry and
both of his accomplices, questioned them, and, unsatisfied with
their answers, searched them. The officer found weapons on their
person, which led to Terry's arrest and eventual conviction on a
concealed weapons charge.

There's a reason why the ruling in *Terry v. Ohio* was 8–1 and the
opinion was written by Earl Warren and joined by Thurgood Marshall. The opinion starts off with a long recitation of fundamental principles of the Fourth Amendment, but then acknowledges
that those principles have to be balanced with practical realities of
"rapidly unfolding" and potentially dangerous situations the police
routinely face.

The court then justifies a stop and frisk as a "minor inconvenience and petty indignity" that can be imposed on citizens by
police officers who have a reasonable suspicion. The frisk is meant
to protect the officers' safety, and there is a strong state interest to
make sure police officers are not harmed.

I should point out that *Terry v. Ohio* was the first Supreme Court
case in history argued by two Black attorneys. Both prosecutor
Reuben Payne and defense attorney Louis Stokes were Black and
were able to argue their positions in front of the first Black Supreme
Court justice in history.

Despite the deep tensions between competing societal goals, tensions that Warren took pains to address, the result in *Terry v. Ohio*
seems obvious and inevitable. The police must have some ability to
question "suspects of crime" in situations where they do not yet have
enough evidence to arrest. And while questioning those suspects, a
search for dangerous weapons that could be used to harm the police
officer seems like a reasonable protection to afford those officers.

The Supreme Court took pains to limit *Terry v. Ohio* to the specific facts of the case before it. The officer had more than a "hunch," having observed Terry over a long period of time. The search was limited to a pat down of Terry's clothing, removing his overcoat to reveal a revolver in his left breast pocket. The weapons found were the very ones Terry seemingly intended to use in the commission of a crime.

I do not think the Supreme Court intended for Terry stops to metastasize into what stop and frisk has turned into. I think that Warren, Marshall, and Payne would be surprised and horrified by what *Terry v. Ohio* has become.

But Louis Stokes knew what would happen. Stokes went on to become Ohio's first Black representative in Congress. And he never gave up arguing that *Terry v. Ohio* was wrongly decided. Stokes saw New York City mayors Rudolph Giuliani and Mike Bloomberg coming a mile away.

New York State's stop and frisk law was passed in 1971. It was a direct attempt to codify legislatively what the Supreme Court ruled as constitutional in *Terry v. Ohio*. It says, in pertinent part:

> a police officer may stop a person in a public place located within the geographical area of such officer's employment when he reasonably suspects that such person is committing, has committed or is about to commit either (a) a felony or (b) a misdemeanor defined in the penal law, and may demand of him his name, address and an explanation of his conduct.

At first, it was more accurate to call the statute New York's "stop and question" law, because section three of the statute was fairly clear that searches of individuals who were questioned should be done only if officers have a reasonable belief they are or could be in physical danger.

But that was before "Giuliani Time."

People now know Rudolph Giuliani as an unhinged crisis performer who goes on television to spout ridiculous theories and threaten Black and brown people. But before his life as a racist spokesperson for Donald Trump, Giuliani was an unhinged crisis performer who used his time as mayor of New York City to spout ridiculous theories and threaten Black and brown people.

Giuliani, and his police commissioner William Bratton, took stop and frisk to unprecedented levels, through the implementation of what they called "broken windows policing." The men argued that aggressively preventing low-level crimes (like the eponymous breaking of a window) somehow prevented the commission of more serious offenses. To advance this policy, police were authorized to stop, question, and frisk people who the cops suspected had committed or *were about to commit* such offenses.

Racial profiling is the inevitable result of the degradation of Fourth Amendment protections. Understand, it is unconstitutional to stop somebody because of their race. (That protection doesn't come from the Fourth Amendment—which was part of the initial Bill of Rights written by the collection of colonizers and slavers who wrote the Constitution—but the Fourteenth Amendment's guarantees of equal protection and substantive due process. We'll fight about that later in this book. Despite what you may have heard on Fox News, being Black is not a constitutionally valid reason to suspect a person of crime.)

Technically, cops are supposed to have a "reasonable suspicion" before stopping a person under *Terry*. That's an easier standard to meet than the "probable cause" standard for an actual arrest, but it's still supposed to be some kind of objective standard. Remember, Terry was observed walking back and forth outside a storefront a dozen times and conversing with potential accomplices.

The problem is that when you set the bar for "crime" as low as

Giuliani and Bratton did, then "reasonable suspicion" becomes a joke. What the hell is a "reasonable" suspicion that you are about to break a window? Unless the police are stopping Mike Trout and frisking him for baseballs and bats, I'm going to question the reasonableness of their actions.

Absent the kind of psychic technology available to Tom Cruise in *Minority Report*, there is rarely an objectively reasonable suspicion that a crime is about to be committed, and that's especially true of low-level crimes for which no planning is required. Cops might think they're a bunch of Sherlock Holmeses, but they're actually some Miss Cleos who turn the occasional lucky guess into a professional grift.

Instead of reasonable suspicion, cops act on their unreasonable implicit (and often explicit) biases. That's why arguably constitutional stop and frisks became nothing more than a Trojan horse for the unconstitutional scheme of racial profiling.

The numbers do not lie about the disparate racial impact of stop and frisk. The program started by Giuliani was continued during the term of his successor, Michael Bloomberg, who defended stop and frisk right up until he briefly, unsuccessfully, and expensively ran for the Democratic presidential nomination in 2020. The racism reached new heights during Bloomberg's regime: in 2011, 685,724 New Yorkers were stopped by police, according to the New York Civil Liberties Union. Not surprisingly, 87 percent of those people were Black or Latino, despite Blacks and Latinos making up only 25 and 29 percent of NYC's population, respectively.

A number of legal actions have been brought to try to put an end to this racist policy. The most important of these was a class action lawsuit against New York City. A federal court in *Floyd v. City of New York* eventually ruled that the city was engaged in unconstitutional racial profiling. Which is nice, I guess. Racial profiling was already unconstitutional, but since so many white people think that racial profiling should be constitutional, it's always nice when a court reminds them that it's not.

It just doesn't do a lot for a Black kid trying to drive across Indiana this evening. The battle against stop and frisk has turned into a battle against racial profiling, which leaves the basic constitutionality of, you know, *stop and frisk* unchallenged. It's a bit like getting angry at your pet tiger that ate the mailman because its dietary choices violated postal guidelines. *Terry v. Ohio* should be overruled because the "minor inconvenience and petty indignity" of stop and frisk will always disproportionately fall on Black and brown citizens. There is no regime of "reasonable suspicion" that can be divorced from the implicit or explicit biases of police officers.

I left out a detail about the *Terry* case. According to Louis Stokes, one of the justices asked Officer McFadden why he approached Terry and the other men. McFadden responded: "In all honesty, I just didn't like them."

5

ATTACK DOGS ARE
NOT REASONABLE

In 2014, Michael Brown was killed by police officer Darren Wilson in Ferguson, Missouri. Wilson shot Brown six times, despite the fact that Brown was unarmed. The slaughter led to weeks of protests, caused a national conversation about police violence, and led to the formation of various social justice movements, including Black Lives Matter.

But it didn't lead to charges. All of the protests and "difficult conversations" in the world couldn't make authorities charge a cop who killed an unarmed man with a crime.

Wilson attempted to stop Brown, and his friend Dorian Johnson, from walking in the middle of the street. Authorities would later say that Brown stole some cigarillos from a local store, but Wilson didn't know that at the time he profiled Brown and decided to stop and question him. After some verbal warnings, Johnson claims that Wilson, while still in his police cruiser, attempted to grab Brown by the throat. An altercation ensued. Wilson claims that Brown attempted to get the officer's gun. Wilson started firing.

He fired twelve shots in total, six of which hit Brown. Brown was left dead in the street like a dog for hours until authorities collected his body.

At a deposition he gave to then St. Louis district attorney Bob McCulloch, Wilson attempted to justify the twelve shots he fired at an unarmed Black teenager. He said: "When I grabbed him the only way I can describe it is I felt like a five-year-old holding on to Hulk Hogan. Hulk Hogan, that's how big he felt and how small I felt just from grasping his arm." (Remember, Johnson says Wilson grabbed the kid's throat, not his arm, but whatever.)

At the time of his murder, Michael Brown was an eighteen-year-old kid who stood six feet, five inches tall and weighed about 290 pounds. Darren Wilson is six feet four, 210 pounds. By way of comparison, the average five-year-old is about three feet five and weighs around 40 pounds. Hulk Hogan is a professional performative strongman who wrestled as a six-foot-eight, 303-pound heavyweight. Wilson did not feel like a five-year-old grasping Hulk Hogan. And lest you think I'm nitpicking about some harmless hyperbole, remember we're talking about Wilson's official, on-the-record justification for shooting a teenager to death.

Wilson's fever dream of a deposition continued. He said that Brown "had the most aggressive face. That's the only way I can describe it, it looks like a demon, that's how angry he looked."

In a civilized country, an officer's inability to tell the difference between an eighteen-year-old Black kid and a demonic giant on steroids would be grounds for immediate dismissal from the force. In a just world, an officer who shot and killed an eighteen-year-old unarmed kid and then admitted in sworn testimony that he briefly thought he was fighting Hellboy would be tried and convicted of manslaughter.

But when it comes to police violence against Black people, justice, civility, and basic common sense are thrown out the window. The police have a license to kill Black people, as long as police argue that they were so afraid they wet themselves. Police are the only people whose own cowardice and hysteria can be used to justify an objective misreading of the facts. When and how much force a police officer is entitled to use is left almost entirely to the discretion of the police officer, which means my constitutional rights and physical safety hinge on whether a guy like Darren Wilson is afraid I'll use my big lips to suck in his soul from ten yards away.

That rule comes directly from the Supreme Court, in a 1989 case called *Graham v. Connor*. There, the Court ruled that a police officer's use of force must be judged from the perspective of an officer at the scene of the crime or altercation. *Graham v. Connor* is why police officers *always* claim they "feared for their life" after they shoot somebody to death. *Graham v. Connor* is why those claims, no matter how ridiculous, make it difficult for good prosecutors to bring indictments against police officers, and easy for corrupt prosecutors to let their law enforcement buddies walk free.

Unlike some Supreme Court cases that had a solid grounding in the law at the time and were warped into causing great harm, *Graham v. Connor* has been a flaming trash decision since the moment it was published. The facts of the case would be horrifying if the modern viewer were able to see it on dashcam footage.

In 1984, a North Carolina diabetic man, Dethorne Graham, went to a convenience store to buy some orange juice to offset his reaction to an insulin dose. He apparently went into the store, took one look at the line, decided the wait was too long, and drove off with his friend.

This behavior raised the suspicion of officer M.S. Connor. Connor happens to be Black, and I point that out only to highlight the fact that Black police officers can be just as racist as white ones. Connor followed Graham and his friend, William Berry, for about a half mile before pulling them over.

Graham, still suffering from an insulin reaction, apparently got out of the car and ran around. Then he passed out on the curb. Connor handcuffed Graham and called for backup. When Graham regained consciousness, he tried to show the officers his diabetic information card, but the officers wouldn't take it, apparently deciding that Graham was drunk. A different friend apparently saw the commotion and, being familiar with Graham's condition, tried to get Graham some orange juice, but the officers wouldn't let him have it. Graham begged the officers for the drink and one of the officers responded, "I'm not giving you shit."

Police eventually slammed Graham's head onto the hood of his car and put him in the back of the police car over Graham's resistance. Graham ended up with a broken foot and several lacerations. Eventually, the officers got around to actually checking with the convenience store, which told them that Graham did nothing unusual. Then the officers let him go.

Graham filed a lawsuit against the police for excessive use of force, under the 1871 Civil Rights Act. That's not a typo. The 1871 Civil Rights Act is, more or less, the statutory provision that makes the Fourteenth Amendment prohibition against racial discrimination a law, in the same way that the Volstead Act is what made the Eighteenth Amendment's prohibition on alcohol a thing.

But instead of applying the *Fourteenth* Amendment to the case, the way Graham asked, then chief justice and hard-core conservative William Rehnquist decided that the *Fourth* Amendment was the proper principle under which to assess police misconduct. The Fourth Amendment prohibits "unreasonable search and seizure," and Rehnquist only asked if Connor's treatment of Graham was "reasonable" under that amendment, as opposed to a violation of Graham's civil rights under the Fourteenth.

By converting Graham's claim into a Fourth Amendment question, Rehnquist nullified the racial discrimination at the heart of his case. Would a white man have been tailed for half a mile for the crime of popping his head into a convenience store? Would cops have refused to listen to a white man's pleas to look at his diabetes information? Would police officers have given a white man a few sips of orange juice before pounding his head into a hood and breaking his foot? Graham was a victim of racial discrimination, and Rehnquist waved it all away by deciding the case on grounds nobody asked him to.

It should go without saying that, having invented an entirely different question, Rehnquist decided to answer it poorly. Rehnquist, citing *Terry v. Ohio*, wrote: "The 'reasonableness' of a particular use of force must be judged from the perspective of a reasonable officer on the scene, rather than with the 20/20 vision of hindsight."

The callback to *Terry* is instructive. In 1968 the Court went out of its way to limit *Terry* to the specific set of facts, where a man was observed casing a storefront and was briefly stopped and frisked to search for weapons that could harm the police officer. But just twenty years later, Rehnquist was out there using *Terry* as justification for cops tailing a Black man from a convenience store and denying him a glass of orange juice while they roughed him up. Once you give cops an inch of daylight under the Fourth Amendment, they will brutalize Black people for miles.

Judging the reasonableness of violence from the perspective of the officer who committed the violence, or the officer who witnessed the violence but did nothing to help, or even the alleged "good" cop who knows damn well that one of his colleagues is a violent hothead but does nothing to stop him, is the entirely wrong way to go. Police officers are agents of the state. They are authorized to have a monopoly of force: they can hit you but you can't hit them back. They can execute on the street—I mean they can literally impose the death penalty upon you without a fair trial or a right to appeal—if they feel you're a danger to others. Holding them to a

standard somewhat beyond what they themselves think is reasonable is not too much to ask.

The Fourth Amendment does not say: "The right of the people
to be secure in their persons, houses, papers, and effects, against
unreasonable searches and seizures, shall not be violated . . . unless
the state employs hysterical racists and cowards who are afraid of
Black people, in which case failure to immediately comply with their
unconstitutional orders is a capital offense." The Fourth Amendment does not say that "only other police officers" can determine
what a reasonable or unreasonable search and seizure really means.
One does not judge what is "food" based on whether or not a dog
will eat it.

Unfortunately, the Court's decision in *Graham v. Connor* has
had the effect of choking off any meaningful solution to police
brutality at the national level. Understand, we do not have one
national police system. The Constitution reserves the police power
to the states, which means that the federal government does not
have broad authority to hold police accountable for acts of violence. But the federalism (which is the term indicating that most
of the legal power in this country rests with states) doesn't end
there. Even within the states, most policing is done at the local
level. We don't have to change one system to address police brutality, or fifty; instead there are over three thousand county sheriffs
and police commissioners in this country, and each one of them
retains a level of autonomy to determine how much the cops are
allowed to beat Black people. Whether you have the right to, say,
know the disciplinary history of the officer who attacked you
depends on which municipality you happened to be in when the
beating started.

Without the Fourteenth Amendment protection that Rehnquist
ripped away, there's no longer a great way for individual victims of
police brutality to bring racial discrimination claims against the

police. Instead, that work now largely falls to the Department of Justice. The DOJ can launch what's called "pattern and practice" investigations to see if a law enforcement entity, like a local police department, is engaged in racially discriminatory behavior—that's what the DOJ did in Ferguson, Missouri, after Michael Brown's murder by Officer Wilson. These investigations often result, as they did in Ferguson, in "consent decrees"—agreements to allow federal monitoring of local police to ensure compliance with the Constitution.

But relying on the DOJ to conduct a pattern and practice investigation every time one murderous cop kills an unarmed Black man is an inefficient process that doesn't always produce results. And it's a process that is wholly dependent on which party controls the Department of Justice. During the Barack Obama administration, Attorneys General Eric Holder and Loretta Lynch both tried to carry out this work. But one of the first things Jeff Sessions did when he was installed by President Donald Trump was to stop pattern and practice investigations, end the use of consent decrees, and make it harder for the ones already in place—including in Ferguson—to be enforced. Trump's next attorney general, William Barr, refused to open pattern and practice investigations in Minneapolis after the murder of George Floyd, or in Louisville after the murder of Breonna Taylor.

Merrick Garland, Joe Biden's attorney general, has brought pattern and practice investigators back. But I promise you the next Republican attorney general will largely stop them again.

While the federal government has limited and relatively weak powers to compel police forces to stop beating and murdering Black people, state and local governments have incredible power. Police—which really only became a standing, uniformed enforcement apparatus in the mid-nineteenth century—are not organized under a constitutional principle or federal statute. They're organized under state and municipal laws. They can be reorganized (or disorganized) by those same authorities.

But state and local governments are just as reluctant to hold police to an objective standard as the Supreme Court is when it comes to use of force. That's because of the incredible power of police unions, especially in municipal politics. Most (white) people have a positive view of the police, and so when one of the union bosses starts screaming about how their officers need to be able to choke the life out of unarmed Black people just to keep white people safe, there are a lot of white people who are inclined to believe them.

A recent battle in California shows how hard it is to get meaningful police reform passed at the state level, even in a "liberal" state. In 2019, the California legislature proposed a new law amending the language about when police could use deadly force. The old standard said police had to "reasonably" believe deadly force was necessary, which is the same standard set by *Graham v. Connor*. The proposed legislation changed that standard to "no reasonable alternatives."

That language would have been an improvement, though it's still not the best. I favor a straight-up objective standard for cops. Their actions should be reasonable with 20/20 hindsight. They should look reasonable on a camera phone. They should appear reasonable to a crowd gathering around asking what the cops are doing. If the cop believes a person has a weapon, that person better damn sure objectively have a weapon. "Oops" is not a good enough answer from agents of the state who shoot Black people armed with cell phones.

And if the cop is objectively wrong or unreasonable, they should be prosecuted. We have a sliding scale of homicides and all other types of crimes, and there's no reason we can't apply such a thing to various levels of police violence. Maybe a cop who shoots "Hulk Hogan" after a fight catches a manslaughter charge, while a cop who shoots an unarmed man seven times in the back, as a Wisconsin police officer did to Jacob Blake, gets charged with attempted murder? Or maybe a cop who uses his gun to kill somebody gets murder, whereas one who merely chokes the life out of an unarmed Black man in broad daylight gets a reckless homicide charge? I can be reasonable about how long these violent police officers need to spend in jail. I am anti-carceral, after all. But the idea that a cop who kills or attacks somebody should walk away without punishment because *other* cops are just as violent and depraved is not a constitutional principle I accept.

My view would be called extreme. But I have two black sons I'd like to survive me, and so I'm a little insistent that the police should not shoot at them. More moderate observers worry that my standard would make police hesitate before gunning down my kids, and for some reason they think police hesitation before opening fire is bad. All I want is for the police to hesitate. I'll live longer.

But, in a world where I have to accept that most white people are going to be more worried about criminals shooting the police than they are about the police shooting my kids, I have to acknowledge the California language as a step in the right direction.

At least, it would have been. But police unions reacted to the "no reasonable alternatives" as if it were a death sentence to their order. They complained that the California standard would be the thing that makes them hesitate and thus somehow get shot by criminals. They complained that the standard would allow courts to come in after the fact and judge them (you think?) for decisions that have to be made in a "split second." Police unions somehow think that having to make decisions quickly is an excuse for shooting the wrong people.

Through their outrage, and help from the Republican party, the unions got California to change the proposed language. The final bill that passed dropped the "no reasonable alternative" standard and changed it to "necessary." Now police can only use deadly force when "necessary."

I cannot think of one person who will be saved in California because police ask "Is it necessary to shoot this Black person?" as opposed to "Is it reasonable to shoot this Black person?" Deep-blue California succeeded only in changing which words the police have to use in their justifications for murder.

The California story goes to show the yawning gap between what is needed to stop police violence against Black people, and what politicians and courts are actually willing to do to stop the murders. Many people understand that the standards for police use of force are a problem, but few seem able to break out of the thrall of letting the police themselves tell them when force was "reasonable" or "necessary."

Bringing the police to heel will require us to stop letting them substitute their judgment for our constitutional protections. It's time to stop asking the foxes for their opinions on the security of the henhouse.

6

WHY YOU CAN'T PUNCH A COP

Why can't I punch a cop? Why can't I punch a cop who is punching me? Why can't I punch a cop who has broken into my home? Why do I, a grown-ass man writing my own damn book, feel compelled to use the word *punch* as a substitute for legitimate self-defense against armed agents of the state, whom this country will not stop from killing me because of the color of my skin? If the law will not protect me from the police, why can't I protect myself?

Students of Western political philosophy will reflexively reach for their copy of *Leviathan* by Thomas Hobbes to answer my questions. In 1651, Hobbes gave one of the best articulations for a government having a "monopoly of violence" over its subjects. If I may reduce one of the greatest works of political thought down to a sentence: If we let people kill each other, literally everybody would do it, so the only way we can have nice things is to let only one man kill people and hope he's not a complete asshole.

Hobbes is not wrong. It's nearly impossible to imagine a functioning society where the state does not have a monopoly over the legitimate use of force. Indeed, our definition of a "failed state" is one where the nominal ruling government no longer has a monopoly on violence. If a local group or gang can maraud across a region, taking what they want and killing who they will, and the state cannot stop them even if it wants to, then that state no longer deserves or is owed any allegiance from its people. The area a government controls through a monopoly of violence is, according to German sociologist Max Weber, the very definition of a state's territory.

And yet even Hobbes called the right to self-defense "inalienable." Even he said that a person had the right to resist agents of the sovereign sent to do them harm. No rational political philosophy can expect a person to comply with their own execution.

The thought that a person should accept their death at the hands of the state is not a concept we get from political philosophy; it's a concept we get from religious philosophy. Jesus went to the cross willingly. Obi-Wan Kenobi let Darth Vader strike him down. These men fell because of their religious beliefs—they thought they would become one with the Trinity or the Force or whatever. Hobbes might have told them to stop acting like punks and start shooting lightning out of their hands. Doing whatever it takes to stay alive is the rational play. Every person has a right to defend themselves against the Emperor, be they in Rome or orbiting the forest moon of Endor.

Of course, the Hobbesian right to self-defense is in conflict with the Hobbesian requirement that the sovereign has a monopoly on violence. Without religion, without shrugging your shoulders and saying, "Be happy when the state murders you because God will give you a mansion in the sky," it's really hard to square state violence, or even incarceration of a state's own subjects with the right of those subjects to resist. When you think about it, "resisting arrest" shouldn't be a crime: it's a goddamn moral imperative to rage, rage against the dying of the light.

Everybody understands the right to self-defense against non-police officers. The right comes from English common law, which is a fancy way of saying the right predates the Constitution and the founding of America, and is incorporated into the American legal system. People have the right to defend themselves (see the discussion of the Second Amendment above for the gun lobby's perversion of this right into a gun, however), and people have a right to defend themselves from deadly force with deadly force.

Self-defense is what lawyers call an "affirmative defense" to a homicide charge. Most people are familiar with the concept of "innocent until proven guilty." But in a self-defense case, the accused is clearly guilty of a homicide: I mean, for God's sake, they killed someone. The burden of proof therefore shifts to the clearly guilty person to "justify" that homicide. The law will allow people to argue a number of justifications, but self-defense is the most basic.

In America, we've taken that ancient right to self-defense and made it more violent and bloodthirsty. The right to self-defense used to include a duty to retreat. That made sense: you can defend yourself from deadly force with deadly force, but if you can safely get away from deadly force, you should by all means do so. But I guess *retreat* isn't performatively masculine enough for the assortment of weekend warriors and ammosexuals who get to make the rules in this country. Most state governments now specifically reject the duty to retreat, and the most deadly form of that rejection has been codified in "stand your ground" laws in many jurisdictions.

Understand, the right to self-defense, as applied in this country, is one of the most provably racist functions of law that we have statistics for, and stand your ground just makes those racial disparities worse. One well-respected study by the Urban Institute's Justice

Policy Center found that white people who kill Black people are 250 percent more likely to have their homicides ruled as "justified" than when white people kill other white people. In stand your ground states, that number jumps to 354 percent—it is 354 percent more likely that white people will be ruled as justified in their killings of Black people.[*]

"Self-defense" is how white people get away with murder. It is a textbook example of a "race-neutral" concept that has been applied with deep prejudice against Black people. It doesn't matter if the Black person was armed, unarmed, strong, weak, fast, slow, or just walking home with some Skittles. If a white person kills that Black person, they always have a chance to "get out of jail free" by claiming self-defense.

Is it any wonder that police use this same trope when they kill Black people? As we've discussed, every single time a cop guns down a Black victim, *the cop* turns around and claims he feared for his life.

If this country wasn't so suffused in racial prejudice, our "no retreat, no surrender" irrationally violent conception of self-defense would work against cops, not for them.

Consider what happened to Kenneth Walker. Walker was at his girlfriend's apartment one night, watching a movie in bed, when three men kicked in the door. Walker did not hear the men identify themselves as police, neither did at least four of his neighbors. Walker's girlfriend allegedly called out repeatedly at the men breaking into her home, and received no answer. Walker reached for his weapon and fired into the dark, resulting in a hail of gunfire from the armed men.

---

[*] A different study looked at 204 homicides in Florida (ground zero for stand your ground) where the stand your ground statute was cited by defendants. It found that people were twice as likely to be convicted—that is, have their stand your ground defense rejected—if the victim was white.

His girlfriend, Breonna Taylor, was killed in her bedroom. Walker was arrested at the scene and charged with attempted murder of police officers. While charges against Walker were eventually dropped (after intense public pressure), the attorney general of Kentucky, Republican Daniel Cameron, determined that the police murder of Taylor was justified, in part because of Walker's actions. Cameron was able to convince a grand jury of his judgment, and the cops were never charged.

The universe in which the cops can break into a woman's apartment and shoot her dead, but her boyfriend cannot fire back at the armed, unknown assailants who killed her, is deeply fucked. Where was Walker's right to self-defense? Where were the ammosexuals speaking out for Walker's right to defend himself? But that is the universe the Supreme Court wants.

We could live in a better place, under a better system of laws. Until recently, the Ninth Circuit Court of Appeals (which is the federal court overseeing California, Hawaii, Oregon, and Washington) recognized a "provocation" rule. The rule meant that if the cops, through their violation of constitutional rights, cause a violent confrontation, then the cops are responsible for all damages resulting from that confrontation. The rule didn't exactly allow people to shoot at the police, but it did put the cops on the hook financially for any destruction or medical bills caused by police violating constitutional rights.

But in 2017 the Supreme Court struck down the Ninth Circuit's rule in a case called *County of Los Angeles v. Mendez*.

The facts in *Mendez* are a gross example of abuse of police power. Angel Mendez and his wife, Jennifer, were homeless, living in a shack in a friend's backyard. The police, searching for an armed parolee, came across their windowless shack while searching the friend's premises. Without a warrant, or even so much as a knock and announcement that they were law enforcement, the police barged into the shack.

Police allege that Mendez reached for a BB gun, which he owned for shooting rats. The cops opened fire, unleashing fifteen shots. Angel was shot multiple times; Jennifer—who was pregnant—was shot in the back and hand. Thankfully, the Mendezes lived. And sued.

At trial, a federal judge found that firing fifteen shots at a family with a BB gun and shooting a pregnant lady in the back was a "reasonable" use of force, under the circumstances. Again, we need a wholesale reinterpretation of our use of force guidelines. But the Mendezes were awarded $4 million nonetheless because the police "provoked" the encounter with their unlawful search of the Mendezes' shack.

The Supreme Court dismissed the jury verdict and overturned the Ninth Circuit's provocation rule. (The case was sent back for reargument where the Ninth Circuit later held up the jury verdict on a different theory.) Writing for a unanimous Court, Justice Samuel Alito ruled that provocation could not lead to liability if the police officer's use of force was itself reasonable.

Essentially, the provocation rule fell victim to this country's insistence on extending "qualified immunity" to agents of the state who violate the Constitution. All qualified immunity does is protect an officer or agent from being personally sued for their constitutional infringements. Everybody familiar with the calls for racial justice and police reform now knows that qualified immunity is a huge problem. Agents of the state, be they police officers or prosecutors or presidents, are immune from personal prosecution and punishment over constitutional violations they commit while carrying out their official duties.

There's some nuance here that often gets overlooked when non-lawyers talk about this concept. First of all, qualified immunity doesn't protect state actors from punishment for things they do outside their official capacity. Senator Rand Paul, for instance, has immunity for actions he takes as a United States senator. But when he's just growing a gross pumpkin patch outside of his house, he could totally be found in violation of any neighborhood ordinances against being a smelly compost person (Rand Paul's neighbor breaking Rand Paul's ribs over Rand Paul's pumpkin patch is, you know, the kind of thing Hobbes was trying to stop).

Qualified immunity also does not inoculate state actors from criminal charges. It does nothing to protect a cop from a murder charge, including in the line of duty. In fact, if cops were more reliably prosecuted and convicted for murder when they killed people, I'd bet very few people would still be worried about qualified immunity.

And qualified immunity does not protect the state itself from liability arising from the misdeeds of its agents. It is actually quite common for a city to be sued and eventually reach a settlement with the victims of their murderous police forces.

Technically, both state and federal officials can be sued for monetary damages for constitutional misconduct. For federal officials, the cause of action was more or less created in a Supreme Court decision called *Bivens v. Six Unknown Named Agents of Federal Bureau of Narcotics*. In both state and federal situations, qualified immunity is an affirmative defense those agents can raise in court to argue that they should not be personally held financially liable for the damage caused by their actions.

You can see why some limited version of qualified immunity should exist. You don't want people suing, say, meter maids for violations of the equal protection clause, just because they slap a ticket on a car that was parked in a handicapped spot by a driver trying to make things easier for her elderly mother. If the driver wants to bring that case, she should bring it against the government that jealously guards those handicapped window thingies instead of the poor schlep meter maid who is just doing their job.

But that decent reason does not justify making the Fourth Amendment damn near unenforceable. Remember, qualified immunity doesn't come into play when the reasonableness of a search is somehow in question. We're not dealing with cops who argue, "I thought shoving the plunger up the Black guy's ass was a reasonable way to probe for narcotics." We're not having a reasonableness argument. We're talking about liability for searches already deemed unreasonable or constitutionally defective.

An officer who violates constitutional rights should be punished in some way, even if that violation doesn't rise to the level of a criminal act. At the very least, the officer should be *worried* that he'll be punished in some way. The people who defend qualified immunity are, once again, the people who claim to be worried that a cop will hesitate before taking action. But if the threat of financial punishment makes a cop think twice before violating the Constitution, I say good. Any tool available to make police think differently before violating the laws is a tool that should be put to use.

Courts have turned qualified immunity into a license for cops to act on their racial prejudices with impunity. Qualified immunity cases come down to whether state agents "violate[d] clearly established statutory or constitutional rights of which a reasonable person would have known." That trash language comes from the 1982 Supreme Court case *Harlow v. Fitzgerald*.

Honestly, how in the hell is "I didn't know I was violating an established constitutional right" a *defense* to police misconduct? Why in the hell should I have to establish that a cop watched enough episodes of *Law & Order* to know that beating the snot out of me was wrong? How is it possible that courts are allowing cops to skate by on their constitutional violations under the theory that the courts themselves haven't done a good enough job of articulating what constitutional rights exist? What kind of white nonsense system leaves cops free to racially discriminate if a "reasonable" cop didn't know their particular method of discrimination was unconstitutional?

Harlow created a Kafkaesque loop where litigants can't argue that cops violated "well established" principles until a court establishes those principles have been violated. The case is like telling people they can't open a bank account without money, but it won't give people money until they open a bank account. And that loop was made worse in 2009 when Samuel Alito, writing for a unanimous court, issued a ruling in *Pearson v. Callahan*. That case made it more difficult for litigants to get established constitutional principles on the record, thus making it functionally impossible to prove that a cop violated one.

The Supreme Court's jurisprudence around qualified immunity is so broken that progressive congresspeople are trying to fix it legislatively. Representative Ayanna Pressley (D-MA) introduced legislation in 2020 to end qualified immunity for police officers who commit brutality or murder. Senator Cory Booker (D-NJ) has put forward similar legislation in the Senate, but of course Republicans have thus far blocked it.

The proposed amendments, while necessary, are merely legislative workarounds for deep constitutional rot. Our Constitution, like that of nearly every other modern nation-state, waves away this inherent conflict between the state's necessary rights to violence, and the citizen's inalienable right to self-defense, by making a distinction between legitimate and illegitimate uses of state power. The government is allowed to use violence to accomplish certain agreed-upon goals, and nobody is allowed to violently object. But the state is not allowed to do just anything.

Who is supposed to stop the state from using its power illegitimately? Well, "the law" is supposed to stop it. I'm not allowed to violently resist illegitimate state action, because *the law* is supposed to prohibit and punish such illegitimate uses of state power.

If a police officer tries to pull me over illegitimately, I'm not supposed to rev my engine and lead the officer on a high-speed chase through town. I'm supposed to pull over, get the guy's badge number, and then go to court and get the guy fired and be paid damages for my trouble. I'm not allowed to punch a cop who is trying to kill me, because the *other cops* are supposed to show up and stop their buddy from illegitimately using his monopoly of violence against me. That's what living in a "nation of laws" is supposed to mean: I don't have to fight the state, and I don't have to wait for God to raise me up in the afterlife, because I can sue the pants off the state right now. I'll take my mansion up front, thank you very much.

But the Supreme Court has functionally eviscerated my right to go to court and make the offending officers buy me a house. As I've mentioned, while Justice Alito is one of the most aggressively pro-police jurists in America, the two decisions I highlighted were unanimous opinions. Even liberal justices accept the premise that cops should be allowed to violate the Constitution, maim or murder civilians, and not pay for it. I'm not allowed to resist the cops, I'm not allowed to sue the cops, all I'm legally allowed to do is beg the cops to not kill me and pray that they don't choke the life out of me over eight minutes and forty-six seconds.

Why can't I punch a cop? Because by the time a cop gets in punchable range it's already too late. As a Black man in this country, I am prey, and the cops are my predators. My country and the courts have authorized these people to hunt me. My country and the courts refuse to place restraints on them to make them less likely to murder me. My country and the courts have left me in a Hobbesian state of nature, but in this jungle the police are far more powerful and terrifying than I will ever be. Like a gazelle running from a lion, if the lion catches me I've functionally lost my battle for survival and my existence is at their mercy. There's no point in kicking at them, because kicking them only pisses them off.

As Cypher from *The Matrix* might say: If you see a cop, you do what I do. Run. Run your ass off.

7

STOPPING POLICE BRUTALITY

There's a scene I love from the first Austin Powers movie. Mike Myers's Doctor Evil character is executing his elaborate plot to kill Austin Powers. It's a spoof of the movie trope where the bad guy makes an unnecessarily complicated contraption for killing the hero, which the hero predictably escapes. Dr. Evil's son "Scott" (played hilariously by Seth Green) questions the plan: "He could get away . . . I have a gun in my room, you give me five seconds I'll get it, I'll come back down here, BOOM, I'll blow their brains out."

Of course, Dr. Evil ignores him. "You just don't get it, do you." And that's the joke. To make movies work, it can never be that simple. Script writers of action movies have to devise convoluted plans of villainy so that it seems plausible for the protagonist to escape.

I hope people can see that we could stop police brutality in five seconds, if we wanted to. It's really not that complicated. The last three chapters of this book point the way, through the Constitution as already written, to end this scourge of police violence against Black people.

The Fourth Amendment does all the work. Here's the text:

> The right of the people to be secure in their persons, houses, papers, and effects, against unreasonable searches and seizures, shall not be violated, and no warrants shall issue, but upon probable cause, supported by oath or affirmation, and particularly describing the place to be searched, and the persons or things to be seized.

Boom. Make stopping people because they're Black an "unreasonable search." Make shooting people because they're Black an "unreasonable seizure." Make "shall not be violated" include actually prosecuting cops and holding them personally accountable when they violate these principles. The way to fix the police was written into our Constitution before there were even police in need of fixing.

The unnecessary destruction of Black lives would stop. Not all at once, but over time, as cops learned to play by the rules that have always been there, they'd adjust their behavior. At the margins, sure, there'd still be some close cases: situations where the suspect really did have a weapon and really was threatening the police or others. There would still be times when reasonable, unbiased people disagreed about whether the police tried to de-escalate the situation, and those close cases would still be fought about in court. And, I imagine, most of those tough cases would still be resolved in favor of the police officer. But applying the Fourth Amendment as I suggest would make police officers think twice before killing Black children. It would make officers hesitate before brutalizing unarmed Black teens who pose no credible threat to the officer. It would make the police liable for shooting Black people in the back. Cops who continued to be racist would risk jail, or poverty. And that risk, that threat of accountability, is what is needed. Black lives can only matter if there is punishment for the people who take them.

There. I've solved police brutality in America. Tell me when to arrive in Oslo for my Nobel Peace Prize.

Of course, we won't be implementing the Fourth Amendment as I suggest, and I won't be getting my $1,145,000 in prize money, because white people want the police to act this way. They want them violent and unshackled from constitutional restraint. Maybe not all white people, all of the time, but enough of them, most of the time. I can't stop police brutality, not because it's difficult to stop, but because too many white Americans want the police to be brutal.

I point, specifically, to Amy Cooper—"Central Park Karen," as she's come to be known. Amy Cooper got into an argument with bird-watcher Chris Cooper (no relation), because Chris asked her to leash her dog, as Central Park rules require. Chris Cooper happens to be Black, while Amy Cooper is white. Amy threatened to call the cops on Chris, and then she did just that, alleging in a faux-hysterical voice that a "BLACK" man was "ATTACKING" her in the park.

In that moment, Amy Cooper was asking the cops to show up and enforce the supremacy of her whiteness. She was in the wrong. Who the hell calls the cops when they are the ones in violation of a city ordinance? A white person does. A white person who knows that the cops are there to protect her privilege, not enforce the law and keep the peace.

Most white people I know like to think of themselves as better than Amy Cooper. Most tell me they were disgusted by her actions and would never call the cops like she did, or any number of so-called Karens have been shown to do, in this era of the camera

phone. But most of them are lying. Most of them are reacting nega-
tively to Amy Cooper's application of her privilege, not the underly-
ing concept upon which it rests.

Most white people want there to be somebody to call when they
feel threatened by Blackness. Sure, many use that power more judi-
ciously than Amy Cooper, but they want the power nonetheless.
And many of those who don't want the police to be at their beck
and call to deal with perceived threats from Black people are the
ones who are concealing firearms to handle any threats themselves,
in the name of "self-defense." As I've explained, even the way we
apply the legal concept of self-defense in this country is inextricably
linked with white violence done unto Black people.

So while police brutality and violence only gets talked about as
a "Black" issue, make no mistake: it's a problem entirely created by
and for the benefit of white people. I don't hold personal enmity
toward the police, any more than I'd hold a personal grudge against
a pack of dogs sent to recapture me after I escaped from bondage.
My issue is with their owner. My issue is with white people who
refuse to keep their goddamn cops on a leash.

There are no good cops or bad cops. There are just shitty white
people.

8

IT SAYS WHAT IT SAYS

Confessions should be unconstitutional. They shouldn't carry any force or effect. They shouldn't be used against defendants who recant later at trial. Criminals who are guilty can, upon the advice of their attorney, enter into a plea bargain with the state where they allocute to their crimes in exchange for leniency or mercy. Admissions of crime voluntarily made to third parties, or even to agents of the state disguised as third parties, can be used as evidence of criminality at trial. But the common practice of police officers or local prosecutors questioning suspects—sometimes coercively, sometimes violently—until they blurt out a statement against their own interest needs to end.

The Constitution, arguably, already prohibits the use of compelling confessions against criminal defendants. The language is right there in the Fifth Amendment. For those playing along at home, the relevant part of the Fifth Amendment says:

> No person . . . shall be compelled in any criminal case

to be a witness against himself, nor be deprived of life,
liberty, or property, without due process of law.

You don't have to jump through a bunch of fancy lawyer hoops
to get from this text to my theory that confessions are unconstitutional. If anything, you have to get willfully obtuse to arrive at the
opposite conclusion: that a confession can be somehow sanitized to
the point where it is not "compelled" by the government, but given
freely and voluntarily by well-meaning criminals who don't want to
put the state through the trouble of finding them guilty.

Think about why the right against self-incrimination is included
in the Fifth Amendment at all. It's there, entirely obviously, to stop
the government from beating confessions out of people. Constitutional scholar Jed Rubenfeld says it plainly in a *Yale Law Journal*
article:

> The core Application Understanding of this Clause
> is well-known: It prohibited the kind of interrogation
> practice found in certain seventeenth-century English
> courts such as the Star Chamber, where an individual
> was placed under oath, asked if he was guilty of a crime,
> and subject to severe punishment for refusing to answer.
> In seventeenth- and eighteenth-century thought, this
> practice put guilty defendants in a tight spot. They faced
> three unattractive options: incriminate themselves and
> go to jail; lie and condemn themselves to hell as perjur-
> ers; or, refuse to answer and go to jail anyway.

Put me in a DeLorean and take me to any time before the Enlight-
enment, and I'll find you a guy who is getting his ass kicked until he
admits to a crime.

Now, most scholars will tell you that the right against self-incrimination as understood by the people who wrote it in the eighteenth century referred to that somewhat limited situation where a person was getting repeatedly punched in the face or having their eyes burned with hot coals or having their entrails removed to compel them to "confess." They'll tell you our modern understanding, which has evolved to view some forms of mere nonviolent coercion violative of the Fifth Amendment, is very different from what Madison thought he was making unconstitutional.

Most scholars are probably right, and I for real don't give a shit. I'll talk about this more when we get to the Eighth Amendment's alleged prohibition against cruel and unusual punishment. Suffice it to say here that I do not care about what the collection of slavers and colonizers who wrote the Constitution thought were legitimate, "voluntary" confessions. The people who wrote the Constitution wouldn't understand the word *coercion* if you wrote the definition on parchment and shoved it up their ass.

If we believe that a person should not be compelled to incriminate himself, then there's no good reason to try to parse legitimate ways to force a person into confessing. This shouldn't be a game where the government tries to invent different ways to trick a person into ceding their constitutional rights, without crossing an entirely made-up line between "enhanced interrogation" and "torture."

Why should one's Fifth Amendment protections change based on how susceptible a person is to government coercion? Are we in the novel *1984*? Does the government have a Room 101 where I will be subjected to my deepest fears? Maybe I'm the kind of guy you could never beat a confession out of, but one threat made against my children would make me confess to murdering Tupac. I wouldn't be the first parent who lied or begged or *confessed to a crime* to save my children. Why should the Fifth Amendment stop the state from, say, waterboarding me, but potentially allow a prosecutor to threaten my kids with criminal charges, unless I incriminate myself?

In the real world, the strength of your Fifth Amendment protections depends on your level of legal education or exposure to the law. I know to never talk to the police without an attorney present, because I've been to law school. Every lawyer, every person who had a lawyer for a parent, every person who made it through a first-year course on criminal law knows not to talk to the police, no matter what the police offer you in exchange for talking. If the police suspect you of a crime, get a lawyer. If the police don't suspect you of a crime, shut up before you talk yourself into becoming a suspect.

The Fifth Amendment is a litmus test of whether you have enough education (from the books or from the streets) to know it exists. And that's not how it's supposed to be. Your constitutional rights aren't supposed to change depending on whether you know they exist.

Everybody has heard of the Supreme Court decision that tried to change that. *Miranda v. Arizona* tried to level the Fifth Amendment playing field so that everybody understood their basic right against self-incrimination. *Miranda v. Arizona* was actually a consolidation of four cases, in all of which the defendants had confessed to crimes without knowledge of their Fifth Amendment rights. For his part, Ernesto Miranda was suspected of raping an eighteen-year-old woman near a bus stop. Police tracked him to his girlfriend's home, questioned him, arrested him, and made him appear in a police lineup. (I can also make an argument that police lineups should be banned: they pressure victims into naming *somebody* responsible, and, despite a mountain of evidence showing that eyewitness accounts are unreliable, juries tend to place a lot of weight on these allegedly "positive" identifications.)

The victim could not positively identify Miranda, but Miranda was nonetheless questioned for some two-and-a-half hours, without an attorney. The police falsely indicated to Miranda that he had in fact been identified by the victim in the lineup, and at one point brought the victim into the interrogation room. Miranda eventually signed a written confession to the crime.

His lawyer, once he finally got one, appealed, and eventually Miranda became the lead litigant in this famous ruling.

The *Miranda* ruling was 5–4 with Chief Justice Earl Warren writing a sweeping opinion requiring suspects to be informed of both their Fifth Amendment rights against self-incrimination and their Sixth Amendment right to an attorney. Warren also laid out a possible procedure to ensure that those rights are communicated—the "Miranda warnings" that you've heard on every cop show on TV:

> You have the right to remain silent. Anything you say can and will be used against you in a court of law. You have the right to an attorney. If you cannot afford an attorney, one will be appointed for you.

Thing is, much as I love Earl Warren and consider *Miranda* to be one of the most important decisions ever handed down by the Supreme Court, this ruling is totally made up.

I think conservatives and originalists cry wolf a lot of times with their ceaseless bitching that liberal justices "make up new laws," acting like legislators instead of jurists. But here, as Justice John Marshall Harlan II pointed out in his dissent, Warren invents from whole cloth a requirement to inform people of their rights. Indeed, if we're now in the business of informing people of their rights, I have some things I would like the cops to say before they search your home, or vehicle, or shoot you in the back for jaywalking or selling loosies.

Miranda is, to put it kindly, untethered from prior Fifth Amendment precedent. It is far more outside the lanes of traditional, precedent-based jurisprudence than cases like *Roe v. Wade* or *Planned Parenthood v. Casey*. The only reason conservatives don't complain about it as much (now) as those other cases is that there's not a culture war to be had over cops beating people into confessions, and *Miranda* has been so popularized by television shows that people think it's actually *in* the Constitution as opposed to something a bunch of liberals made up one day.

Even modern conservatives only agree with *Miranda* now because it is popular. In 2000, the Supreme Court affirmed *Miranda* in a case called *Dickerson v. United States*. There, by a vote of 7–2 (with Antonin Scalia and Clarence Thomas dissenting, because of course), Chief Justice William Rehnquist said that *Miranda* was now "part of our national culture" and so shouldn't be overturned, even though it represented a constitutional "invention" by Warren.

I'd argue the additional reason conservatives have seemingly made their peace with *Miranda* is because they've seen how easy it is for cops to overcome while they're trying to deprive people of their Fifth Amendment rights.

My issue with *Miranda* is not that it's made up, it's that it didn't go nearly far enough. As long as we're inventing constitutional procedures, I'd have invented one that stopped the cops from lying.

Aside from its unnecessarily limited scope, *Miranda* actually gives law enforcement a pathway to violate rights. While Warren's opinion did talk about looking at the "totality of the circumstances" of an interrogation to determine if rights were violated, in practice, the Miranda warnings have become a dumb and reductive prophylactic that law enforcement uses to sanitize otherwise unconstitutional interrogation tactics.

As long as law enforcement tells the suspect they have a right to an attorney, the police can basically keep questioning the suspect until the suspect makes a clear and unmistakable ask for a lawyer. In the meantime, the cops can tell the suspect all sorts of straight-up lies: about what they'll do to them if they request an attorney, about what their friends are saying in the next room, about evidence that may or may not exist that points to the suspect's culpability. Once the police recite the Miranda warnings, they are free to go back to lying, intimidating, and coercing confessions.

This takes us right back to the idea of Fifth Amendment rights being a litmus test for legal education, instead of inalienable rights given to all regardless of their knowledge of the law. The people who continue to answer police questions without a lawyer present are behaving irrationally, mostly because they don't know any better. As a result, they're being taken advantage of by law enforcement in a way that sidesteps their constitutional rights.

Now, you might think that it's okay for cops to take advantage of criminals, especially dumb ones. At the heart of all of our discussions about the Fifth Amendment is the belief, explicitly stated or implicitly held, that cops should be allowed to do whatever it reasonably takes (within a subjective definition of *reasonableness*) to bring criminals to justice. Ernesto Miranda (probably) raped somebody.* The other defendants consolidated into Miranda's case were all suspects in serious crimes. Oftentimes, the people arguing that their Fifth Amendment rights have been violated are not the easiest people to defend.

More than that, most people believe confessions are true. Most people do not understand how easily a reasonable person can be compelled into giving a false confession, absent actual physical tor-

---

* Miranda had his confession thrown out by the Supreme Court and received a new trial. At that new trial, he was convicted again of rape, this time on the strength of his girlfriend's testimony, who claimed that Miranda confessed his crimes to her while he was in a jail the first time. To recap: Miranda confessed to a crime, which landed him in jail, which resulted in him making a confession to a third party, which was used against him even after the initial confession that led to his jailhouse confession was thrown out. Miranda was paroled some years later and stabbed to death in a bar in Phoenix. When questioning suspects for that murder, police were compelled to read those suspects their Miranda rights. One suspect skipped town, and nobody was ever arrested or charged for Miranda's murder.

ture or some kind of well-defined mental incapacity. Most people believe that the truly innocent person will maintain their innocence right up to their death, but the guilty person's conscience will eventually lead them to admit to their crimes and seek the salvation and forgiveness of God.

Most people aren't Black. Most people have never been Black children. Most people cannot conceive of the intense and terrifying pressure that can be brought to bear on unrepresented and unprotected Black youths, and how that can make a person willing to tell the white man whatever they want to hear.

Most people think what happened to the Central Park Five was wrong but have not thought critically about how to prevent it from ever happening again.

The Central Park Five are Antron McCray, Kevin Richardson, Yusef Salaam, Raymond Santana, and Korey Wise. They were all sixteen or younger when they were rounded up, along with seven other Black and brown boys, on suspicion of committing various crimes in Central Park on the night of April 19, 1989. One of those crimes was the brutal beating and rape of Trisha Meili, the "Central Park Jogger." Under the lead of Linda Fairstein, who was head of the Manhattan District Attorney's "sex-crimes" unit, the boys were questioned for hours, without an attorney or their parents present.

Eventually, all five boys "confessed" to some aspect of the crime against Meili. They were convicted and sent to prison. In 1989, then real estate developer Donald Trump took out a full-page ad in four New York newspapers, demanding that New York State reinstate the death penalty, in response to the attack on Meili.

We know now that the boys were wrongly accused, and that their confessions were entirely fabricated. We know that because in 2002, serial rapist Matias Reyes was captured and confessed to the attack on Meili after he met Korey Wise in prison. This is why they're now called the Exonerated Five.

Reyes confessed to acting alone, but we don't just have to take Reyes's word on the matter. First of all, his confession was given with the advice of counsel, instead of the confessions wrested out of the Exonerated Five without an attorney present. Additionally, DNA evidence, sought only after Reyes's confession, confirmed that Reyes's DNA, and nobody else's, was at the crime.

Since we now know that the Exonerated Five were innocent the whole time, why did they confess to raping Meili?

Well, first of all, they didn't actually confess to the rape. After hours and hours of interrogation, the kids still never said that they raped anybody. Instead they "confessed," falsely, that they were involved in the attack on Meili, but not the rape. In fact, some of the kids literally confessed to facts the police knew were false at the time. They were confessing to things that were contradictory to what the other boys were confessing to.

In the exoneration report prepared by Assistant District Attorney Nancy Ryan in 2002, she says these inconsistencies were obvious at the time of their confessions:

> The significant weaknesses in the defendants' statements lie in the details they provide in describing the attack on the jogger. Taking the statements individually, those details appear to give them power. But a comparison of the statements reveals troubling discrepancies. Using their videotaped statements as the point of comparison, analysis shows that the accounts given by the five defendants differed from one another on the specific details of virtually every major aspect of the crime— who initiated the attack, who knocked the victim down, who undressed her, who struck her, who held her, who raped her, what weapons were used in the course of the

assault, and when in the sequence of events the attack
took place.

The kids were inventing stories to sound like mere witnesses,
rather than primary perpetrators, possibly convinced this would
allow them to testify against whoever the real perpetrator might be.
As Ryan writes:

> All five of the defendants implicated themselves in a
> number of the crimes which had occurred in the park.
> None of them admitted actually raping the Central Park
> jogger, but each gave an account of events in which he
> made himself an accomplice to the crime.

But Fairstein and the police turned it around on the boys. Instead
of charging one of them (falsely) with rape and using the (false)
statements of the others against them, they charged all five boys
with some kind of group gang rape that none of them even *falsely*
confessed to.

To be clear, there is no evidence linking the Exonerated Five to
any part of the attack on Meili, or any crime committed in Central Park that night. There's no evidence connecting actual rapist
Reyes to any of the boys; Reyes subsequently confessed to acting
alone, and that's how he appears to have carried out the other violent rapes he committed. People sometimes forget that when police
and prosecutors hone in on the wrong people, when they coerce
false confessions, they allow actual criminals to go free and commit
additional crimes.

Despite what have now been legally and scientifically proven to
be false convictions, no charges have been brought against Linda Fairstein or any of the cops who, we now know, coerced false

confessions out of five teenage boys, thereby letting an actual serial rapist go free. Fairstein is an author now: she writes crime novels. The lead character, Olivia Benson, on the popular television show *Law & Order: Special Victims Unit*, is inspired by Fairstein. I must have missed the episodes where Benson charges five Black kids with a crime they didn't commit in violation of their constitutional rights.

Fairstein was dropped by her publisher after Ava DuVernay's Netflix series *When They See Us* brought renewed attention to the plight of the Exonerated Five, but nothing legally bad ever happened or will ever happen to Fairstein. Prosecutors have qualified immunity too. Even when one like Fairstein violates constitutional rights and helps to falsely imprison kids for a decade, she can't be sued for damages.

The Fifth Amendment, even one supercharged by a robust application of *Miranda v. Arizona*, does squat to protect Black people from prosecutors like Fairstein. There are too many people in law enforcement who treat the right against self-incrimination like a technical obstacle to overcome, instead of an ancient right that is not to be violated. There are too many people who think the right to counsel is a trick to subvert justice, as opposed to the linchpin to make sure justice is done. There are too many people who think that five Black teenagers arrested in Central Park probably did *something* wrong, and it's the teenagers' job to prove white people wrong about them.

The way to stop this is not to add more procedural hoops for law enforcement to jump through on their way to secure a false or coerced confession. The way to stop this is to take confessions off the table entirely. Stop giving police and prosecutors a "prize" for successfully tricking or intimidating a suspect into speaking against their own interest *if they do it just right*. Stop inventing canons of law rife with loopholes cops can use to smuggle in beatings or threats of beatings while trying to induce the "voluntary" admissions of guilt. Stop the good cop/bad cop routine and television veneration of "closers," who can magically get people to confess to crimes without ever once asking to see their lawyer because the showrunner didn't budget for the Constitution.

If the Fifth Amendment recognizes the right against self-incrimination, then we should stop asking people to incriminate themselves. Why is that hard to understand?

9

THE TAKING OF BLACK LAND

In 1825, John and Elizabeth Whitehead divided their Manhattan, New York, farmland into two hundred lots and began selling it off. I know it's hard to imagine Manhattan as ever having farmland, but "the city" remained densely clustered on the southern tip of the island well into the nineteenth century.

The first three lots of the Whiteheads' land were bought for $125 by a shoeshiner named Andrew Williams. Williams was a Black man, and the Whiteheads were among the very few white landowners who would sell to Black people back then.

Williams was a member of the New York African Society for Mutual Relief. The group sought to help Black people buy real estate and was moderately successful at helping the Black middle class gain a foothold in New York. Other Black families began buying land from the Whiteheads in the area around Williams's new plot. A Black store clerk named Epiphany Davis bought twelve lots for $578. The African Methodist Episcopal Zion Church bought six lots, and the village became even more desirable to Black middle-class families. Irish immigrants, another group of "undesirables" the Whiteheads were willing to sell to, bought many of the other lots.

The Whiteheads ended up selling half of their plots to Black people. The little enclave they made was known as Seneca Village. According to census data in 1855, Seneca Village had 264 residents, three churches, three cemeteries, and two schools.

Seneca Village was a home of political power for Black people, as well. Remember, in 1855, there were no Fourteenth or Fifteenth Amendments. There was no guaranteed right to vote for African Americans, even free ones living in the North. To be eligible to vote in New York State in the 1850s, Black men needed to be a male landowners in possession of $250 worth of property and have state residency for three years. Neither the property nor residency requirements applied to white men. Seneca Village was a way for some Black men to meet that property requirement. Of the hundred Black people eligible to vote in New York State in 1845, ten lived in Seneca Village. Five years, later, in 1850, of the seventy-one Black property owners in New York City, 20 percent lived in Seneca Village.

By 1857, however, the entire area had been razed to the ground. The homes and churches were demolished, and the people were scattered. Seneca Village did not fall to some natural disaster, or even the ubiquitous mob of angry whites that show up, again and again, throughout American history to lynch Black people who seem to be getting ahead. No, Seneca Village was destroyed because in 1853 New York passed a law allowing for the construction of Central Park.

Seneca Village was located in what is now thought of as the west side of Central Park. Its boundaries extended from about Eighty-Second Street to Eighty-Ninth Street, between what is now Central Park West and where Seventh Avenue would be if it extended straight through the park. Seneca Village was a small and arguably unnecessary part of the 775 acres of land set aside by legislature to create the park.

The government had the authority to buy or "take" the land for Central Park, under the doctrine of eminent domain that is enshrined in the Fifth Amendment of the Constitution. Eminent domain is the theory that all land, even private property, can be acquired by the government if it is in the public interest. The relevant part of the Fifth Amendment reads:

> No person shall be . . . deprived of life, liberty, or property, without due process of law; nor shall private property be taken for public use, without just compensation.

Eminent domain is such a core concept of sovereignty that the U.S. Supreme Court has said that it doesn't even *require* a constitutional provision. But *compensation* for exercising that inherent sovereign authority does require some constitutional language.

To understand eminent domain, you have to appreciate that if you start from first principles, all land is "public." All land is just there, owned only by whoever or whatever happens to be standing on it, and can physically defend it, at a particular time. It's all God's land, if you're into that sort of thing. Or the king's land, if you lived in pretty much any pre-Enlightenment society.

"Private" property has surely always existed in some form—I'm certain that some of the ancient art we've uncovered and put in our museums was actually early modern "Beware of Bear" signs fashioned by cavemen who were sick of being solicited at their homes. But as a standing inalienable legal concept, fully private property that rulers are not allowed to violate at will is new (geologically speaking) and kind of weird. Entire treaties on government (including the only one most people have ever heard of: John Locke's second treatise on government) have been written to explain, more or less, why private property should exist at all. Private property is not the natural or inevitable result of settled society.

Different legal systems treat the concept of private ownership differently. Take, for instance, the initial "purchase" of Manhattan Island by the Dutch. In 1626, Peter Minuit, director of New Netherland, reported that he bought Manhattan for sixty guilders (about twenty-four dollars, according to nineteenth-century historians). It would be too glib and easy to say that the indigenous peoples who sold him the land didn't understand private property. As Arizona State law professor Robert Miller makes clear, the people likely did have a fully functional concept of property "exclusivity." But we would probably call the land deal a "lease" not a "purchase." In his book *Law in American History*, University of Virginia law professor G. Edward White makes the case that the native Lenape people were "not relinquishing the island, but simply welcoming the Dutch as additional occupants." It was the colonizers who didn't understand or respect the deal.

Unlike private property, eminent domain does flow naturally and inevitably from the concept that ownership exists only insofar as the state is able to secure and defend the territory. If the state needs your land for some public purpose, and you can't raise an army to oppose the state, your land is forfeited. Living in a state that is willing *to pay for* private land it needs to take is just a modern invention for property owners who could otherwise get screwed if they happen to live on land the state needs. Dutch jurist Hugo Grotius, whose *On the Law of War and Peace* from 1625 is one of the first real texts of international law, wrote: "The property of subjects is under the eminent domain of the state. . . . But when this is done the state is bound to make good the loss to those who lose their property."

That's the nice way of saying: "There wouldn't be a West India Company without these fortifications, but here, take some money and go." The Dutch didn't really "own" Manhattan in 1626, because they couldn't defend Manhattan in 1626. Indeed, "Wall Street" is so named because there used to be a defensive freaking wall there. The wall was built by slaves the Dutch also "bought" and brought with them to defend the settlement of New Amsterdam from attacks by the indigenous Americans, the British, or pirates.

Now, I would love to tell you what James Madison, author of the Fifth Amendment, meant by "just compensation." But I can't. I can't even tell you why eminent domain is tacked onto this amendment and not some other. I can tell you that Madison's initial proposed language was: "No person shall be . . . obliged to relinquish his property, where it may be necessary for public use, without just compensation." Congress changed it to its final version, but I can't tell you why. No record of whatever debate may have occurred exists. No Federalist Paper focuses in on this particular topic.

What I can tell you is that when white people want your shit, they will take it, and Black people will rarely be justly compensated for the destruction of their wealth.

Fighting against eminent domain has become a bit of a cause célèbre for libertarian forces on the right. They've even given it one of their cool, right-wing names, so that their entire objection can fit on the bumper sticker on somebody's truck. They call eminent domain actions "takings." Get it? The government is "taking" your stuff; who could support that, right?

Much of the heat on the right is over what constitutes a taking at all. Eminent domain certainly refers to physical takings: you had some land and now you don't. But arguably eminent domain should also come into play when the government dictates how you are allowed to use your property. These are called "regulatory takings," and they happen when, say, the government declares your private property a national historical site and thus prevents you from demolishing it and building a CVS. How much compensation is the government required to give out then?

Another large area of contention happens when the government takes only part of your property. Let's say that the government wants to place a few wind turbines on part of your land. The private property owner can still live there, so is it a taking at all? What if the wind turbines are super noisy? What if they "cause cancer" (author's note: they don't). What if they're really quiet but super ugly? What is the just compensation for ruining your view?

If you know anything about Republicans, you understand why the right-wingers get up for this fight, and you can see why liberals are generally on the side of the government when it comes to eminent domain. We need things like wind turbines and historical sites much more than we need libertarians bitching and moaning about whether they received enough of a vig from the government for their troubles.

If this were a Republican book, I would spend the next thirty minutes of your life telling you about a 2005 case called *Kelo v. City of New London.* Conservatives complain about this case more than Pharaoh complained about Yahweh. The case is about a white lady, Susette Kelo, who didn't want to sell her pink house. In a twist to the standard eminent domain case, New London, Connecticut, wanted to acquire her land to then sell it to a private developer, which created a Supreme Court battle. In a controversial 5–4 decision, the liberal wing of the court, joined by Anthony Kennedy, ruled that taking private property and then selling it to private interests for economic redevelopment was indeed a constitutional use of the government's eminent domain power.

Conservatives went nuts. They made a fucking movie about this lady and her stupid house. Parts of the house were moved and "rededicated" at a new site, and it's now some kind of monument to the fight against big government overreach.

Reluctantly, I agree with the Republicans about this issue. Clarence Thomas, in dissent in *Kelo,* said that the majority was converting the "public use" allowed by the Fifth Amendment into any vague promise of a "public purpose." And, God help me, I think Thomas was right about that. The government should not use its powers of eminent domain to essentially acquire land on the cheap for business interests, just because those businesses promise that there will be some public purpose behind their profit motive. For instance, I don't think the government should be involved in acquiring land to build sports arenas that will be owned by wealthy team owners and used to pump the valuation of their sports franchises into the billions.

My issue with *Kelo* is that centering this issue on a white home-owner and the legal distinction between public "use" versus "purpose" ignores entire Black and brown communities that have been wiped off the damn map by the government's use of eminent domain. Where's the movie about Seneca Village? Where's the movie about the Black and Latino renters who get crushed every time the local team wants a new stadium? Where's the movie about all the people and communities who were destroyed by former New York City parks commissioner Robert Moses?

Yeah, if we're going to talk about eminent domain, we're going to talk about how many of our roads, highways, and beaches were figuratively built on top of the bones of Black and brown people who used to live there. I'm sorry I just can't get up for this law-yer fight between public use and public purpose, when the govern-ment's definition of public "use" is so often merely "playthings for white people," as if that's an acceptable constitutional definition of the term.

The first time I heard about eminent domain was in college, where I read Robert Caro's seminal book *The Power Broker: Robert Moses and the Fall of New York*. Robert Moses is responsible for so much of how modern cities look and feel, and not just in New York because his methods were imported and copied throughout the country. Moses was a destroyer of Black and brown communities. And eminent domain is what allowed that asshole to be racist at an industrial scale.

If I may summarize one of the greatest modern biographies ever written in two sentences: Robert Moses was a deeply racist man who built highways, bridges, parks, beaches, and even housing projects by bulldozing the hopes, dreams, and often literal homes of people in his way. His main tactic for acquiring land for his projects was identifying vulnerable minority or immigrant communities, declaring their homes and land "blighted," and then using the government's power of eminent domain to evict people from their homes over their objection and for a fraction of what their communities were actually worth.

Declaring a community "blighted" or a home "condemned" is a favorite trick of the government when it wants to avoid paying just compensation for the land it takes. It's what Moses did, repeatedly, throughout New York City in the 1930s, '40s, '50s, and into the '60s. Moses would target a community, have state assessors declare it a "slum," and acquire the land through eminent domain at cut-rate prices. And it's a method many cities and states would copy under the guise of "urban renewal."

Urban renewal laws authorize the state to seize land it has designated blighted and deteriorated in some way. The New York State urban renewal law is codified at Article 15 of New York Consolidated Laws, Section 500. Look at how the law describes the purpose of the policy at Section 501:

> There exist in many municipalities within this state residential, non-residential, commercial, industrial or vacant areas, and combinations thereof, which are slum or blighted, or which are becoming slum or blighted areas because of substandard, insanitary, deteriorated

or deteriorating conditions, factors, and characteristics, with or without tangible physical blight. The existence of such areas constitutes a serious and growing menace, is injurious to the public safety, health, morals and welfare, contributes increasingly to the spread of crime, juvenile delinquency and disease, necessitates excessive and disproportionate expenditures of public funds for all forms of public service and constitutes a negative influence on adjacent properties impairing their economic soundness and stability, thereby threatening the source of public revenues.

As Yoda might say, "Mudhole? Slimy? My home, this is." Clearing out "the slums" and replacing run-down and dilapidated-looking buildings with fresh, shiny, economically productive buildings and infrastructure sounds like a great plan, unless you are the person being cleared out. Then, not only are you being displaced from your community, your "just compensation" becomes slum prices, leaving you only enough money to go and try to find a different slum to live in. The government usually doesn't pay people in so-called blighted communities what their homes are worth, and never pays them what the land would be worth after all the happy-clappy urban renewal takes place.

This is why eminent domain so often takes advantage of vulnerable people and communities. The government doesn't actually want to pay a fair price for the land and doesn't want to fight legal battles against well-connected and powerful communities who can protect their property and interests in court.

"Condemnation" is what happened to Susette Kelo's property, before the government took it.

But again, this tactic didn't just start happening in 2005, and to white people. We can go all the way back to the creation of Central Park a century and a half earlier and find the same tactics at play.

An enormous park measuring 775 acres (today the park is actually 843 acres) in the middle of the island was not actually the first plan for an open green space in New York City. The first suggested site was a parcel of land, about 150 acres, along the East River between what is now Sixty-Sixth Street and Seventy-Fifth Street, known as Jones's Wood. In 1851, the New York State Assembly and Senate both passed resolutions to take Jones's Wood property through eminent domain. It was happening.

But the wealthy white landowners—John Jones's heirs, and another wealthy New York family named the Schermerhorns, whose property was included in some of the proposals for the park—didn't want to sell the land. Understand, neither the Joneses nor the Schermerhorns lived *on* the property full-time. Remember, this is the 1850s and the Upper East Side might as well have been a Mars colony. The Joneses' and the Schermerhorns' primary residences were downtown, where any self-respecting wealthy New Yorker would live. These people just didn't want to sell their undeveloped "country" estates uptown to the city for a public works project.

So the families sued New York State to block the state's taking of their land.

Did I mention the Joneses and Schermerhorns were white? They were white. And since they were white, all of the stuff I said earlier about the foundational principles of state sovereignty that eminent domain rest on, all of the stuff I said about how, legally speaking, the concept of eminent domain is so ingrained into the very conception of property that you scarcely need constitutional language acknowledging it, all of that stuff comes with the caveat of *unless you are wealthy and white.*

Of course the Joneses and Schermerhorns won their lawsuit against the state. Of course they did. A court ruled that the state resolution to acquire the property through eminent domain violated the due process rights of the rich white people. Apparently the resolution allowed the state to back out of the deal but didn't allow the Joneses and the Schermerhorns the same right. I'd point out that of course the Joneses and the Schermerhorns had no right to "back out" of the deal, because the state was using its unquestionable sovereign power to force the families into taking the "deal" whether they liked it or not, but now I'm just shaking my fist at white judges who have been dead for 150 years.

And so, instead of displacing two white families who didn't even use their land as their primary residence, the city went forward with a new plan that included displacing over two hundred Black people in Seneca Village who had built up an independent Black community on some of the only land they were allowed to purchase. All of the tricks that would later be deployed against Black communities in the twentieth century were used against the people of Seneca Village in the nineteenth century. The newspapers called their land a "swamp." The media called the people living there "squatters" (even though, again, 20 percent of the Black homeowners in all of New York City lived there), and, of course, the papers referred to their community as a "n***er village."

The residents of Seneca Village also went to court to object to the government taking their land, but unlike the wealthy white families, they lost in court every time. The landowners were paid an average of $700 per lot. Andrew Williams, that shoeshiner-turned-landowner who bought the first lots from the Whiteheads, was paid $2,335 for his three lots and house, even though he initially asked for $3,500 in "just compensation." Even when taking his land and destroying the community he helped to found, the state couldn't be bothered to pay the man what he asked for.

The Time Warner Center is a relatively recent construction just off Columbus Circle in New York City that sits right at the southwestern entrance to the park. It sits on about two acres of land and is valued at approximately $1.5 billion.

New York City should go and find all the descendants of Seneca Village and pay them what their land is actually worth. I bet the government would be more cautious and fair when using its power of eminent domain if the compensation were ever just.

10

A JURY OF YOUR WHITE PEERS

The right to a trial by jury in criminal cases is one of the oldest rights in our legal tradition. It's considered one of the defining features of democratic self-government. The ancient Athenians had public jury trials. The Romans had them. English kings, perhaps as far back as Henry II, reintroduced some form of jury trial by the twelfth century. By the 1700s, William Blackstone (the OG of legal pundits) wrote in his *Commentaries on the Laws of England* that the jury trial was an indispensable barrier between the rights of the people and the whims of the king because "the truth of every accusation . . . [must] be confirmed by the unanimous suffrage of twelve of his equals and neighbors, indifferently chosen and superior to all suspicion."

In America, the right to a jury trial was written into the constitutions of each of the thirteen original colonies, both before the American Revolution and after the formation of the new country. And, of course, it's written into the U.S. Constitution itself, in the form of the Sixth Amendment, which guarantees "the right to a speedy and public trial, by an impartial jury of the state and district wherein the crime shall have been committed."

I'm often surprised by how much faith people place in juries as a check on arbitrary, despotic uses of state power. I mean, do people just not know how arbitrarily despotic juries can be? I cannot reliably get a random sampling of twelve people to read a whole article before calling me an asshole based on my headline. But I'm supposed to trust twelve randos pulled off the street to figure out if I murdered somebody? They don't even have to be experts at anything? In fact, they generally have to be twelve people we found who literally had nothing better to do? This is the best system thousands of years of human civilization have been able to come up with?

Of course, I happen to be Black. The prospect of being judged by twelve potentially malicious white people doesn't immediately seem better to me than being judged by one potentially malicious white person in a robe. The right to an impartial jury has never really applied to people who look like me: not at the founding of the country, not after the Civil War, not after the Civil Rights Movement, and not today. I don't have a right to an "impartial" jury; I only have a right to a jury composed of white people who can answer the question "Are you racist? Yes/No" without shouting the n-word or firebombing a Black church.

For Black people, the Sixth Amendment is a cruel joke. The point of a trial by jury, if there is one, is to be judged by a community of your peers. But Black people are and have always been regularly brought up on charges by a white prosecutor, in front of a white judge, to have their guilt or innocence judged by an all-white or predominately white jury. That's not "impartial" justice; it's white justice imposed on Black bodies by a system that treats white people and their experiences as the default.

And it's certainly not a jury of your peers. Can you imagine a white banker accused of tax fraud sitting in front of an all-Black jury of "peers"? Can you imagine a white cop accused of murder being subjected to an all-Black jury? It doesn't happen. This country doesn't let a panel of all Black people judge white people involved in a freaking reality television dance competition. There is scarcely a situation in American life where any white person this side of Eminem is subjected to the final judgment of Black people, but Black people are subjected to the final judgment of white people all the damn time.

It would be one thing if Black people faced naturally occurring, predominantly white juries. If the only Black guy in town had to stand trial in front of his all-white neighbors, so be it. But predominately white juries are not the natural result of population dynamics mixed with "bad luck." Instead, those juries are the manufactured result of the criminal justice system purposefully excluding Black people from the jury pool.

White people, of course, used to explicitly exclude Black people from sitting on juries. Like nearly everything else in the Constitution, the Sixth Amendment didn't even pretend to apply to Black people, free or otherwise, for the first seventy-five years of this wretched country.

But after the Civil War, with the adoption of the Fourteenth Amendment and its promise of equal protection under the law, courts decided that directly excluding Black people from the jury pool was no longer okay. In 1880, the Supreme Court decided a case called *Strauder v. West Virginia*, which held that laws making Black people ineligible to serve on juries violated the Constitution. It's important to note here that the Court ruled the legal exclusion of Black jurors as a violation of the Fourteenth Amendment's grant of equal protection, not the Sixth Amendment's promise of an impartial jury.

But that wasn't really an issue in 1880 because racist white people were more than capable of keeping Black people off juries without the official statutory power to do so. The tool prosecutors used, and still use, to ensure all-white (and almost always all-male) juries is the peremptory challenge.

Here's a quick primer on how you get on a jury, for those who have yet to have the honor. First, eligible jurors are summoned to the courthouse for a day or more using a "reasonably random" method. This assemblage of eligible jurors is called the venire, or jury pool. If any cases need juries that day, the court selects people from that jury pool to sit on the jury (sometimes called a petit jury of twelve people used for trials, to distinguish it from a grand jury used for indictments to determine who needs to go to a trial).

But, unlike the larger jury pool, getting onto a trial jury is not done by random lot. The judge and lawyers, for both parties, are allowed to question potential jurors, ostensibly to test for bias against the people on trial, or potential witnesses, or issues likely to arise at trial. This process is called voir dire.*

During voir dire, potential jurors can be rejected for any reason, or for no reason at all. When a lawyer rejects a juror without having to state the reason for the rejection, it's called a peremptory challenge.

The right of lawyers to dismiss jurors via peremptory challenges for no stated reason goes back almost as far as juries and public trials themselves. The thought is that a lawyer might know the

---

* Why does the law use so many French terms to describe the jury process? Well, that's because while most people think of lawyers throwing around esoteric Latin phrases (and they do sometimes), our common law system comes from England, not Rome. And the English system used a lot of French words and terms because of the Norman conquest of England in 1066. It's called "law French," and words like *jury, tort, mortgage, bailiff,* and even *attorney* all come from that tradition. In areas of the law that are particularly old, like jury selection, you'll see more French. I usually try to resist using this archaic jargon, but some of the cases I want to talk about use these terms, so I have to explain them and, well, that's why William is conquering my keyboard right now.

juror is biased for reasons that can't be fully articulated but are true nonetheless. Because voir dire is not a forum to put jurors on trial, and there's no time or resources to check the character and moral standing of every potential juror, lawyers in the courtroom must be given wide latitude to exclude potentially unfit jurors. Maybe the juror looked like they were unserious and falling asleep during voir dire. Maybe the juror's answers just sounded untruthful, despite the lack of any evidence to impugn their character. Maybe the lawyer just gets a "bad feeling" about the juror.

Or, you know, maybe the juror is Black. After *Strauder v. West Virginia* outlawed the explicit statutory exclusion of Black jurors, lawyers were easily able to keep Black people off juries through the use of peremptory challenges. (Lawyers did the same thing to potential women jurors, both before and long after the Nineteenth Amendment gave women the right to vote.)

And that's the way things were for about a hundred years after *Strauder*. Black people would show up for jury duty only to be rejected via peremptory challenge in criminal cases, especially cases involving a Black defendant. These challenges allowed the system to discriminate against Black people who wanted to sit on juries and discriminate against Black people accused of crime. They allowed prosecutors to render the Sixth and Fourteenth Amendments inoperative for Black people, based on their own gut feelings before a trial.

The Supreme Court kind of tried to address this problem in 1965, in a case called *Swain v. Alabama*. But *Swain* focused on the exclusion of Black people from the jury *pool*, not on exclusion from the actual jury. All the Court really did in *Swain* was acknowledge that the systemic exclusion of Black people through peremptory challenges *could be* a violation of the equal protection clause, without giving defendants who were convicted by actual all-white juries any real way to object to how the jury was selected. A constitutional right that people have no way of accessing through litigation is just, like, a suggestion.

Finally, in 1986, the Supreme Court decided to put some teeth behind the super cool thought experiment that maybe Black people should not be summarily excluded from juries. That case is called *Batson v. Kentucky.* Just so people don't lose sight of how recent this decision is: the *Challenger* space shuttle blew up on live television before Black people had a tool to avoid being excluded from criminal juries in America. Barack Obama, the first Black president, was twenty-four years old before Black people had a reasonable chance of getting on a jury. Black people were brought to these lands in 1619, and Janet Jackson released *Nasty* before randomly excluding Black people from the jury process—an institution that's been around since Athens—was ruled unconstitutional in any meaningful way.

The next old white Republican who wants to talk to me about "law and order" can kiss my black ass.

But I digress. The case of *Batson v. Kentucky* would have never happened without the fairly extraordinary efforts of James Batson.

Batson, a Black man from Louisville, Kentucky, was charged with burglary. The evidence against him was light, and Batson went to trial. Batson's trial resulted in a hung jury: there was one Black juror on Batson's panel, and that juror would not vote to convict.

The prosecutor in the case, Joe Gutmann, decided to retry the case. This time, Gutmann used his peremptory challenges to exclude all four of the Black jurors who showed up in the jury pool. Batson was actually present at the voir dire when the potential jurors were being questioned. He told his lawyer to object to Gutmann's discriminatory use of his challenges. The lawyer said there was nothing he could do, and Batson, famously, told him to "object anyway."

He did but was shut down. Batson was convicted by an all-white jury.

On appeal, a white public defender named David Niehaus became interested in how it could possibly be constitutional for prosecutors to so brazenly reject Black jurors from being empaneled on petit juries. Niehaus moved to have the entire jury discharged as a violation of the Sixth and Fourteenth Amendments. It was Niehaus, a random public defender from Kentucky, who ended up arguing this seminal case in front of the Supreme Court.

Niehaus and Batson won. The Supreme Court ruled, 7–2, that using peremptory challenges to exclude jurors because they are Black violated the equal protection clause. Just as importantly, the Court ruled that defendants have a right to object to exclusion of Black jurors, and if they do, the burden shifts to the prosecution to provide a race-neutral reason for the exclusion of Black jurors.

We now call these hearings "Batson challenges." And Batson's logic has been extended to include women as well, from the 1994 case *J.E.B. v. Alabama ex rel. T.B.* (That decision was 6–3. So, to recap: until 1994 it was technically legal to use peremptory challenges against women *because* they are women. And, in *J.E.B.*, both Justice Sandra Day O'Connor and Justice Ruth Bader Ginsburg had to sit there and listen to arguments about why they could be summarily excluded from common criminal juries solely on the basis of their gender. Three of their male colleagues agreed with those sexist arguments, to their faces.)

Batson challenges became the first real tool to examine a lawyer's potentially discriminatory use of peremptory challenges, and force lawyers to come up with some reason for excluding jurors other than race or sex.

Which, of course, they do, all the time. A reoccurring theme in constitutional law is that racist white people are not stupid, and they never take a constitutional setback as an opportunity to be less racist going forward. If you tell them they can't be racist in one way, they'll find some other way to achieve the same racist results. And because courts are slow and infected by racist white people themselves, it might take decades or, as in the case with jury selection, a century for courts to catch up with the new way white people have figured out to be racist.

The problem with *Batson* is that white courts are inclined to accept any old allegedly "race-neutral" reason for excluding Black jurors. Lawyers have cited jurors' employment status, "body language," and pretty much anything else you can think of. A 1993 *University of Michigan Journal of Law Reform* article captured a number of cases where the prosecutors excluded Black jurors who "looked like" the Black defendant as the "race-neutral" reason accepted by the courts. Frankly, you have to be a piss-poor attorney not to be able to come up with some "race-neutral" reason to get rid of Black people. There are literally training videos on YouTube you can find that teach lawyers how to get around Batson challenges. *Batson* is both one of the most important modern civil rights victories and a complete fucking joke all at the same time.

Thurgood Marshall saw all of this coming from a mile away. Marshall concurred in the judgment in *Batson*, but he wrote separately. It's one of my favorite Marshall opinions:

> I join JUSTICE POWELL's eloquent opinion for the Court, which takes a historic step toward eliminating the shameful practice of racial discrimination in the selection of juries. The Court's opinion cogently explains the pernicious nature of the racially discriminatory use of peremptory challenges, and the repugnancy of such discrimination to the Equal Protection

Clause. The Court's opinion also ably demonstrates the inadequacy of any burden of proof for racially discriminatory use of peremptories that requires that "justice . . . sit supinely by" and be flouted in case after case before a remedy is available. I nonetheless write separately to express my views. The decision today will not end the racial discrimination that peremptories inject into the jury selection process. That goal can be accomplished only by eliminating peremptory challenges entirely.

The majority opinion in Batson assumes that lawyers acting in bad faith will be distinguishable from those acting in good faith. Marshall assumes white people gonna white.

Marshall was right.

But I think the way to attack peremptory challenges is not through the equal protection clause, but through the Sixth Amendment itself.

The Sixth Amendment's right to an impartial jury, chosen from "the state and district wherein the crime shall have been committed," has been interpreted by courts to mean that the Sixth entitles a defendant to a "fair cross section" of jurors from their community. But courts have routinely limited this fairness to the jury pool as a whole—the venire—and not the actual petit jury selected for trial.

Again, if Black people were being judged by a fair representation of their community, everybody could live with it. Everybody could agree that the ancient right to a jury of peers was satisfied if the people of the actual community where the crime was allegedly committed sat in judgment of the suspect. But courts have interpreted the Sixth Amendment to be nothing more than a bait and switch. The Supreme Court has said: "The Sixth Amendment requirement of a fair cross section on the venire is a means of assuring, not a *representative* jury (which the Constitution does not demand), but an *impartial* one (which it does)."

What the fuck does that mean? How in the hell does a fair cross section of my community in the jury pool "assure" me of an impartial jury at trial, if that fair representation does not make it onto the actual trial jury? Saying *"Here are all the Black people who could have been on your jury"* really doesn't do me a speck of good if I'm in the defendant's chair. How is representation crucial to impartiality at one stage, but not the other? That's like saying I have the right to go into the whole 7-Eleven, but I'm only allowed to buy malt liquor and condoms. What is this man talking about?

Sorry, the man talking is Antonin Scalia, and the case I'm quoting him from is 1990's *Holland v. Illinois.* Holland was the test case designed to attack the constitutionality of peremptory challenges to exclude Black jurors, regardless of the race-neutral reason invented by the prosecution. But Scalia rejected the argument in a 5–4 opinion.

Thurgood Marshall dissented:

> The Court decides today that a prosecutor's racially motivated exclusion of Afro-Americans from the petit jury does not violate the fair-cross-section requirement of the Sixth Amendment. To reach this startling result, the majority misrepresents the values underlying the fair-cross-section requirement, overstates the difficulties associated with the elimination of racial discrimination in jury selection, and ignores the clear import of well-grounded precedents. I dissent.

Marshall would retire only a year and a half after this dissent. And the increasingly conservative court has never again come as close to rejecting peremptory challenges.

At the dark heart of making the Sixth Amendment meaningful in any way for Black people lies an argument that white people, even white liberals, are reluctant to make: white jurors cannot sit in impartial judgment of Black people.

Nobody really wants to say that, so we run ourselves through a bunch of equal protection analysis about the fairness of the objections to Black jurors, to make the conversation more palatable. But the real argument is that a Black person cannot get an *impartial* jury if that jury is all white.

I know white people understand this argument because, again, there is not a time in this country where white people let twelve Black people judge them for anything. You won't see a goddamn boxing match where the panel of ringside judges are all Black if one of the combatants in the ring is white. White people reject implicitly the notion that their actions or, God forbid, crimes can be judged exclusively by a community of Black people. I've had white people tell me with a straight face that I'm not even allowed to judge *whether a white person has been racist to me personally.* Like I'm the one who is too "biased" to adjudicate the situation impartially. If I could have one white superpower, it would be the fucking nerve of these people.

And yet white people, most of them, think that it's at least theoretically possible for an all-white jury to sit in impartial judgment of Black people. White people don't bat an eye when they see a gang of whites sitting in judgment of a Black person's actions: in the courtroom, in the boardroom, or even just on a stupid Facebook post. I don't think a lot of white people even notice just how often they've been part of a mob of whites judging Black people: be it on a sports call-in show or piling on a Yelp review.

The result of allowing peremptory challenges, the result of failing to provide for a fair cross section of the community at trial, is that Black people are denied the constitutional entitlement to a jury of their peers. We don't have it under the Sixth Amendment or any other provision of law. We are just entitled to the same lynch mob of white people that has always shown up throughout history and claimed the authority to take our lives away.

At least now we get to object. Maybe next century white people will decide their Constitution requires them to listen to those objections. Juries have been around for a while and don't appear to be going anywhere, so I guess we still have time to work this out.

11

IT'S NOT UNUSUAL TO BE CRUEL

The moral argument against the death penalty is actually a lot harder to make than the legal objection to the practice. I feel like anti–death penalty folks, like me, sometimes get that backwards. To us, murdering unarmed, defenseless people, often painfully, feels like a moral nadir that should be obvious to others.

But it's not. Most people have no problem killing people *who deserve it*, or at the very least looking the other way while the people who deserve it are killed. The entire scope of recorded human history bears that out. People kill other people all the time, and nearly everybody can be convinced to kill somebody else.

And not just in a "him or me" situation. Like, unquestionably, nearly everybody alive would kill another person who was trying to kill them. That's a *given* of the human condition. But beyond what we'd tell ourselves are "defense" killings or "justifiable" homicides, there's a broader number of people we'd kill who are "too dangerous to live." Would you kill baby Hitler? Of course you would. You'd be a selfish asshole not to. Dude is going to be responsible for millions and millions of deaths and you wouldn't stop him before he got started because of, what, your immortal soul? Fuck you and your precious soul. Take one for the team and kill baby Hitler before he murders us all.

In our popular culture, we don't hesitate to glorify the killing of people who deserve it. The good guy almost always kills the bad guy. Thanos gets snapped, Sauron gets melted, John Wick kills the guy who killed his dog, and that guy's dad, and maybe one third of New York City who got in his way. That's just how movies work. In fact, when the bad guy is not killed, when they're merely captured or arrested, the entire theater knows: "Oh, they're setting up a sequel."*

To oppose the death penalty on moral grounds is to deny two of the most fundamental human emotions: fear and revenge. We kill criminals as punishment for all the harm they've caused to society, or out of fear that they will escape and cause additional harm in the future. Those are entirely natural human concerns.

It's not even morally clear why I, or any person who is not the victim, should get a vote in all of this. I mean, as far as I know, nobody on death row owes me money. I'm not on the hunt for the one-armed man who killed my wife. If the people who were wronged by a condemned man want to see that man put to death, who am I to say, "Actually, that's morally wrong, you should let him live." Who died and made me Jiminy freaking Cricket? If killing a person who is trying to kill you is more or less okay, how is killing a person who *successfully* killed your family wrong?

---

* Kids, "movie theaters" were places where people went to watch Netflix or Disney Plus with other strangers, before the coronavirus pandemic. In much of our art and literature, the conflict is not "resolved" until the antagonist is dead. It's easier to name the exceptions (nobody kills Prince Humperdinck in *The Princess Bride*) than it is to name the times a villain paid the ultimate price.

Compared to the moral argument that will leave you searching for a philosopher's stone, the legal argument against the death penalty is easy and straightforward. First of all, it's against the law. It's against one of the *first laws*, if you come from and believe in the Judeo-Christian tradition. Moses was the first lawgiver, and one of his first ten rules (some would call them commandments) he claims God told him is *"Thou shalt not kill."* Again, killing is kind of what people do, so most religious traditions go on to create enough exceptions to the "no killing" rule to drive a genocide, but arguably the law has been against killing people since the invention of *laws*.

Of course, that's just a story we tell each other. The first historically verifiable lawgiver was all about killing people: King Hammurabi of Babylon codified twenty-five different crimes that were punishable by death. By the seventh century BCE, the Athenian code made all crimes, literally all of them, punishable by death. They called it the *Draconian Code of Athens* and the name was not in error.

But the law's historical bloodlust is still overcome by the very point of law itself: to have rules that can be relied upon as opposed to whims that are applied in an arbitrary and capricious fashion by a despot. Capital punishment, as applied in our legal system, has none of the characteristics of good laws. It's not reliable: we literally convict and condemn innocent people all the time. It's not repeatable: similar crimes are treated as capital offenses or not depending on minor aggravating factors, the random geography of where the crime took place, or the good graces of the judge or jury that happens to hear the case. And, most importantly, it's not just or fair: the death penalty is carried out more frequently against poor defendants and even more frequently against Black and brown defendants. It's entirely rational to believe that the death penalty is theoretically legal, but whatever the hell we're doing is not.

Our Constitution addresses capital punishment in the Eighth

Amendment, but it doesn't even try to establish a consistent, reliable standard for a question as fundamental as "When can the state kill us?" Instead, it gives us this—the Eighth Amendment, in full:

> Excessive bail shall not be required, nor excessive fines imposed, nor cruel and unusual punishments inflicted.

Well, that's not really helpful. The Constitution defines neither *cruel* nor *unusual* (nor *excessive bail*, which is a whole different problem). Instead of making a rule, it offers a platitude the framers themselves didn't even come up with on their own (the exact language "cruel and unusual" is copied and pasted from the 1689 English Bill of Rights) and seems to assume that judges or juries will figure the whole thing out in the fullness of time. Say what you will about the Draconian Code of Athens, but at least it's an ethos.

A standard as vague and subjective as "cruel and unusual" is one begging future generations to figure things out for themselves. In 1787 it was normal and appropriate to beat children with tree branches and condemn people for witchcraft. Now, we're not supposed to do those things. Times change. Standards and practices change. The Eighth Amendment is a little bit of a "living constitution" written into the old parchment. It's a facially subjective standard that can be applied to our own situation as we see fit.

Unfortunately, we share the country with people who will not let us have nice things. These people are called originalists, and they will not allow our polity to function rationally. They think the Constitution can be only as good as the worldview of the small-minded slavers and colonists who wrote it, and because of that they insist the death penalty must be constitutional.

Originalists say that James Madison and Alexander Hamilton and John Jay and all the people who did the thinking and the selling of the new American Constitution clearly envisioned a society where capital punishment was a thing. Originalists will tell me that the state was well in the business of executing people when the Constitution was written, and yet the framers didn't specifically outlaw the practice. They'll tell me that the Eighth Amendment, which specifically prohibits cruel and unusual punishments, could not possibly have been referring to capital punishment, because convicts were murdered by the state, in every state, both before and after the Constitution was ratified. They'll point out that the English Bill of Rights, where the amendment was copied from, was written by people who chopped off their own king's head merely forty years earlier. They'll say that the very most the Eighth Amendment prohibits is torture, not executions.

I say: I don't give a shit. To my mind, the Eighth Amendment is the cleanest battle to be had with originalists. It's the easiest place to drop out all of the legalistic claptrap and doctrinal fencing to get down into the guts of the thing. The framers wrote something down. That something is vague. Originalists say that we can understand what they really meant by looking at what they did. I say I don't give a fuck about what those depraved assholes actually did. I will stipulate that the people who wrote the Constitution had a sense of humanity that was so underdeveloped they could eat sandwiches while watching a man being hung from the neck until death. But so what? The Constitution does not require me, or my country, to be forever hobbled by their sociopathy.

Indeed, we are not hobbled by eighteenth-century thought bubbles when it comes to what we define as capital *crimes*. There's no great accounting of how many crimes were punishable by death in America at the time the Constitution was ratified, because for the most part putting people to death was squarely in the purview of state law. But, at the time of the founding there were well over two hundred crimes punishable by death in England, including crimes as common as stealing and as nonserious as cutting down someone else's tree. Over time, here in America, the states have been able to cull the number of offenses that could get a person executed, without the need of an entire constitutional amendment.

It makes no sense that we've been able to remove ourselves from an eighteenth-century view of who gets punished but remain locked in an eighteenth-century view of how to punish people. That goes beyond the death penalty. For instance, some form of solitary confinement has been viewed as a fairly standard and appropriate punishment since forever. But now, with our modern understanding of, you know, human psychology, studies suggest that solitary confinement is especially cruel. It's torture for your brain. James Madison did not understand this and likely wouldn't have cared if he did. Why in the hell should that matter now? *We* know. We are the ones who know. And we are the ones who have the option of making cruel punishments, like solitary confinement, unconstitutional. To not do so because some old dead white people didn't have the knowledge or decency to do the same is not an alternative theory of legal interpretation. It's the promulgation of evil hiding behind the banality of cowardice.

A modern understanding of the Eighth Amendment would read it to outlaw the death penalty. That point is so obvious it has literally been done before. In 1972, in a case called *Furman v. Georgia*, the Supreme Court decided the death penalty statute in Georgia violated the Eighth Amendment mainly because it was applied in an arbitrary and capricious manner.

Furman is interesting because it's a one-page, per curiam (which means unsigned) opinion holding the Georgia statute unconstitutional, followed by two hundred pages of concurrences and dissents as the justices try to work out why or why not. Only justices William Brennan and Thurgood Marshall ruled the death penalty unconstitutional in all circumstances. Justice Marshall wrote:

Perhaps the most important principle in analyzing "cruel and unusual" punishment questions is one that is reiterated again and again in the prior opinions of the Court: *i.e.*, the cruel and unusual language "must draw its meaning from the evolving standard of decency that mark the progress of a maturing society." Thus, a penalty that was permissible at one time in our Nation's history is not necessarily permissible today.

But the rest of the majority did some version of trying to parse what the framers really meant by "cruel and unusual" to arrive at the position that the death penalty was theoretically legal but practically unworkable as applied in Georgia.

It shouldn't surprise anyone that *Furman* was but a temporary pause on the death penalty. Capital punishment was reinstated just a few years later, in 1976, in a case called *Gregg v. Georgia*. The Supreme Court reversed itself on the very thin logic that Georgia's new death penalty statute included enough procedural protections to make it okay for Georgia (and Texas, and Florida, which soon followed suit) to start killing people again.

Gregg was a 7–2 case, with only Brennan and Marshall dissenting. But *Furman* and *Gregg* have basically set the stage for the last forty years of death penalty fights at the Supreme Court. Marshall argued that the death penalty was an anachronistic holdover from our barbaric past, but the current argument against the death penalty doesn't take Marshall's "maturing society" position. Instead, the modern way of fighting the death penalty is to argue that each individual punishment is unnecessarily cruel in some specific way, without arguing that killing people is the thing that is cruel.

It's worked, after a fashion. Advocates have successfully forced the state to move from hangings to firing squads to gas chambers to electric chairs to, now, lethal injections. Over the last few years, manufacturers of drugs used in executions have started depriving state governments of their preferred cocktails of death. This forces states to try to use different drugs, in different cocktails, and every time the state does, people who haven't already been killed have an opportunity to appeal to the Supreme Court and argue that the new method of execution constitutes cruel and unusual punishment. The withholding of death drugs by the people who make them is one of the best stories about corporate responsibility we have in the modern era. It's one of the best examples of the market taking steps to correct a failure in government.

Predictably, conservatives are sick of it. They're sick of what they deem as legal tricks to keep people alive. There's actually a movement afoot in this country to bring back firing squads because too many prisons can't get their lethal drugs. "Just shoot it till it stops moving" is how conservatives like to handle their problems anyway. Conservative courts are annoyed that condemned men and women keep coming to the court asking for mercy, and that annoyance has manifested itself in a series of increasingly harsh decisions from the Republican majority on the Supreme Court.

The most cruel, the most needlessly fucking sadistic ruling, came from Justice Neil Gorsuch in 2019's *Bucklew v. Precythe*.

Russell Bucklew was a murderer, convicted and sentenced to death in the state of Missouri. Missouri is one of those states that lost its preferred death cocktail when manufacturers stopped selling the state prison system the drug, so it had to cobble together a new cocktail based on whatever it had lying around. It figured something out (damn near any drug will kill you if they give you too much of it): a lethal dose of the sedative pentobarbital.

The problem, from Bucklew's perspective, was that pentobarbital would be extremely painful. Bucklew suffered from a rare condition called cavernous hemangioma, a vascular issue. He argued that the pentobarbital could react adversely in his system, and, aside from killing him, would cause him extreme pain before he died.

Have you ever seen a movie where somebody who is about to be executed asks, "Will it hurt?" Usually the hero (or antihero if we're supposed to like him) will say something like "You won't feel a thing," and the character who is about to die gives a weak smile and sigh of relief and prepares himself for the inevitable. Now, imagine that executioner saying, "It'll hurt like a bitch and frankly I don't give a damn." That will give you an idea about Gorsuch's majority opinion in *Bucklew*. He wrote: "The Eighth Amendment forbids 'cruel and unusual' methods of capital punishment but does not guarantee a prisoner a painless death."

What a bastard, what a heartless-bastard thing to write while condemning a man to die painfully.

Gorsuch goes on to create an entirely new standard for Eighth Amendment objections. This is what originalists do when confronted with an area of law that was originally vague or open for interpretation: they make some shit up. Here, Gorsuch decides that to qualify as "cruel and unusual," pain has to be "superadded" on top of however the state decides to kill you. Gorsuch writes:

> While the Eighth Amendment doesn't forbid capital punishment, it does speak to how States may carry out that punishment, prohibiting methods that are "cruel and unusual." What does this term mean? At the time of the framing, English law still formally tolerated certain punishments even though they had largely fallen into disuse—punishments in which "terror, pain, or disgrace [were] superadded" to the penalty of death.

He then goes on to list various methods of execution the Eighth Amendment was understood, at the time, to prohibit, versus methods it was understood to permit. He divines that superadded pain is the thing that distinguishes forms of acceptable death from cruel death, then and now, and argues that the burden is on prisoners to somehow invent ever less painful ways to die that the state can readily implement without delay to execute them.

But Gorsuch is wrong about the Eighth Amendment, not just the theory of what it should and shouldn't permit, but in terms of how it was practically applied at the time it was adopted. People don't notice he's wrong, because he's wrong in the way that originalists almost always are when describing the fairy tale they've invented around the founding of America. He forgot about the slaves.

Quoting William Blackstone's *Commentaries on the Laws of England*, Gorsuch writes about methods of execution that would have "readily qualified as cruel and unusual" to a reader at the time of the Eighth Amendment's adoption:

> These included such "[d]isgusting" practices as dragging the prisoner to the place of execution, disemboweling, quartering, public dissection, and burning alive, all of which Blackstone observed "savor[ed] of torture or cruelty."

Instead, what unites the punishments the Eighth Amendment was understood to forbid, and distinguishes them from those it was understood to allow, is that the former were long disused (unusual) forms of punishment that intensified the sentence of death with a (cruel) "'superadd[ition]'" of "'terror, pain, or disgrace.'"

But that's a lie. All of those methods, and more, were used to kill Black people, and would have been readily identified as acceptable methods to kill Black people to most of the white people reading the Eighth Amendment at the time of its ratification. These punishments were not "long disused" by the time of the founding. They were used all the time, and would continue to be used all the time, against Black people. Don't even get me started on the eighteenth-century punishments thought to be normal and acceptable to inflict on Black people when the white people wanted to keep them *alive*. You'd take being burned at the stake any day over what some of these slavers could come up with when they still wanted to *protect their investment*.

From the perspective of the framers, what distinguished a cruel and unusual punishment from an allowable and normal punishment was not the method of execution, but the victim who was executed.

And it is that *original public purpose* of the Eighth Amendment that conservatives want to take us back to. Of course our society has evolved past the need to execute prisoners. A 2019 Gallup poll found that 60 percent of Americans favored life in prison over the death penalty. Of course we should not be executing people when we can't even be sure that they are guilty, and the fact that 165 people have been freed from death row because they've been proven innocent since 1973 should make us despair at how many innocent people may have been put to death. Of course a system that is more likely to kill you if you are Black or brown, or merely poor and cannot afford the best legal representation, fails to pass the basic standards from which law derives its power and authority.

The state-sponsored arbitrary murder of its own citizens who may or may not have committed a crime cannot be made legitimate through an invented definition of the word *cruel* that wasn't even used by the savage slaveholders who wrote the word down 250 years ago. Come on. I struggle accepting that originalists even believe the bullshit that comes out of their own mouths. "Oh, the Constitution totally requires us to distinguish between superadded terror and regular old terror when figuring out whether we can inject a drug into your bloodstream that will cut off oxygen to your cells and thus effectively suffocate you from the inside out. That's because the same people who would whip, mutilate, rape, and let dogs dismember enslaved humans only prohibited punishments that added unnecessary terror, pain, or disgrace."

Naw. That's not a real argument. That's too stupid to be a real argument. The real argument being made by originalists, and all the pro–death penalty people going all the way back to the founding, is that these people deserve to die. They're saying Russell Bucklew and all other death row inmates deserve to die and nobody should give a shit if it hurts.

Their legal grounding for that argument is actually a piece of crap. It makes no sense to have a legal definition of *cruel* centered upon what some eighteenth-century assholes thought that word should mean, especially when they changed their definition of the word based on the race of their victim. It's monstrous for the state to kill people when the state regularly convicts the wrong people of crime. And it's unethical to kill people based more on the effectiveness of their legal counsel than the severity of their offenses.

But arguing against the death penalty as a thing that cannot be done in a civilized society is a little different than arguing against it as a moral failure. Consider, again, Bucklew.

Stephanie Ray wanted to end her relationship with Bucklew. When she told him, he threatened her with a knife and cut her jaw. She fled, with her children, to a friend's house. Later, Bucklew caught up to her there. He shot the friend in the chest, killing him, and shot at the children (missing them, thankfully). He carried Ray to a secluded spot and violently raped her at gunpoint. He was apprehended, but he then somehow escaped the local jail, went back to Ray's home and beat Ray's mother with a hammer before he was apprehended again.

If you want a moral argument for why Bucklew should live, you'll have to pull out your copy of *A Black Guy's Guide to the Bible* (many of you have one, you probably just call it the *New Testament* in your house). I've got nothing for you there.

All I can tell you is that Russell Bucklew was put to death by the state of Missouri on October 1, 2019. Legally, that was the wrong result. The Constitution allows us to be better than this.

12

THE MOST IMPORTANT PART

In a sense, I've been explaining the Constitution with one hand tied behind my back. I've been looking at our rights and protections through the lens of the Bill of Rights—the ten amendments originally appended to the Constitution—as the originalists do. I've been trying to explain why originalists are wrong, on their ground and on their terms, on the things they claim to care about.

I really do believe that the Eighth Amendment, on its face, renders capital punishment unconstitutional. I really do think that the right to an impartial jury enshrined in the Sixth Amendment must mean the right to a representative jury of one's community. I absolutely believe that the Fourth Amendment's protection against unreasonable search and seizure means that the cops cannot harass, arrest, or murder me, simply because the officer has a "hunch" about the color of my skin. I can make a textualist and even originalist case against the kind of white supremacy infused into our Constitution. I've been to Federalist Society events; I can argue with them inside the paper bag that borders constitutional inquiry into the intentions of the small-minded white men who wrote the thing.

But my understanding of the Constitution does not have to be limited to the document as originally written, nor the first ten amendments as the framers originally understood and implemented them. That original Constitution, the one drafted at the Constitutional Convention in 1787, ratified by the thirteen colonies, and venerated by conservatives as if it were gospel, is dead. It was shot at Bull Run. It burned in the Battle of the Wilderness. It bled the ground red at Gettysburg. As a Black person, I do not even acknowledge the legitimacy of the original Constitution, much less think our modern rights and responsibilities can be understood only through its lens.

The Union survived the Civil War, but its slavers' Constitution did not.

If I'd been in charge, I'd have written an entirely new document. I'm sure that everybody knows that the original document counted slaves as "three fifths" of a free individual, but I'm not sure that most people appreciate how deeply cynical this clause was, beyond the obvious racism.

First of all, the actual text referred to three-fifths of "all other persons," because the slavers who wrote it didn't want to put the word *slaves* in their precious document. It's one of the most obvious indications that the founders knew damn well that slavery was wrong and didn't give a shit. But when you dig deeper, you realize that the three-fifths clause was put in there to help the slavers and the slave states. The Northern states out-peopled the Southern states, and so, rightly, the Southerners were worried about a federal government controlled by the states in the North with more people in them. You know, like a democracy or something. To counteract the places with the most people, the slave states put a bunch of antidemocratic loopholes in their Constitution, while also trying to inflate their own numbers by counting slaves who—by their own evil logic—had no right to representation. But they couldn't just say that slaves should be counted as full people, because then why are they holding *people* in bondage? So they counted slaves as three-fifths of a person to give *their captors* more congressional representation.

A document *that* flawed, one animated by such evil, and one that so spectacularly failed that the country fought a live-ammo Civil War less than a hundred years after its conception, should have been thrown out with the bathwater. That's what they did in South Africa. In South Africa, they didn't just track changes and strike through the old apartheid constitution. You can't make Freddy Krueger friendly by giving him a new hat. Instead, they wrote an entirely new document, in a constitutional convention that represented all of the people, and they took two years to do it. Adopted in 1996, the South African Constitution now stands as a model for the world, while we have a "constitutional crisis" every time a Republican president figures out a new way to commit crimes.

But nobody asked me. Instead, white Northerners thought their precious slavers' document was fixable with a few amendments—amendments that they passed without the help and over the objections of their defeated Southern cousins.

The real debate between liberals and conservatives on the Supreme Court, the true argument, when you drop out the legal jargon and hot-button culture-war issues, is the debate over whether or not the new amendments worked to redeem the document. Conservatives, fundamentally, act as though they did not. They act like the post–Civil War amendments were mere updates to the original slave document. We still have a white supremacist's Constitution—we just have to count Black people as full people for the purposes of congressional representation, is all. Not much has changed.

Liberals, conversely, act like the new amendments changed everything. Writing about the Thirteenth, Fourteenth, and

Fifteenth Amendments—collectively known as the Reconstruction Amendments—Eric Foner in his book *The Second Founding* explains the profound changes brought about by the new rules. He says:

> They forged a new constitutional relationship between individual Americans and the national state and were crucial in creating the world's first biracial democracy, in which people only a few years removed from slavery exercised significant political power...the amendments both reflected and reinforced a new era of individual rights consciousness among Americans of all races and backgrounds. So profound were these changes that the amendments should be seen not simply as an alteration of an existing structure but as a "second founding," a "constitutional revolution."

As a matter of interpretation, analyzing any constitutional clause without straining it through the Fourteenth Amendment's guarantee of equal protection and due process, or the Fifteenth Amendment's distribution of the voting franchise, is an exercise of intellectual apartheid. Without the Thirteenth, Fourteenth, and Fifteenth Amendments (and the Nineteenth Amendment, which finally acknowledged women's fundamental right to vote), the Constitution is a violent piece of shit that can be used to justify or allow the legalized supremacy of white men over all others. Those four amendments do not perfect the original Constitution; they're not the final pieces of the puzzle that complete a picture by filling in some obvious holes. Instead, they recast the entire document, destroying the slave state that the founders wrote into existence and replacing it with something new, something heterogenous, and something still flawed yet not utterly unredeemable.

Which is why the entire conservative legal project, since ratification of those amendments during Reconstruction to the present day, has been to limit the scope and effectiveness of this "new" Constitution. It doesn't matter if the conservatives call themselves Democrats (as they did after the Civil War) or Republicans (as they have since the New Deal or so). It doesn't matter if the conservative legal theorists say they're in favor of federalism or judicial restraint or originalism and textualism. Their goals are and have been the same no matter what they are calling themselves this morning. They want the right to vote to be limited to the people who agree with them. They want to exclude fairness from the question of due process. And they want equal protection to be one input among many, as opposed to a required outcome of just laws.

It's not complicated. If conservatives seem to excel at coming up with snappy names and bumper sticker slogans for their legal theories, it's because their goals are banal and simplistic enough to fit on the back of a truck. It's pretty easy to dress up "whites win always" with legalese and sell it back to an audience of white people, especially when Thomas Jefferson and James Madison have already done most of the work.

At the founding, all political and economic power in this country was given to white men. Almost all of the other amendments and common law updates simply change the balance ever so slightly on which white men get to be in control of any particular instrument of power. But the Reconstruction and Nineteenth Amendments say that white men have to share that political and economic power with everybody else. And not merely as a theoretical proposition either; those amendments demand that power is actually shared among our multicultural society, or else the government ceases to be legitimate.

Of course, conservative white men object to that. They don't like *sharing*. I mean, have you met a conservative white man? They're still flummoxed by the concept of letting a woman finish her sentence. You think sharing the wealth and power of a global hegemony is something they'd just roll over and accept? The only time conservative white men have agreed to share power is when other white men make them do it at the point of a gun. And whenever those more enlightened whites lose the will and the nerve to keep stuffing equality and fairness down the throats of their objecting brothers and cousins, conservative forces retrench, recalibrate, and reemerge with new strategies to violently reassert white male dominance, and new legal theories to justify their supremacy.

Sometimes those theories are even adopted by other minorities or women who are willing to sell out everybody else in order to snatch up whatever scrap of power or cash the white men are willing to drop from the table.

But make no mistake, the Reconstruction and Nineteenth Amendments offer a complete repudiation of white male supremacy, if legislatures and courts would only apply them to our republic. Hell, I could make a case that the only amendments I need in order to run a free and fair society are the Fourteenth and the First. Seriously, try me:

I want to buy some slaves.

Sorry, that's a violation of equal protection of the laws and substantive due process.

I didn't say Black slaves, I said any old slaves.

Yeah, still. There's no fair process by which you could acquire people as chattel.

Okay, fine, well I don't want to let everybody vote.

That sounds like a violation of equal protection to me.

Fine, they can vote but they can't live next to me.

And that's a violation of substantive due process in home buying.

Shut up!

Dude, First Amendment.

What if I wanted to take everybody's guns? I bet you'll say that's a violation of substantive due process too.

No, that's cool. Go right ahead.

Name me a structure of white supremacy, and I can show you how equal protection or substantive due process obliterates it. Show me an artifact of institutionalized bigotry or sexism that is upheld through force and effect of law, and I can tell you how to constitutionally destroy it. I cannot make people less racist. I cannot change hearts and minds. But I can make damn sure that racists and misogynists don't have the protection of law while they're doing their racism and misogyny in the name of the government.

Just, like, read it. Read the first section for God's sake. It does most of the things:

Amendment XIV

Section 1.

All persons born or naturalized in the United States, and subject to the jurisdiction thereof, are citizens of the United States and of the state wherein they reside. No state shall make or enforce any law which shall abridge the privileges or immunities of citizens of the United States; nor shall any state deprive any person of life, liberty, or property, without due process of law; nor

deny to any person within its jurisdiction the equal protection of the laws.

Here, I'll even annotate it for you.

All persons born or naturalized in the United States,
and subject to the jurisdiction thereof, are citizens of
the United States and of the state wherein they reside.

Everybody born here is a citizen. Everybody. There are not people
who are less citizens just because of where they came from, or how
recently they became citizens, or where their parents were born.

No state shall make or enforce any law which shall
abridge the privileges or immunities of citizens of the
United States.

All citizens have the same rights. Those include economic rights,
contractual rights, and speech rights. And those rights cannot be
taken away just because they live in a crappy state.

nor shall any state deprive any person of life, liberty, or
property, without due process of law.

You know that promise we made in the Declaration of Indepen-
dence about the pursuit of life, liberty, and happiness? The thing
we said once and then completely ignored when it came to Black
people? Well, we're serious about it now. Sorry we didn't make that
clear the first time.

nor deny to any person within its jurisdiction the equal
protection of the laws.

We can't have laws that only protect white people. We can't have a country that only works for white people. We just can't. We just fought a freaking war. Stop it.

The Reconstruction and Nineteenth Amendments, on their textual face, obliterate the structures of white male supremacy this nation was founded upon. They obliterate whatever new structures white guys will think of next. These amendments are supposed to win the debate on whether we're going to be a racist country or not.

And so originalists deploy one final trick from their big bag of bad ideas. They say that the Reconstruction Amendments must be interpreted according to the original public meaning of the people who wrote them after the Civil War. Instead of going higher, instead of looking at the ideals the Reconstruction Amendments represent, originalists again try to hobble them by limiting them to what dead white people may have thought. Originalists try to lock the country into an eighteenth-century kind of understanding of racial equality, and when that fails, as it must in the face of the Reconstruction Amendments, they argue with a straight face that we should be locked into a nineteenth-century white man's idea of racial justice.

It's fucking insulting. The people who wrote and voted for the Reconstruction Amendments were the best generation of white men America had yet produced, but they were still racist, sexist, flawed white men.

Here's your boy, Abraham Lincoln, speaking at Cooper Union:

> I will say then that I am not, nor ever have been, in favor of bringing about in any way the social and political equality of the white and black races, [applause] that I am not, nor ever have been, in favor of making voters or jurors of Negroes, nor of qualifying them to hold office, nor to intermarry with white people; and I will

say in addition to this that there is a physical difference
between the white and black races which I believe will
forever forbid the two races from living together on
terms of social and political equality. And inasmuch as
they cannot so live, while they do remain together there
must be the position of superior and inferior, and I as
much as any other man am in favor of having the superior position assigned to the white race.

And Lincoln was a great man. Not as great as his congressional
contemporary, the abolitionist congressman John Bingham, who
actually wrote the first section of the Fourteenth Amendment and
demanded the inclusion of sweeping language that guarantees the
right to all, but pretty great as nineteenth-century white people go.
Ulysses S. Grant, who as president would be in charge of executing the Reconstruction Amendments, actually owned slaves. And
again, Grant was a great white man for his time—the Emancipa-
tion Proclamation and the Thirteenth Amendment were probably
no more than unenforceable thought bubbles without Grant. But
the conservative plea that we center the legal rights and privileges
of everybody else on what the best available white men could imagine in the 1860s and '70s is ridiculous.

Equality and fairness must meet the standards of our modern
definitions of those ideals, or else the entire American experiment
is illegitimate. I mean that without hyperbole.

Understand, Black people did not get a vote in the drafting, adoption, or ratification of the Constitution in 1787. We did not get a
vote in the drafting, adoption, or ratification of the Reconstruction
Amendments. We did not consent, tacitly or otherwise, to this slave
state. And we were systematically denied political power in this
country until roughly 1964 (and I'm being *generous* to this country
by starting the clock in '64 with the passage of the Civil Rights Act,

as opposed to, like, 1984 and Jesse Jackson forcing the left-wing party to acknowledge the electoral strength of Black folks).

There is no political or legal philosophy of democratic self-government that contemplates people living under the yoke of laws as they would have been interpreted by their captors. Either equal protection and fundamental fairness mean something radically different now than they did then, or Black people are an occupied people in this land, still waiting for our chance to break free.

I'm not a radical, because I believe the former *must be* true. I believe that equal protection means what it says—that racist laws are unconstitutional, even if the legislators don't write "I hate n***ers" into the law—not what Neil Gorsuch thinks John Bingham really meant. I'm not a Black Nationalist, because I believe the Reconstruction and Nineteenth Amendments could redeem this whole bigoted and misogynist enterprise.

But white people won't let them. It really is that simple. I say the Fifteenth Amendment must mean that the votes of Black people cannot be suppressed by voter ID laws, and white people tell me no. I say that Black political power cannot be gerrymandered away by racist white legislatures, and white people tell me no. I say that the Fourteenth Amendment's grant of equal protection of laws must protect me from racial harassment by the cops, and entitles me to equal pay for my talents, and promises me that my peaceful protest will be treated with the same permissiveness the cops accord to a mob of white insurrectionists storming the nation's Capitol, and white people tell me no, no, no.

These amendments are a tonic white people refuse to drink. They can cure the Constitution of its addiction to white male supremacy, if white people would just take the medicine.

13

CONSERVATIVE KRYPTONITE

The Fourteenth Amendment was ratified by the states on July 9, 1868. But its guarantee of rights was almost immediately undercut by the Supreme Court. Then, as now, when the Supreme Court is controlled by conservatives, even a constitutional amendment cannot stop it from denying equal rights and social justice to all. Nothing decent can overcome a conservative court. That's something that modern liberals and progressives should always remember.

The conservative attack on the Fourteenth Amendment started with economic rights. The amendment says:

> No state shall make or enforce any law which shall abridge the privileges or immunities of citizens of the United States.

That suggests that any rights, including economic rights, held by any citizen must be held by all citizens, but the Supreme Court didn't see it that way.

The case that invented this distinction was called the *Slaughter-House Cases*. Decided in 1873, this case dealt with, well, slaughterhouses. The state of Louisiana granted a monopoly to a company called Crescent City Live-Stock Landing and Slaughter-House Company to run all slaughterhouses downstream of New Orleans. In exchange for the monopoly, Crescent City was supposed to comply with health and safety regulations and allow independent butchers to work on their premises, at fixed rates. Some of the white people put out of business, or forced to work at Crescent City, by this law argued a violation of their Thirteenth and Fourteenth Amendment rights to equal protection from this kind of economic favoritism.

But the Court said no. The *Slaughter-House Cases* was the first case interpreting the Fourteenth Amendment, and the Court ruled that it only applied to Black people—"the slave race," as the Court called us—and, regardless of race, the Fourteenth Amendment did not provide for equality of economic privileges for all people. Instead, the Court found that the other "privileges and immunities" enshrined in the Constitution (like the First Amendment's right to free speech and free association) constrained only the federal government. State governments, it ruled, were free to discriminate and deny those rights to their own citizens.

The view that other constitutional rights do not apply to the states was eventually rejected. Even though the Court, to my knowledge, has never had an opportunity to explicitly "overturn" the *Slaughter-House Cases*, by the early twentieth century its logic was dismissed. Today, most of the Constitution, including the original Bill of Rights, is thought to apply to state governments as well as the federal one.

But the argument that the Fourteenth Amendment protects economic equality, in addition to political equality, never recovered from the *Slaughter-House Cases*. You don't see poor white people suing for *their* rights under the Thirteenth or Fourteenth Amendment. You don't see Black people making, say, antitrust arguments against Facebook under the Fourteenth Amendment's grant of privileges and immunities. The closest thing we have to an argument like the ones made by the plaintiffs in the *Slaughter-House Cases* is from college athletes trying to get compensation or endorsement contracts while supporting the multibillion-dollar industry known as "amateur" sports. And those athletes are consistently rejected by courts.

So, right out of the gate, the Fourteenth Amendment was significantly limited by the Supreme Court. The amendment could have been a tool to stop all kinds of white-owned monopolies that crowd out Black-owned businesses. It could have been used to bring about increased economic opportunity for all. But it never turned out that way.

Part of that is because civil rights advocates and Fourteenth Amendment defenders at the time had bigger problems than *Slaughter-House*. The Civil Rights Act of 1875 was a big, sweeping bit of legislation that promised to affirm the "equality of all men before the law." The law banned discrimination in public accommodation and transportation. That meant restaurants, buses, and hotels all had to treat people equally. Most importantly, the 1875 act allowed people to sue for their rights in federal court, as opposed to state courts, which in the South were controlled by former slavers.

The legislation marked the last time white lawmakers would give a shit about Black people for nearly a hundred years. In 1877, Rutherford B. Hayes was installed as president after a disputed election where the validity of the Electoral College was called into question. A special commission decided the election in favor of Hayes, a Republican, with the help of Southern Democrats, but there was a catch. Hayes had to agree to remove federal troops from the South, which he did, thereby marking the effective end of Reconstruction.

By 1883, the Supreme Court overturned much of the 1875 Civil Rights Act, including all of the protections against discrimination in public accommodations and transportation. The Supreme Court, in a case called the *Civil Rights Cases*, ruled that the Fourteenth Amendment could not prohibit "private" discrimination.

Without troops left in the South to protect Black people who were trying to exercise their rights, without states willing to write laws prohibiting discrimination in their own territories, and without a federal cause of action so that Black people could object to the discrimination they were facing, the Jim Crow era was off and running. State governments didn't even have to pass laws formally discriminating against Black people; they could just let so-called "private actors"—like private restaurants or private hotels—do all the work for them.

But, of course, states did pass laws discriminating against Black folks, because if there's one thing about racists, it's that they're never satisfied with being ahead. They need total subjugation of Black people to make them feel good about themselves.

As early as 1870, just two years after the Fourteenth Amendment was ratified, Virginia passed a law requiring segregated public schools. All kinds of segregation laws were passed (and not just in the South) that should have violated the Fourteenth Amendment, even under the disastrous and wrong logic of the *Civil Rights Cases*. Georgia passed a law prohibiting amateur "Negro" baseball teams from playing "within two blocks" of any playground or school for white children (and prohibited white teams from playing within two blocks of colored playgrounds). Florida passed a law segregating housing for juvenile delinquents. Damn near everybody passed anti-miscegenation laws. All of these laws involved state actions, not private businesses conduct. They all should have been unconstitutional, even under the precedent of the *Civil Rights Cases.*

It all came to a head in 1892. That's when Homer Plessy bought a first-class ticket on the East Louisiana Railway for a trip from New Orleans to Covington, Louisiana. Plessy was Black, but he sat in the part of the train that was reserved for whites. The conductor asked Plessy to move. Plessy refused. He was then forcibly ejected from the train and sent to jail.

Plessy was a plant. He was not discernibly Black, his racial classification as "Negro" was owed to the infamous "one-eighth" rule of blood purity. Plessy had been approached by civil rights advocates specifically to challenge Louisiana's Separate Car Act of 1890. It was a classic Jim Crow law: trains were required to make one passenger car or section available for white passengers, and an "equal, but separate" accommodation for colored passengers—a plain violation of the Fourteenth Amendment's equal protection clause. Plessy's physical characteristics reduced the entire law to the bald, discriminatory intent of Louisiana's state. The only reason Plessy was ejected from the train car was because he was one-eighth Black. To reject his claim—to argue that legislating different treatment based not on the "color" of one's skin but on their racial classification was valid—would be to admit that the Fourteenth Amendment wasn't worth the parchment it was written on.

And the Supreme Court did just that. In a 7–1 decision the Court upheld the Louisiana law mandating segregated train cars. Here's the critical part of the majority opinion:

> The object of the amendment was undoubtedly to enforce the absolute equality of the two races before the law, but, in the nature of things, it could not have been intended to abolish distinctions based upon color, or to enforce social, as distinguished from political, equality,

or a commingling of the two races upon terms unsat-
isfactory to either. Laws permitting, and even requiring, their separation in places where they are liable to be
brought into contact do not necessarily imply the inferi-
ority of either race to the other, and have been generally,
if not universally, recognized as within the competency
of the state legislatures in the exercise of their police
power.

What's going on here is the interplay between three competing
spheres of rights: political rights, civil rights, and social rights.
Political rights are the rights to participate in the democracy: the
right to vote, or hold elective office. Civil rights are the rights to
participate in the economy: the right to own a home, or buy land.
Social rights are the rights to participate in society: the right to get
married, or throw a party.

The Court here interprets the Reconstruction Amendments to
protect only *political* rights. According to the logic of this Court,
Black people had the right to participate: they could vote or have a
trial or travel on trains. But they had no civil rights. No white man
was bound to sell Black people a home, or a first-class train ticket.
No white man was bound to employ Black people, or pay them an
equal wage if they did. And Black people certainly had no social
rights: they could be segregated or ghettoized or discriminated
against at will.

The core logic of Plessy is that laws that are facially race-neutral
are constitutional, even if they have a discriminatory effect. So a law
prohibiting Black baseball teams from playing with white baseball
teams is "facially race-neutral" because arguably it restricts white
teams as much as Black teams. This is a logic that conservatives will
come back to, again and again.

Here, Louisiana argued that it wasn't violating the equal

protection clause because its law treated black people and white people the same. Both races get their own section of the train.

Of course, those accommodations were never actually equal. The back of the train was never as nice or well maintained as the front of the train. Getting your food from the kitchen was never the same as sitting down at a table to eat. If things were actually equal, how would a lazy, mediocre white man come to feel he was still *better than* every Black person? The "equality" bit was always just a legal fiction: when white people see actual equality, they turn angry or violent. Come on. Twenty-first-century white people got so pissed off that a Black person got an equal employment opportunity as president that they turned to a vicious, bigoted, stupid person to save them, and stuck with him even as he helped get everybody sick. But you want to tell me that nineteenth-century white people really thought they were just in favor of "separate *but equal*" accommodations on a train? Or in a school? Please.

Plessy was decided in 1896. Its logic of "separate but equal" was used as the legal justification for the entire Jim Crow era. It's how the South, and many places and institutions in the North, justified the denial of civil rights to Black people. *Plessy* was the law of the land for almost sixty years, until it was overturned in the 1954 case *Brown v. Board of Education of Topeka.*

Now, conservatives will tell you that Plessy's logic has been roundly rejected. They'll say that laws requiring racial segregation are facially unconstitutional. They might even quote Justice Earl Warren from his *Brown* opinion where he says: "separate educational facilities are inherently unequal." But conservatives are trying to pull a fast one; they're trying to hide the racist evil they actually believe in by making a big show of one form of discrimination they've been forced to reject. In reality, *only* the "separate but equal" logic of Plessy has been rejected by conservatives. But the part where racists think the Fourteenth Amendment does not protect social rights? Conservative assholes still believe that. The part where they think that laws that are neutral (or "equal") according to the law's bare text should be interpreted without looking at the clear discriminatory impact of those laws? Modern originalists believe that the most.

The mere existence of *Plessy* really puts modern originalists in a bind. Again, their goal is to limit the Reconstruction Amendments to the original intent and public meaning of their white male writers. But that becomes an untenable position if the original intent and public meaning of the Fourteenth Amendment allows for the kind of segregation and racism of the Jim Crow era. If the nineteenth-century Supreme Court thought that equal protection didn't actually protect civil rights, and none of these other nineteenth-century white politicians did anything to stop them, then how can looking at original meaning and intent possibly be a valid way to interpret the Constitution or its amendments?

Clearly, the Fourteenth Amendment means more and does more than what the white people living at the time it was adopted thought it could mean and do. Looking to Jim Crow–era white society for guidance on how to bring about racial equality, of all things, is insane. A theory of constitutional interpretation and justice, supported by originalists, that *requires them* to look to and value the intents and purposes of unabashed, unrepentant white supremacists is obviously, irreparably racist. Originalists try to dress up their theories with a bunch of fancy words and legal jargon, because what they actually believe in plain terms is provably stupid. "Racial equality only means what white people, and white people only, some of whom actually owned slaves, thought it could mean a century and a half ago." Get the fuck out of my face with that nonsense.

You have, perhaps, seen some modern originalist judicial nominees struggle with this issue, when pressed about it at their confirmation hearings. The question "Was *Brown v. Board of Ed.* rightly decided?" has been put to some recent nominees, and some of them have struggled to answer. It's not just that Republicans are intent on nominating unreconstructed white racists who would be totally cool with bringing back segregation given the chance (although, that *is* part of what is going on). It's that they don't want to give up their originalist bona fides and admit that sometimes the original intent of slavers and colonists was just wrong.

The thing is, the originalist judges who struggle with *Brown v. Board of Ed.*, the ones who can't seem to decide if the case overturning one of the most racist decisions in U.S. history was "rightly decided," those people are the dumb ones. They're the stupid originalists who downloaded the white supremacy widget that is originalism but didn't watch the YouTube video on how to make it work.

The Court's decision in *Plessy* was wrong on its face even at the time it was decided. It is relatively easy to make a fully originalist case against *Plessy*, because *Plessy* was so wrong that even other white people knew it (not that those white people cared enough to do anything about it). The authors of the Reconstruction Amendments clearly envisioned the protection of political *and* civil rights as part of the package. For equal protection to mean anything, it had to mean the right for Black people to enter into contracts, civil or otherwise.

The Civil Rights Act of 1866 (not to be confused with the Civil Rights Act of 1875) explicitly protects the civil rights of Black Americans, including the right to contract, and creates a federal cause of action to sue for racial discrimination in contracts that we still use to this day. While that act was proposed in 1866, it was not enforced until 1870. According to Congressman John Bingham—who, you'll remember, is the guy who wrote the Fourteenth Amendment—Congress did not have the power to advance the 1866 Civil Rights Act *until* the states ratified the Fourteenth Amendment. This is evidence that the people who wrote the damn thing literally thought they were protecting the civil rights of African Americans, whether they lived in former slave states or not.

Smart originalists cling to this history like a life raft. It allows them to argue that all *Brown* did was *restore* the original public meaning to the Fourteenth Amendment, not update that meaning for the modern era. They act like Bingham is the only relevant white man the way Batman uses Commissioner Gordon when he needs to say "#NotAllCops."

And while defending *Brown* requires originalists to admit that seven sitting Supreme Court justices were deeply, irrevocably wrong, they can still point to one who wasn't. Justice John Marshall Harlan I (not to be confused with his grandson, Justice John Marshall Harlan II, who also served on the Supreme Court) wrote in dissent in *Plessy*, and he gave originalists a line they often repeat:

> Our Constitution is color-blind, and neither knows nor tolerates classes among citizens. In respect of civil rights, all citizens are equal before the law.

Harlan's dissent in *Plessy* has been fully adopted by originalist ideology. Indeed, in a *UCLA Law Review* article, University of Houston law professor Ronald Turner points out that the most famous originalist, Antonin Scalia, has repeatedly aligned himself with Harlan's dissent in *Plessy*. Even in his book, *Reading Law: The Interpretation of Legal Texts*, which Scalia co-authored with scholar Bryan Garner, they write:

> The Thirteenth and Fourteenth Amendments . . . can reasonably be thought to prohibit all laws designed to assert the separateness and superiority of the white race, even those that purport to treat the races equally.

Justice John Marshall Harlan took this position in his
powerful (and thoroughly originalist) dissent in *Plessy
v. Ferguson.*

Let's check the rest of that "thoroughly originalist" dissent, shall
we? Here's the paragraph leading up to Harlan's declaration that
the Constitution is color-blind:

The white race deems itself to be the dominant race in
this country. And so it is in prestige, in achievements,
in education, in wealth and in power. So, I doubt not, it
will continue to be for all time if it remains true to its
great heritage and holds fast to the principles of constitutional liberty.

As I keep saying, even the "best available" nineteenth-century
white men were racist assholes.
But wait, there's more:

There is a race so different from our own that we do
not permit those belonging to it to become citizens of
the United States. Persons belonging to it are, with few
exceptions, absolutely excluded from our country. I
allude to the Chinese race. But, by the statute in question, a Chinaman can ride in the same passenger coach
with white citizens of the United States.

"What the fuck are you talking about? The Chinaman is not the
issue here, dude. I'm talking about drawing a line in the sand, dude.
Across this line, you do not . . . Also, dude, *Chinaman* is not the preferred nomenclature. Asian American, please." (For this and other

important philosophical interpretations about "the rules," please see Walter Sobchak in *The Big Lebowski*.)

Scalia is, of course, correct. Harlan's dissent is thoroughly originalist. Because the original intent of the Fourteenth Amendment by the white supremacists who passed it was to confer a bare minimum of political and civil rights to Black people, but none of the social rights.

We can see this again in the 1866 Civil Rights Act. Here's Congressman James F. Wilson, of Iowa, who introduced the bill on the House floor, explaining what the act was meant to do, according to the *Congressional Globe*:

> It provides for the equality of citizens of the United States in the enjoyment of "civil rights and immunities." What do these terms mean? Do they mean that in all things civil, social, political, all citizens, without distinction of race or color, shall be equal? By no means can they be so construed.

If you want to flummox an originalist, don't ask them about *Plessy v. Ferguson* or *Brown v. Board of Ed*. The smart ones can square that circle. Instead, ask them about *Loving v. Virginia*. Ask them whether the Fourteenth Amendment protects "social" rights. Ask them if Black people have a constitutional right to be treated equally in society.

Because social equality is what *Loving* is all about. Richard Perry Loving was a white man born in Central Point, Virginia, in 1933. When he was seventeen, he met then eleven-year-old Mildred Delores Jeter, who was also from Central Point, Virginia, through a family friend. Mildred was of mixed race: her parents identified as part African American, part Native American.

But for the white authorities in Virginia, she was "Black" and that was all that mattered. The two dated, on and off, for a number of years before deciding to get married in 1958, after Mildred became pregnant with their child (she already had one child from a previous relationship).

They couldn't get married in Virginia. The state had passed an "Act to Preserve Racial Integrity" in 1924, specifically to ban interracial marriages. Laws banning interracial marriage had been ruled constitutional, despite the Fourteenth Amendment, in a case called *Pace v. Alabama* in 1883. All the states in the former Confederacy erected such laws.

It's important to remember that the reason Southern states passed anti-miscegenation statutes was because white people and Black people were getting married to each other. And some white people hated it. Interracial marriages threaten the entire (stupid) logic of white supremacy, because if enough people did it, then gosh, eventually you wouldn't even be able to tell who was *really* white, would you?

Despite the best efforts of the ruling whites, interracial unions continued in spite of the laws, and entire communities that were either comprised of or tolerant of mixed-race families developed. Central Point, Virginia, was one of those places. It was a community where races co-mingled.

Richard and Mildred got married in Washington, DC, where they were legally allowed to do so, but then returned to their community in Central Point to live as husband and wife.

One night in 1958, authorities barged into their home while they were sleeping. Local law enforcement broke down their door and "caught" the couple in bed. "They asked Richard who was that woman he was sleeping with," Mildred Loving later told an interviewer. "I said, 'I'm his wife,' and the sheriff said, 'Not here you're not.'"

The Lovings were arrested and charged with violating Virginia's ban on interracial marriages. Initially they pled not guilty, but after a short bench trial, they changed their pleas to guilty. Judge Leon Bazile sentenced them to one year in prison, but suspended the sentence provided they left Virginia and never returned together for twenty-five years. Judge Bazile wrote in his opinion:

> Almighty God created the races white, black, yellow, malay and red, and he placed them on separate continents. And, but for the interference with his arrangement, there would be no cause for such marriage. The fact that he separated the races shows that he did not intend for the races to mix.

I point that out just because I find it comforting, sometimes, to remember that racists are also extremely dumb. Like, look at this fool. Riddle me this: if God wanted the races kept on separate continents, and only human free will flummoxes that divine segregation, *then why do the continents move*? Why did "God" shove the "Malay continent" right up the ass of the "Yellow continent" as evidenced by the existence of the Himalayas? Bet you didn't think of that. I bet you don't even know why mountains exist in the first place, you ignorant, racist fuck.

Sorry, Bazile is dead and presumably can't hear me over the sound of his own torments.

The Lovings moved to DC and lived with a cousin but were unhappy. They were still so tied to their community that Mildred went home to Central Point, without her husband as the court order mandated, to give birth to two of her children. Mildred's cousin suggested that she write to then attorney general Robert F. Kennedy about her family's plight. She did, and Kennedy found an ACLU lawyer, Bernard S. Cohen, to appeal their case to the Supreme Court.

In 1967, Cohen and the Lovings had their day in front of the Supreme Court of the United States. There, the Commonwealth of Virginia made all of the usual arguments defending segregation. The state said that the law treated Blacks and white equally, insofar as they were equally prohibited from marrying each other. Chief Justice Earl Warren summarized the state's position:

> The State argues that the meaning of the Equal Protection Clause, as illuminated by the statements of the Framers, is only that state penal laws containing an interracial element as part of the definition of the offense must apply equally to whites and Negroes in the sense that members of each race are punished to the same degree.

The Court rejected these arguments, unanimously.

> There can be no question but that Virginia's miscegenation statutes rest solely upon distinctions drawn according to race. The statutes proscribe generally accepted conduct if engaged in by members of different races. Over the years, this Court has consistently repudiated "[d]istinctions between citizens solely because of their ancestry" as being "odious to a free people whose institutions are founded upon the doctrine of equality."

And that was the end of anti-miscegenation laws in the United States of America. Well, not really. Anti-miscegenation laws remained on the books in many Southern states for a very long time. Alabama had its anti-miscegenation law on the books until 2000! It was repealed by voter referendum, and 40 percent of the people voted to *keep* the law banning interracial marriages, even though it had long ceased to be a valid legal prohibition.

Still, *Loving* is one of the most important decisions in the history of the country. It aligned the Fourteenth Amendment not just with the protection of civil rights, which the Court did in *Brown v. Board of Ed.*, but with the protection of social rights as well. The right to participate in society with equality and dignity is also protected by the Fourteenth Amendment, and that is what *Loving* stands for.

Which is why the case is kryptonite for originalist logic. Because if there's one thing most nineteenth-century white men who wrote, debated, and adopted the Fourteenth Amendment were dead set against, it was the social equality of the races. I could make an argument that the Fourteenth Amendment wouldn't have even been ratified if the white men supporting it thought it meant their daughters could marry Black people. There is no originalist understanding of the Fourteenth Amendment that comports with the Supreme Court's unanimous opinion in *Loving*. Either our understanding of the Fourteenth Amendment "evolved" to include a rejection of racist anti-miscegenation laws, or it didn't. If the Fourteenth Amendment doesn't evolve, Alabama could force people to submit "pure-blood" certifications from Ancestry.com before issuing marriage licenses, and we'd need a whole different constitutional amendment to stop them. Originalism has no satisfactory answer for *Loving*, and originalists expose the whole intellectual bankruptcy of their ideology when they try to fashion one.

And boy, do they try. Steven Calabresi, the man who founded the Yale Law School chapter of the Federalist Society and who is one of the guys the originalists deploy to do their "big think" arguments, wrote a 2012 law review article that tried to square originalism with *Loving*. It's notable for its intellectual dishonesty and desperate reliance on an actual dictionary. Yeah, I'm not making that up. Despite all of the evidence that the people who wrote the Fourteenth

Amendment did not at all intend to authorize interracial marriage, Calabresi argues that the "original public meaning" of the Fourteenth totally included the equal protection of marriage, because of the dictionary definition of the words used. That's no different than looking up an eighteenth-century list of "punishments" and determining that since slavers used to shove fireworks up the backsides of misbehaving slaves and light them, that such a punishment is neither cruel nor unusual. But, this is what passes for intellectualism in the modern conservative movement.

Equally disingenuous but less intellectually pathetic is Antonin Scalia's defense of *Loving*. Scalia writes that *Loving* was correctly decided because anti-miscegenation laws were "designed to maintain White Supremacy." He writes: "A racially discriminatory purpose is always sufficient to subject a law to strict scrutiny, even a facially neutral law that makes no mention of race."

It would be tempting to take Scalia at his word—that he actually believes it's necessary to apply strict scrutiny to a law that has a racially discriminatory purpose—if not for the context in which he wrote that.

But that's a line I pulled from Scalia's dissent in *Lawrence v. Texas*. That 2003 case dealt with Texas's "anti-sodomy" law. Police, in response to a (made-up) call about a domestic disturbance, busted into the home of John Geddes Lawrence Jr.[*] They found him engaged in a consensual sex act with another man, Tyron Garner. They were arrested and charged with a violation of Texas's Homosexual Conduct Act and held in jail overnight. They pleaded no

---

[*] Lawrence actually hosted two men that night, Garner and a man named Robert Eubanks. Eubanks apparently left the apartment to "go to a vending machine" but was actually infuriated that Lawrence and Garner were flirting. He called the cops alleging there was "a black man going crazy with a gun." Eubanks later pleaded guilty to making a false police report.

contest to the charges and appealed their convictions. Their case eventually ended up at the Supreme Court.

There, by a vote of 6–3, the Supreme Court invalidated the Texas law and anti-sodomy laws generally. Justice Anthony Kennedy wrote the majority opinion and found that anti-sodomy laws violate the due process clause of the Fourteenth Amendment.

Scalia's dissent rests on the fallacy that discriminating on the basis of race is wrong but discriminating on the basis of sexual orientation is okay. And his argument that some discrimination is okay is literally the same logic used by the court in *Plessy*, and the same logic advanced by the Commonwealth of Virginia in *Loving*.

> Finally, I turn to petitioners' equal-protection challenge, which . . . [o]n its face . . . applies equally to all persons. Men and women, heterosexuals and homosexuals, are all subject to its prohibition of deviate sexual intercourse with someone of the same sex.
>
> . . .
>
> The objection is made, however, that the antimiscegenation laws invalidated in Loving v. Virginia . . . similarly were applicable to whites and blacks alike, and only distinguished between the races insofar as the partner was concerned. In Loving, however, . . . the Virginia statute was "designed to maintain White Supremacy." Id., at 6, 11. A racially discriminatory purpose is always sufficient to subject a law to strict scrutiny, even a facially neutral law that makes no mention of race.

It's simply not an intellectually honest opinion. Scalia can't use literally the same logic as the majority in *Plessy*, and then have anybody credible believe that he actually would have voted with the lone dissenter in that case. And he can't ignore the views of the white people who ratified the Fourteenth Amendment—views that were specifically opposed to interracial marriages—in *Loving*, and then suddenly tell me that their views are critical when trying to make a case for bigotry against gay people in *Lawrence*. I will stipulate that the people who ratified the Fourteenth Amendment hated Black people marrying white people *and* gay people marrying each other. Scalia has to tell me why that hatred should matter in one case but not the other. Because all the Fourteenth Amendment says is that the country cannot deny any "person" the equal protection of laws, and since I'm not a raging homophobe, I'd like us to use a modern definition of the word "person," thank you very much. Tell me I'm wrong.

And Tyron Garner is Black, by the way. Indeed, it is unlikely Lawrence would have gotten into any trouble at all had he been caught that night having sex with a white man. *Loving* and *Lawrence* are functionally the same case; they are logical twins.

The operative difference between *Loving* being decided 9–0 and *Lawrence* being decided 6–3 is that conservatives have successfully adopted a new language to couch their bigotry. That language is now called originalism. I absolutely believe that the three dissenters in *Lawrence* would have dissented in *Loving* if they had been on the Court at that time. I absolutely believe that the current Court, packed as it is with conservatives, would rule against Lawrence, 5–4, if they caught the case today. Conservatives have the votes, now, to do evil they could only dream about twenty years ago.

The current Supreme Court has more in common with the court in *Plessy* than the court in *Loving*. The only real difference between conservatives in 1896 and the ones we have today is that the Federalist Society teaches them how to edit out their bigoted slurs.

14

REVERSE RACISM
IS NOT A THING

Having explained why I think a robust interpretation of the equal protection clause of the Fourteenth Amendment could be used to cleanse this country of much of its legalized bigotry and racial discrimination, I would be remiss if I didn't point out that in reality you can, of course, discriminate against most people, most of the time, for most any reason, or no reason at all.

Speaking just for me, I'm prejudiced against dumb people. Not uneducated people, who I feel simply haven't been given the chance at education and knowledge, but dumb people, who have had all the education and knowledge thrown at them, only to see it bounce off their information-resistant brains. Like Republicans, for instance. If you go to a good school and have access to good professors and good books and you come out as a *Republican*, I'm prejudiced against you. I assume you're defective, in some way. I wouldn't want you to marry into my family. Like, I can't look at Yale Law School graduate and U.S. senator Josh Hawley without assuming he's at least one-eighth fucking idiot, you know.

Discriminating against dumb people is not controversial. Employers, arguably, do it all the time. Public colleges and universities do it too. Oh, we might quibble on the criteria for *dumb* but, as a general rule, denying someone a job or opportunity because they aren't smart enough to have it is legal and clearly constitutional. In fact there are all kinds of discriminations that do not trip any constitutional wires: firefighters have to be strong, pilots generally need to be able to see, underwear models have to look good in their underwear.

One way to think about our equal protection laws are as a long-running argument about what kinds of discrimination our society will allow, and who we can discriminate against.

The government can never discriminate against an individual person. That is directly in the Constitution, Article 1, Section 9: "No Bill of Attainder . . . shall be passed." A "bill of attainder" is a law directed at a specific person. Sadly, for me, a law that said "Nobody named Josh Hawley can be a U.S. senator" would be unconstitutional on its face.

But laws can discriminate against classes of people, and laws do discriminate against classes of people all the time. Indeed, there are only a few classes of people who *cannot* be discriminated against. We call them "suspect" or "protected" classes. In my travels around the internet, I've found the concept of protected classes to be one of those things that really confuses or angers the white "economic grievances" crowd. Federalist Society heroes hate being reminded that white people are not a protected class. Incels (involuntarily celibate) white boys on Twitter do not understand why racist dickheads aren't a protected class either.

The equal protection clause still gives the government wide latitude to pass laws that discriminate against most classes of people, but only a limited and highly controversial ability to discriminate against suspect classes. I'd like to give you a clean definition of what constitutes a suspect class, and, given the importance of that distinction in the law, you'd think there would be one. But there's not. There's no definition that everybody agrees to, and certainly no definition that survives whatever conservatives think to do to this area of the law next.

In general, suspect classes (which can also be called protected classes, because, again, this is an area where courts have decided, "Let's wing it") are groups that can be labeled by their race, religion, national origin, or immigration status. Some argue that being "historically singled out for discrimination" is key to the classification. Some argue that people of a "discrete and insular minority" should be considered members of a suspect class. Others think that the classification should be given to people based only on "immutable characteristics."

More or less, the difference between suspect classes and everybody else is why a policy like affirmative action is facially constitutional. As a class, white people are not suspect. Please don't drag me out of my home and lynch me over a fire, white folks who feel suddenly aggrieved. I'm just the messenger.

No matter what your definition of *suspect class* is, it's hard to fit all of white-dom into it. White people have not been historically singled out for discrimination and torment because of their immutable characteristics. They're not a minority (as of this writing). They're neither discrete nor insular. Lots of white people like to act like they are the "default" people in this country and, well, the law treats them as such.

Now, you could make an argument that there are certain kinds of white people who are members of a suspect class, and that's an argument I and a lot of liberals and progressives love to make. I'd love to see a legal ruling that counts poor people as a suspect class.

But the thing that pisses off some white people is that I won't make an argument that whiteness is the thing that is suspect (as opposed to poverty, for instance). Because whiteness is not suspect. Not in this country. Not ever. To call white people a suspect class is to render the entire phrase meaningless.

These classifications are given meaning by courts who use them to decide how to review laws under the equal protection clause. It turns out: not all laws are created equal. Laws, rules, and ordinances that target suspect classes trigger "strict scrutiny" review by courts. State actions that don't involve suspect classes are given what's called "rational basis" analysis by courts.

That's a lot of jargon. It's a little like explaining how a car works from the perspective of a mechanical engineer: "The four-stroke internal combustion engine mixes fuel, usually refined gasoline, with oxygen to produce internal explosions that power two to twelve torque-producing cylinders." Most people can get by just knowing: that pedal means stop, that other pedal means go. Here, *strict scrutiny* means "stop." If the government does something and the courts apply strict scrutiny, usually that's the ball game, and the government has to stop what it's doing. Everything else means "go."

But it's worth unpacking the jargon a little bit, because courts use it to hide what they're really doing.

Let's start at the top. Federal courts, comprised as they are of unelected old people who are appointed for life and are thus unaccountable to the people, are supposed to assume that most legislative acts are constitutional. Remember, the fact that the Supreme Court has any right at all to declare a legislative act unconstitutional is *kinda* made up. The Supreme Court claimed the power of judicial review—which is the power to invalidate laws—in the 1803 case known as *Marbury v. Madison*. In that case, Chief Justice John Marshall just announced that the Supreme Court could declare a law or order unconstitutional, even though that's not technically written in the Constitution.

That's fine by me; somebody's got to do it. But most people agree that the Court should use that power sparingly. Courts are supposed to give what's called "deference" to the elective bodies. For the most part, if the legislature or executive has a reason for doing something, courts should defer to their will.

This level of judicial review is called rational basis. If the government has the authority to pass a law, and that law has a "legitimate state interest," and the law passed is "rationally related to that interest," the law should be upheld. Seatbelt laws are a fine example of a law that survives rational basis review: the state has a legitimate interest in public safety, and wearing seatbelts is rationally related to keeping people alive, therefore seatbelt laws are constitutional, notwithstanding the idiotic complaints of always-wrong libertarians who claim a constitutional right to die in whatever way seems best to them. (The same logic should apply to, say, mask mandates during a pandemic, but I didn't want to use a *controversial* example of the government's constitutional authority to use basic science when it passes laws.)

But sometimes courts empower themselves to look at the government's rules more skeptically, with less deference to the wisdom of legislatures. This level of judicial review is called strict scrutiny. Under strict scrutiny review, the state has to show a "compelling governmental interest." And then the state must prove its law is "narrowly tailored to achieve that interest." Note the word changes! Courts need a *compelling* interest instead of merely a *legitimate* one, and now they need the law to be *narrowly tailored* instead of simply *rationally related* to the interest at hand.

Again, all of this is kind of made up. One court said: "We're going to review this with heightened scrutiny," and another court said, "Ooh, I like that, let's do that also, but can we change the adjective to *strict*?" and so on, until we have this entire canon of common law defining wildly different standards for when the court can use the power it gave to itself. There's nothing *in* the Constitution that requires courts to have different modalities for judicial review, and there's certainly nothing requiring courts to define those different standards the way they have.

If it were up to me, I'd change my "standard of review" based on the diversity of the legislature passing the law or regulation. *Did minorities and women get a say in this ordinance?* If so, sure, as long as it's not clearly stupid, it should probably be constitutional. *Did y'all really pass this with an all-white or disproportionately white legislature? Really? What year is this?* If so, I'm not inclined to give you people any deference at all.

But, it's not up to me. Courts have gone almost 240 years without giving a shit about what I think (or, more importantly, what people similarly situated to me think), and I imagine they'll go for 240 more so long as we're not all swallowed by the rising seas.

There is, however, a catch. Courts really apply strict scrutiny review to only two areas of law: laws that might violate the Fourteenth Amendment, and laws affecting the freedoms of speech, association, and religious affiliation enshrined in the First Amendment.

Strict scrutiny in the speech context could apply to damn near anybody. But in the equal protection context, strict scrutiny kicks in only for laws targeting members of a suspect class. Hence the legal importance of that classification.

As if all of that weren't random enough, courts have also created something called quasi-suspect classes, which are entitled to (wait for it) "intermediate scrutiny." The Supreme Court first applied this new scrutiny to laws that discriminate due to gender in a case called *Craig v. Boren.* There the Court held that while gender does not create a suspect class, laws discriminating between the gender classifications are "disfavored." The Court has also extended quasi-suspect class status to bastards (like, literal bastards, actual people whose "legitimacy is questioned at birth"). Intermediate scrutiny is said to require the state to show "important" government interests, and the law must be "substantially" related to that interest.

Get it? *Suspect class* triggers *strict scrutiny*, which requires *compelling* government interest with laws *narrowly tailored* to meet those goals. *Quasi-suspect class* triggers *intermediate scrutiny*, which requires *important* government interests with laws *substantially* related to those goals. And *nonsuspect classes* get *rational basis*, which requires *legitimate* government interests with laws *rationally* related to those goals.

All of this is bullshit. It's bullshit so the courts can argue that they have some objective, doctrinal reason for their decisions, because judges and justices don't like to admit that they are being "outcome determinative" in their rulings. "Oh, no, it's not that I hate women, I just think that their quasi-suspect class status does not entitle them to strict scrutiny when they bitch and nag. . . . I mean, go ahead and file lawsuits objecting to statutes that deny them equal access to health care. Golly gee, I'm just a judge here to call balls and strikes, not make policy."

In reality, judges and courts are being subjectively outcome determinative all the time. If courts like the outcome the law produces, the law will magically survive even strict scrutiny review. And if judges or justices don't like the law's outcome, well, then, they can make the laws fail even under a rational basis standard.

I can prove that. Because the first time the Supreme Court articulated strict scrutiny review was in the 1944 case *Korematsu v. United States*—the World War II Japanese internment case. The Court ruled that Franklin Delano Roosevelt's Executive Order 9066—which provided for the forced "relocation" of Japanese Americans living on the West Coast—should be reviewed under strict scrutiny, but concluded that the government passed the strict scrutiny test because of the government's national security interest. Speaking for the majority, Justice Hugo Black said:

It should be noted, to begin with, that all legal restrictions which curtail the civil rights of a single racial group
are immediately suspect. That is not to say that all such
restrictions are unconstitutional. It is to say that courts
must subject them to the most rigid scrutiny. Pressing
public necessity may sometimes justify the existence of
such restrictions; racial antagonism never can.

Spare me the platitudes, I don't know how you get more racially antagonistic than forcibly removing people from their homes
and *concentrating them in camps*, just because of their race. Justice Black's *Korematsu* decision was animated by the same racist
rationale that governed the Court's decision in *Plessy v. Ferguson*,
albeit without Justice Harlan's flair for derogatory racial slurs in the
dissent.

I'm sure the *Korematsu* Court thought itself much more evolved
than the *Plessy* Court. I know the current Court thought itself
much more evolved than the *Korematsu* Court. Chief Justice John
Roberts even explicitly overruled *Korematsu*, in *Trump v. Hawaii*,
a case where the Supreme Court used *Korematsu*'s exact logic to
uphold Donald Trump's Muslim ban. The Supreme Court excels at
using new jargon to smuggle in the same old bigotry.

If these doctrinal standards of review were "real," a reasonably
intelligent person should be able to tell me where to put the LGBTQ
community. Are they a suspect class, a quasi-suspect class, or no
distinct class at all? Go ahead, noodle it out, I'll wait . . .

If you ask me, the LGBTQ community is clearly a suspect class.
Members of that community have been historically singled out for
discrimination, have an immutable characteristic (any "conversion
therapy" acolytes reading can kiss my ass), and are members of a
distinct minority.

But Justice Anthony Kennedy apparently disagreed with me.

Kennedy, who for all intents and purposes is a tolerance hero for his tie-breaking decisions recognizing gay rights (striking down anti-sodomy laws in *Lawrence v. Texas*, invalidating the Defense of Marriage Act in *United States v. Windsor*, striking down laws banning same-sex marriage in *Obergefell v. Hodges*) never went the last yard to give the LGBTQ community protected class status. He thus never fully protected the community within the equal protection clause. In fact, at times he struggled to make a cogent argument for why the LGBTQ community should have equal protection under the Fourteenth Amendment at all. Writing in *The New Republic*, Brian Beutler went so far as to call Kennedy's opinion in the *Obergefell* case a "logical disaster":

> Kennedy alluded to the existence of an equal protection argument, but, as Roberts wrote in his dissent, "The majority [did] not seriously engage with this claim. Its discussion is, quite frankly, difficult to follow." Roberts is correct. Kennedy failed "to provide even a single sentence explaining how the Equal Protection Clause supplies independent weight for its position." This was Team Marriage Equality's strongest ground, and Kennedy surrendered it against a mostly unarmed adversary. In the end, Roberts offered the Court's only real equal protection argument (or counterargument) and it was weak by necessity. "[T]he marriage laws at issue here do not violate the Equal Protection Clause, because distinguishing between opposite-sex and same-sex couples is rationally related to the States' 'legitimate state interest' in 'preserving the traditional institution of marriage.'"

I wouldn't go so far as to say that one of the most important gay rights victories was bad, but, in terms of the fight still to come, *Obergefell* was one of the biggest missed opportunities in modern constitutional history. This was no *Loving*. Kennedy's opinions leave the LGBTQ community exposed to less tolerant conservatives who can simply claim—as Roberts does, as Scalia always did—that the state has a legitimate interest in discriminating against gay people, and that legitimate interest is all they need.

Kennedy was no originalist, but he certainly was a Republican. He's certainly conservative. And, as I've said, the entire conservative project has been to limit the scope and effectiveness of the Fourteenth Amendment since the moment it was ratified. That's why Kennedy did what he did in these cases. He was able to stamp out a couple of specific examples of discrimination against the LGBTQ community without empowering the Fourteenth Amendment to do even more. His decision in *Masterpiece Cakeshop v. Colorado Civil Rights Commission*, discussed earlier, is scarcely intellectually possible if he had granted protected class status to the LGBTQ community in any of his other gay rights cases. But by keeping the equal protection clause on the sidelines, he had no problem finding that the bigoted baker was the *real* victim in that case.

That's why this jargon matters. It's something that judges and justices can hide behind when issuing rulings that the public would otherwise recognize as facially bigoted. These terms aren't "objective." Judges and justices can manipulate these terms to say, or not say, whatever they want, as their desired outcome requires.

Imagine understanding all of that and concluding that the most important equal protection fight we have on our hands is to make white conservative college professors a protected class. Imagine understanding even half of that and thinking: *But what about discrimination against white people?* Or men. Or some mediocre child of a B-list celebrity who's trying to get into USC? I literally cannot get the courts to agree that intentional state-sponsored bigotry against gay people violates the freaking Constitution, but I'm supposed to stop and consider the class status of discrete and insular white people living in Appalachia who feel left behind by the culture.

White people complaining of "reverse racism" need to help themselves to a number and stand at the back of the line. White people are still too busy legislating bigotry against actual minorities and trying to manipulate the equal protection clause to justify it. Let's fix that first, and then we can talk about various "economic grievances."

15

THE RULE THAT MAY OR MAY NOT EXIST

I have two children. Two little boys. As I write this, they are eight and five, though it often feels like I'm living through a real-life "Team Edward vs. Team Jacob" saga from the Twilight movies. I've got one brooding emo and one loyal hothead, and I'm often being asked to choose between them. One of them smacks the other one during some game neither of them should be playing, and they come to me demanding redress for the perceived injustices that have befallen them.

The five-year-old can handle himself, so I'm always tempted to just let them fight it out. My parenting philosophy is no different than my legal philosophy: everything starts in the Hobbesian state of nature, and I am entitled to some kind of prize for leaving it and entering society.

When dealing with my kids, the prize is quiet. Two boys fighting for physical control of one iPad is a recipe for a lot of noise. So I'm usually convinced to intervene in their conflicts. At least until the other iPad finishes charging.

I try not to be arbitrary. I know that a generation of sitcom dads has popularized the use of arbitrary power by beleaguered parents as a comedic art form, and I can play it that way for a laugh. But, I never want my kids to get comfortable acquiescing to arbitrary power from authority figures. That way lies middle management. I try to indulge them when they complain that something is "not fair." I don't take the easy way out; I don't think I've ever once asked them, "Who said life was supposed to be fair?" I try to explain to them my reasons for this decision or that one, at their level, in terms they can understand. And sometimes, when they point out that a current decision cannot be squared with a past ruling, I let them win. I've been talked into letting them stay up for an extra hour so many times that my eldest treats "bedtime" as the start of negotiations, not the end of his day.

But like I said, my ultimate goal, almost always, is to get them to shut the fuck up. I don't actually care about their fucking problems. They're small children living in a suburban home under a roof that never leaks with a fridge that never runs dry. They don't have "problems." They have an assortment of privileged complaints about the rapidity of their wish fulfillment. My kids literally think they're better off than Prince William's kids, because I've told them (lying, I assume) that the royal family won't let their children have video games. My (idiot) children would *gladly* trade rule of all England for an extra hour of *Super Mario Odyssey*.

Because I want all child-related conflicts to end as quickly as humanly possible, I do not guarantee nearly any rights to my kids. I don't always give them the right to speak, for instance. They certainly have no right against self-incrimination: in fact, they better incriminate themselves, before I find out what they did on my own. And, obviously, they're not entitled to any equal protection. Children are not a suspect class in my house, and "You are the older one so really it's your fault" is a line of argument my eldest is already very familiar with. My kids are going to be shocked when they read the Constitution: they're going to realize that both of their lawyer parents knew about all this stuff, yet consistently denied them basic human rights.

But one constitutional right I try to give them, all the time, is their right to "substantive due process." Rules are indeed supposed to be "fair," and I've decided that my children are entitled to a reliable, consistent, repeatable answer every time I deprive them of life, liberty, or the Nintendo Switch.

I'm going to pause for a moment to allow any originalists reading this to finish cursing and pick up this book that they've just thrown against a wall. They're *big mad* right now, because I've just said that the one constitutional right I give my kids is a thing that they do not believe is in the Constitution.

Arguably, substantive due process flows from the Fifth and Fourteenth Amendments, which both say that no person shall be deprived of "life, liberty, or property, without due process of law."

But there's not a universally agreed-upon definition for what "substantive due process of law" even means. Substantive due process is like an avenging Chupacabra: it might be a kind of dog, it might be a kind of cat, it might not even exist, but when it shows up in the night, it's going to suck the blood out of whatever it thinks deserves it.

I think the least controversial definition of the thing is that substantive due process protects *unenumerated* rights. The Constitution explicitly protects some rights, but it must protect other rights in order for the protection of the explicit rights to make any sense. For instance, the Constitution protects freedom of speech, but it doesn't explicitly protect freedom of sight. And yet, a government policy of gouging out the eyes of political dissidents would seem brazenly unconstitutional. The freedom of the press is not secured "because of Braille." The government shouldn't be able to say: "The

First Amendment is not troubled, for we left them their tongues." We don't need an entire additional constitutional amendment to explicitly protect the right to have eyes. Forced blinding is substantively violative of the due process clause of the Constitution. The end.

As Voltaire might say: "If substantive due process did not exist, it would be necessary to invent it."

That's because substantive due process is really about fundamental fairness. The best way to understand substantive due process is to compare it to the other kind of process, "procedural due process."

Procedural due process concerns itself only with whether the process is fair according to its own rules. Taking a number to be served at a deli is procedurally fair. I take the ticket, the guy behind the counter calls out a number, when he calls out my number, I am served, regardless of my race, color, or creed. Fair. A violation of that procedural due process would be somebody cutting ahead of me in line, or somebody going up when their number was not called and being served anyway. That's not procedurally fair and, in Brooklyn, that may be legal justification for assault (this may be a good time to reiterate that I'm not currently a licensed attorney).

But what if I'm at one of those gentrified delis where, instead of having a person call out the number, they just post it on a screen? And what if I've had my eyes gouged out, because, in this iteration of the multiverse, sight is not fundamentally protected? Does the deli still have a fair process?

Procedurally, yes: I came in, got my number, and had an opportunity to be served when my number came up. Substantively, no: I have no eyes and I'm still hungry. Even though I have no constitutional right to a sandwich, I must have some fundamental right to be served when it's my turn. At the very least, arguing that I was afforded due process by the screen I can't see would be a cruel joke that only Antonin Scalia would find funny.

Substantive due process demands actual fairness, not just technical fairness. Predictably, conservatives hate it. Conservatives reject
a view of the law that guarantees fairness. And conservatives hate
unenumerated rights, because unenumerated rights could be whatever I (or five justices on the Supreme Court) say they are. Today I
claim an unenumerated right to have eyes. Tomorrow I might claim
an unenumerated right to reasonable accommodations should my
sight be taken from me. In the future, I might claim an unenumerated right to have Geordi's visor from *Star Trek* made available to me, free of charge, from a universal health care provider.
"Where does it end?" asks the conservative jurist. What's the point
of winning the birth lottery if the government is just going to step
in and level the playing field? Conservatives are always worried that
protecting too many rights might one day lead to a society that's
fundamentally fair.

What's frustrating here is that conservatives do have a glint of a
point. There must be some limiting principle to the unenumerated
rights protected through substantive due process. It can't just mean
whatever five unelected, unaccountable judges say it means. I don't
have a fundamental constitutional right to, say, have consensual sex
with my mother, right? Surely the same principle that prevents the
state from gouging out my eyes does not require that the state recognize mother-fucking marriages?

You don't even have to slide all the way down to the Oedipal end
of the slippery slope to get to the problem of unchecked substantive
due process. You just need to look at a 1905 case called *Lochner v.
New York*.

The case involved New York's Bakeshop Act, which limited the
number of hours bakers could work to no more than sixty hours in
a week and no more than ten hours in a day. Business owner Joseph
Lochner "permitted" one of his employees to work more than sixty
hours, and was fined under the statute. Lochner objected.

The Supreme Court ruled, 5–4, that New York's statute violated the due process clause of the Fourteenth Amendment by taking away the worker's "liberty" to work himself to the bone for capitalist paymasters. That's not a direct quote, but you take my point. The Court found that the employee had a fundamental right to contract that could not be abridged by a law designed to prevent employers from abusing their workers.

Between 1905 and 1937, courts used *Lochner* logic to invalidate over two hundred regulations on the grounds of violated economic rights. This sad historical period is known as the *Lochner* era, and, had it persisted, the New Deal would never have been a thing. But in 1937, Franklin Delano Roosevelt announced his plan to pack the Supreme Court with justices more amenable to his New Deal, worker-protecting regulations. And, also in 1937, Justice Owen Roberts broke with *Lochner*-supporting conservative justices and sided with the liberal faction to uphold the constitutionality of a minimum wage law. How closely linked these two events were is still a debate among legal scholars that I do not care about enough to have an opinion on. The important thing is that the Lochner anti-worker era stopped.

Lochner is, for the most part, a dirty word in polite legal company. For a long time, both liberals and conservatives agreed that the case was wrongly decided. The revulsion to *Lochner* was such that one could argue that the Warren Court during the civil rights era went out of its way to avoid mentioning *Lochner*, or using the phrase *substantive due process*, while issuing rulings that fit squarely in the framework of protecting rights not specifically enumerated in the Constitution. *Lochner* is sometimes called "anti-canon."

It's a classic liberal mistake: *conservatives used a tool for evil, so instead of using that same tool for good, let's never use tools.* Sometimes, I swear, it can seem like liberals spend all their time inventing ways to get their asses kicked.

Conservatives, on the other hand, are shameless. They say that

Lochner is bad and that substantive due process does not exist, but they will absolutely use Lochner-era logic to come to the Lochner-era conclusion that the only "people" who have rights in this country are corporations.

Indeed, the current conservatives on the Supreme Court are leading a *Lochner* resurgence in their eagerness to, once again, gut labor laws and regulations on businesses. In his article "A New *Lochner* Era," *Slate*'s Mark Joseph Stern describes Samuel Alito's majority ruling in *Janus v. American Federation of State, County, and Municipal Employees*—a 2018 case that severely limited the effectiveness of public sector unions—like this: "Justice Samuel Alito's majority opinion in *Janus* is the most egregious example of Lochner-ism in modern judicial history." He continues:

> *Janus* isn't shy about reviving *Lochner*. Alito's opinion points out that "into the 20th century, every individual employee had the 'liberty of contract' to 'sell his labor upon such terms as he deem[ed] proper.'" To support this proposition, he cites 1908's *Adair v. United States*—a defining decision of the *Lochner* era. Both *Lochner* and *Adair* rested on the premise that the Constitution protects an individual's right to sell his labor at any cost. This doctrine trammeled minimum wage and maximum hour rules, as well as laws safeguarding workers' right to unionize. *Janus* restores this premise in a slightly altered form, replacing "liberty of contract" with "associational freedoms." The upshot is the same: Laws designed to benefit labor's ability to act collectively are inherently suspect.

This is why conservatives cannot be taken at their word when they argue that substantive due process doesn't or shouldn't exist. Every time he decides to open his mouth on the subject, the notoriously reticent Clarence Thomas writes something like what he wrote in a 2011 case called *Perry v. New Hampshire:*

> [T]he Fourteenth Amendment's Due Process Clause is not a "secret repository of substantive guarantees against 'unfairness.'"

But did Thomas sign onto Alito's opinion in *Janus?* Of course his hypocritical ass did. He signed on in full: he didn't even write a concurring opinion reiterating his legally famous line about what the Fourteenth Amendment really means. Thomas, and the rest of the conservatives, absolutely believe substantive due process exists; they just think the Fourteenth Amendment is hiding rights for businesses they think are people, instead of minorities they wish were not.

If conservatives had a limiting principle for substantive due process, I'd listen to it. But they don't really; they just have a limiting principle on who should benefit from its existence.

Basically, conservatives treat the due process clause as if it's an evil djinn. It technically has to grant you three wishes—life, liberty, and property—but it hates you and is constantly trying to interpret your request in the most literal, least generous way so it can deny you the benefits of the very thing you asked it for. "You asked for the right to marry, you didn't say anything about the right to start a family: request for adoption denied, gay people. Mwahahaha."

Meanwhile, liberals treat the due process clause like it's the genie from Aladdin. Not only will it grant you your wishes of life, liberty, and property, it'll grant you whatever you need to make those things actually work. The genie wants to be your friend and wants to help you live your best life. Just don't let Samuel Alito steal the lamp, or else he'll use the genie to rule on high as the most powerful being on Earth.

I'll stipulate that neither of these approaches is perfect, but what kind of sick bastard thinks conservatives have the better view of things? What kind of wounded soul thinks that the conservative version is the way things are supposed to work?

For my part, I will keep telling my children that substantive due process is a thing. I will keep giving them the right to fairness.

Recently, my boys were playing the video game *Minecraft* together. My five-year-old likes to play *Minecraft* in the creative mode, where you just run around, gather supplies, and build things. My eight-year-old likes to play in survival mode, where many things can kill you and you mainly build things to stay alive. The five-year-old can't keep up in survival mode, so they were fighting. The older child came up with what he thought was an elegant, fair solution: they'd split their *Minecraft* hour, half of the time in creative mode, and the second half in survival mode. The eldest even agreed to let the youngest take his creative half hour first, which made him feel particularly magnanimous and smug.

Overhearing this deal from another room, I rushed in to tell them no. The five-year-old, I said, "has a right to enjoy his video game time without getting murdered." It's not easy to explain substantive due process to an eight-year-old, but damn it, I tried. It is important that they understand that technical equality is not necessarily fairness, and that sometimes such procedural equality can even be the opposite of fairness.

I'll keep trying. I'll keep trying to get them to think about rules substantively instead of procedurally. I'll keep trying to make them into the kinds of people who are outraged at unfairness, instead of desensitized to the suffering of others. I'll do whatever I can think of to make sure they grow up to be anything other than like Clarence Thomas.

16

THE ABORTION CHAPTER

No, the right to an abortion is not explicitly guaranteed in the text of the Constitution. Nowhere in the main document, or its twenty-seven amendments, does it say "Congress shall make no law restricting a woman's right to choose." Moreover, the right to privacy—from which reproductive rights, including the right to contraception, stem—is also not in the text of the Constitution. There's no amendment saying "The right to privacy shall not be abridged."

If you think that matters, I can't really help you. Of course reproductive rights are not textually enshrined in the Constitution. The white men who wrote the Constitution did not think women were people deserving of the same political, civil, and social rights as men. They didn't allow women to vote, didn't allow them to own property, and didn't allow them to sit on juries or hold public office. They thought girls could be married off, against their will, to secure social or political favors from other families. Once married off, they thought wives could be beaten and raped. *Marital rape* was an oxymoron *until the 1970s*, to give a sense of what is and is not *textually* protected in the Constitution. Every state in the union had laws making an exception to rape if the rapist and victim were married. The last of these marital rape exception laws didn't come off the books until 1993.

And that's how the men who wrote the Constitution treated the women they liked. Those were the rules for white women. Black women could be raped with total impunity and sold for higher prices to the white men most interested in raping them some more.

Did these white men perhaps care about children? No, they did not. Children, the ones who survived infancy anyway, could be put to work in the fields or beaten with sticks if they misbehaved. Again, girl children could be married off at the behest of their father. And, despite hobbling the economic opportunities for women and mothers, the framers of the Constitution provided no social safety net whatsoever for widows and orphans. Protecting children was just not something the framers thought the federal government had the power to do (put a pin in that thought).

And again, that's how white men treated children they liked. We know how they treated children they didn't like. Black children were no more than profit centers. Labor to be raised for the market like a lamb to be fattened for slaughter.

Horrifically, that view often extended even to the slavers' own children who were the offspring of violent rapes. The white men who founded this country were perfectly willing to let their own children, conceived in hate, be born into bondage.

It's a feature of chattel slavery, as practiced in the Americas, that scarcely has a historical analogy, and I think is too easily overlooked. White slavers regularly treated their own bastards as slaves. White neo-Confederates love to point out that "slavery" was practiced throughout much of the world, throughout much of human history, but this idea that slavery was a condition you could *inherit from birth* was not common in ancient slave-loving Rome or other slave-based societies. That idea was market-tested and industrialized in the New World.

Here, white Americans were not demanding that their bastards join the clergy, as was common in Europe. Or the army, as was common in the ancient world. Or defend a seven-hundred-foot-tall ice wall from zombies, grumkins, and ice dragons. Here, they were enslaving their own bastard children, condemning them to some of the most brutal bondage the world had ever known. And grandchildren. And also, of course, the children and grandchildren of every other enslaved woman who happened to get pregnant.

So, tell me again why I should care which rights these vicious assholes happened to think women had. Tell me again why the failure of these fucking rapists and/or rape apologists to recognize any explicit right to bodily autonomy should matter one bit to the polity in which we now all live. Don't you dare say "the rights of the unborn" to me. Don't you dare fix your lying mouth to tell me that these people who condemned their own progeny to bondage and torment, for the sin of being conceived in the womb of a colored woman—a woman they would continue to work and rape while she was pregnant with their child—gave one damn about the health and safety of "the unborn."

If we're going to talk about the constitutional right to an abortion, we're going to talk about it from first principles. And the first principle that the people who wrote the Constitution missed is that women are people. Full, equal, people. If you believe that, and I know a lot of men don't, but if you believe that women are people, then the right to privacy and all the reproductive rights that flow from it is a fairly straightforward thing.

The right to privacy was first recognized by the Supreme Court in a 1965 case called *Griswold v. Connecticut*. The case dealt with an 1879 Connecticut statute that banned the use of any drugs or medical devices that could lead to contraception. In 1961, Estelle Griswold, then the head of the Connecticut branch of Planned Parenthood, and Yale School of Medicine gynecologist C. Lee Buxton opened a birth control clinic. They counseled married couples on birth control and prescribed the best methods for those couples.

Their clinic opened on November 1, 1961. They were arrested on November 10, 1961.

Would these two have been arrested if they were handing out, say, condoms to single men, instead of birth control pills to married women? It's hard to say. I think the right answer is "absolutely not," but "probably not" could be more accurate. Consider that the Connecticut law in question is what's known as a Comstock law, which refers to a slew of federal laws and state laws that were passed during the U.S. Grant administration.

Anthony Comstock was an "anti-vice, Christian reformer," which I guess is a nice way of saying that he was such a tight-ass he could crush a lump of coal into a diamond. The man was apparently revolted by the "vice" he witnessed in New York City—especially advertisements announcing the availability of contraceptives—and made it his mission functionally to destroy everybody's good time.

I just don't get these people like Comstock, who we see again and again throughout human history. I don't understand these people who look at two consenting adults fucking and think, "Oh no, something must be done about this!" Who are these people, and how are there always so many of them? No matter what society you live in, there are deep social, economic, and political problems that need to be addressed. And yet there are *always* some people in that society who are willing to ignore all of those problems and make it their life's work to stop two people from getting busy in a Burger King bathroom. Of all the things to care about, some people invariably choose to care about recreational sex or the possibility thereof. Clothes were a fucking mistake. They send the wrong message.

Anyway . . . Comstock was successful (of course), and in 1873 Congress passed what came to be known as the Comstock Act, which made it illegal to use the federal mail to disseminate "obscene" materials. That included shipping contraceptives—including birth control or condoms—across state lines, as well as using the mail to distribute things like racy letters. I'm not joking: the Comstock Act made sexting illegal back when sexting required two weeks of delayed gratification and legible penmanship. Then they made Comstock a goddamn postal inspector! I'll bet all the money in my pocket that Comstock was "reviewing" potentially violative letters with a gallon of whale oil under his desk and a handkerchief.

The Comstock Act was then buttressed by a number of state laws making obscenity and contraception illegal in the various states, including the 1879 law passed in Comstock's home state of Connecticut.

None of these laws seemed violative of the Constitution by the people who passed them. And remember that the generation that passed the Comstock laws was the same generation that passed the Reconstruction Amendments. One of the clear failures of the Reconstructionists is that they remained unreconstructed sexists. Comstock himself was a Union infantryman in the Civil War. There's no original public meaning of any of the amendments that supports a right to contraception.

Still, by the time of *Griswold* in 1965, many of the Comstock laws had been scaled back. Margaret Sanger, the founder of Planned Parenthood, fought Comstock laws in court throughout the 1920s and '30s, and won some rights for women to use "birth control," a term she is largely responsible for coining. It also must be said that Sanger was an inveterate racist who sometimes tried to sell birth control as part of a larger eugenics plan eventually to eliminate the "Negro race."

So let me say once again, for the people in the back: I do not give one wet shit about the original intent of white folks. Their motives were horrible. Their intentions, barbaric. The public they allowed to have a voice well understood the horrible, barbaric meanings of their laws. And none of it should inform what rights we now have today, unless you are interested in bringing back the shitty, monstrous societies created by long dead white people.

The rights Sanger and others gained for women's contraceptives paled in comparison to the rights men had to control their reproductive decisions. During World War II, despite the statutory prevalence of various Comstock-type laws, condoms were distributed to every man in the military. Personally, I have little doubt that if Griswold and Buxton were handing out condoms and spermicide, nobody would have arrested them for violating a law that was nearly one hundred years old by the time they opened their clinic.

But they weren't just handing out condoms. Because on May 11, 1960, the Food and Drug Administration approved the first birth control pill.

At the risk of stating the obvious, and devolving into some cishet gender norms just because I'm talking about archaic legal restrictions written only with such norms in mind, condoms still leave much of the reproductive choice with the man. He can put one on, or not. Yes, of course the woman can ask or demand condom use, and men are supposed to respect that demand. But men weren't always even legally bound to respect such wishes in 1960. Again, marital rape wasn't even an illegal thing until the lifetimes of most people reading this book. Condoms, fundamentally, still give men a large amount of control over the decision to reproduce.

But the pill shifts reproductive choice back to the woman. It's not just about "liberating" women to have recreational sex (though it certainly does that), it's about giving women control over their reproductive systems. The pill allows the woman to decide if she wants to have kids (or additional kids), not her husband or lover.

The man doesn't get a vote, and (if she can get the pill and keep it secret) the man can't legally force her to bear his child. The man doesn't even get to know. Armed with the pill, a woman has just as much physical power to veto reproduction as a man.

That's why Griswold and Buxton were arrested after just ten days. It's not because they were handing out contraceptives; it's because they were handing out equality.

If you proceed from the premise that "women are people," the idea that women-people have a constitutionally protected right to control their own reproductive system is entirely obvious. Men-people get to do it. Even beyond the obvious point that biological men can engage in any sex act they like without risking having to pass a bowling ball through their penis nine months later, the facts on the ground show that men can get access to more or less reliable contraceptives even when laws ostensibly prohibit them. If a soldier could get a pack of condoms before whoring his way through Paris in 1945, denying his wife a birth control pill in 1960 seems like a point-and-click violation of the equal protection clause of the Fourteenth Amendment.

If I had decided *Griswold*, it would have been maybe a three-sentence opinion:

> Women, being people, have a right to control their reproductive system, as men-people do, through the use of contraceptives, which men-people seem to always be able to get their hands on when they really need to fuck a prostitute while on shore leave. This right flows from the Fourteenth Amendment's guarantee of Equal Protection, which we now recognize includes the right to have sexual intercourse without internal reproductive consequences. We note that men-people have technically enjoyed this right to sex-without-

incubation for five-to-seven million years, depending
on when you start the clock on anatomically modern
humans.

But the actual Court, by a vote of 7–2, took the scenic route to
get to the right result in *Griswold*. Instead of deciding the case on
equal protection grounds, the white guys on the Supreme Court
did their usual thing of acting like the Connecticut contraception
ban was "facially neutral" even though it plainly was not in either
force or effect.

Instead of equal protection, Justice William O. Douglas divined
a right to privacy from the so-called penumbras of other constitutional amendments. This is from his majority opinion: "The forego-
ing cases suggest that specific guarantees in the Bill of Rights have
penumbras, formed by emanations from those guarantees that help
give them life and substance. . . . Various guarantees create zones
of privacy."

I know it sounds made up. Every liberal in law school has been
dunked on by some facetious conservative dickhead (it's always a
man) who incredulously asks which rights are emanating from a
liberal penumbra today.

But I explained substantive due process before I started talking
about the right to privacy for exactly this reason. Remember, in
1965, *substantive due process* was still a dirty phrase, made guilty
by its association with the *Lochner* era. What Douglas is doing
here is applying substantive due process logic in a place where it is
entirely appropriate. Many of the rights explicitly protected in the
Constitution don't make sense unless this unenumerated right to
privacy is also protected. What good is a protection from unreasonable *searches* if there is no protection from being unreasonably
monitored? What good is the right to form an association, if the FBI
can just wiretap any meeting it doesn't like? What freedom do we

really have if the government can shove a camera up your hooha to see if there's any funny business going on?

Of course privacy is a thing. The Constitution scarcely makes sense without it. Conservatives who mock the right to privacy are ironically the same people who think homeowners can shoot people to death should somebody invade their "castle." The right to privacy is just a substantive function of the due process clause. Douglas is just calling it something else because he doesn't want to use that phrase.

Justice Byron White was not as bashful. His concurring opinion states:

> In my view, this Connecticut law, as applied to married couples, deprives them of "liberty" without due process of law, as that concept is used in the Fourteenth Amendment.

None of the justices adopts my equal protection framework. Because, you know, once you start giving women equal protection of laws, the whole damn patriarchy starts to crumble. You'll note that *Griswold* applied to married women; it took a while for the court to extend its logic to unmarried women, but that extension would have happened immediately under an equal protection framework. God forbid they gave women suspect class status, triggering strict scrutiny of discriminatory laws and practices. Then they might even have to start paying women equally.

The decision not to give women protected class status or an equal protection right to contraception does matter, not so much for *Griswold*, but because of another case: 1973's *Roe v. Wade*. You've probably heard of it. But, in case alien archaeologists are reading this book (please, O Great Singularity, let this be the tome on late-republic American law they find, and not some trash written by

Antonin Scalia), *Roe v. Wade* recognized a constitutional right to abortion under the right to privacy and the due process clause of the Fourteenth Amendment. The Court's logic in *Roe* is the same as the Court's logic in *Griswold*, but in *Roe* the Court went out of its way to recognize a "legitimate state interest" in limiting abortions for the benefit of the health of the mother and "protecting the potentiality of human life."

Here's that part from the majority opinion of Justice Harry Blackmun:

> We repeat, however, that the State does have an important and legitimate interest in preserving and protecting the health of the pregnant woman, whether she be a resident of the State or a nonresident who seeks medical consultation and treatment there, and that it has still another important and legitimate interest in protecting the potentiality of human life. These interests are separate and distinct. Each grows in substantiality as the woman approaches term and, at a point during pregnancy, each becomes "compelling."

With respect to the state's important and legitimate interest in potential life, the "compelling" point is at viability.

You see what they did there? Remember, discriminatory laws are okay if they are rationally related to a "legitimate" state interest. Laws discriminating against suspect classes are okay if they are narrowly tailored to address a "compelling" state concern. Here, the Court is basically saying that most abortion restrictions after the first trimester are okay, and at fetal viability, nearly any can be justified.

It's almost like the protected class here is the fetus, and not the born, human, woman-person whose body is attached to it.

All of that came to a head in 1992 in *Planned Parenthood v. Casey*. It's *Planned Parenthood*, not *Roe*, that actually defines abortion rights in this country, such that they are. At issue were a host of abortion restrictions legislated by the state of Pennsylvania in the late '80s. They included "informed consent" before having an abortion (which mainly just involves some asshole trying to talk the woman out of her decision), waiting twenty-four hours before getting the procedure (again, just making people feel bad about it), obtaining parental consent if the patient is a minor (because, you know, anytime you can make teenage pregnancy harder, why not), and requiring married women to notify their husband before having the procedure (I already explained what anti-contraception laws are really about).

The Supreme Court, 5–4, upheld the fundamental right to an abortion, as articulated in *Roe*, but created a new standard for abortions. The Court asked if state abortion restrictions created an "undue burden" on women seeking the procedure prior to viability. It defined *undue burden* as a "substantial obstacle in the path of a woman seeking an abortion before the fetus attains viability." The majority (which included a woman on the Supreme Court for the first time in history, Justice Sandra Day O'Connor) determined that all but the husband notification passed this new test. Everything else—the informed consent, the waiting period, treating women like they're hysterical children who are about to cut their own hair without fully appreciating what they're doing—all of that stood.

I'd slam the majority more, but the dissenters would have overruled *Roe* altogether. I guess infantilizing women is better than turning them into incubators with mouthparts? The Republic of Gilead knows no bounds, I suppose.

The conclusion of *Planned Parenthood* is impossible to reach if you start from the principle that women are people and thus entitled to the same people rights as men. I say that even to those who think that the fetus is a person entitled to some rights. That's because we never, ever, limit a man's access to medical care based on how it will impact any other person. No man is ever denied medical care because of how that care might affect somebody else. You could be a fucking rapist and still get treated for erectile dysfunction. They never say, "I won't help you mask your genital herpes until I receive a signed consent form from your sexual partners." John Wilkes Booth broke his leg while (wait for it) shooting the goddamn president, and a doctor (rightly) set his leg so he could hobble on with his escape.

Where the fuck was his twenty-four-hour waiting period?

Forced-birth activists always like to tell stories about the growing fetus. *At thirty weeks it can cry tears like Jesus and think, "Why doesn't Mommy want me?"*

But instead of anthropomorphizing the fetus, let's never lose sight of the actual person in this story, the woman, and what the state is trying legally to force her to do.

Most women won't know they're carrying the state's legitimate interest for the first couple of weeks, but once the state's interest disrupts their menstrual cycle, a simple home test can detect the invasion of the state. By six weeks or so, the woman might start becoming violently ill. As the state's interest grows, a woman's bones will soften and her joints will stop functioning properly. By the end of the first trimester, she'll have created an entirely new organ, the placenta, which will start leaching nutrients from her bloodstream and feeding it to the state's interest. To compensate, the woman will start producing up to 50 percent more blood to transport oxygen around the body. Some of that extra blood can pool in weird places and be uncomfortable.

By the second trimester, most women can feel the state's interest kicking at them from the inside. I'm told that it's not particularly painful, but what is painful is the back pain. Women are putting on roughly a pound a week at this point, and the human back isn't really designed to carry the excess weight brought on by the state. It can also become difficult to sleep; the woman may experience leg cramps and heartburn, and she'll need to urinate frequently as the state's interest pushes some of her other organs out of the way and crushes down on her bladder.

By the third trimester, when the state's interest has developed from "legitimate" to "compelling," the woman who bears it will have trouble traveling, working, or just moving around easily. Given her burdens, one might expect the state to take a more active role in providing care and money to the woman so that its compelling interest may have its best chance at success. But the state does not. Many women continue to work so that they may provide for the state's compelling interest out of their own pockets. Many countries encourage women to take time off from work at this point, but in America we provide no federally mandated financial assistance to women bearing the state's interest to term.

Childbirth is still the ninth leading cause of death among women aged twenty to thirty-four in this country, and that itself is an amazing success story. In the not-too-distant past, childbirth killed many more women and is still today the leading cause of death for young women in parts of the developing world. That's because, if everything goes well, after about nine months or so, the state's compelling interest will erupt from its female host, tearing through her vaginal cavity in an experience so painful that the woman's brain will actually release drugs into her neural system in hopes that she doesn't fully remember the severity of what she experienced once it's over. The experience is so painful because of a basic design flaw in *Homo sapiens*: the baby's head is almost too big for the human birth canal. Humans are the only mammal that can't regularly give live birth alone. Women need help to do it.

Or so I've heard. I'm a man so I don't have to worry about the state renting out my insides until its compelling interest stretches my dick like a snake vomiting a live pig. Hell, I even stayed "north of the border" for the birth of my two kids. But, from what I've heard, it sounds bad. It sounds like the kind of thing a legitimate government could never even ask a person to do, much less force a fully human person to do if they were unwilling. If somebody ever got me pregnant, I'd punch him right in the fucking mouth and demand an abortion under my *Eighth* Amendment rights against cruel and unusual punishment.

Planned Parenthood's framework doesn't even make sense if you assume that women are people and thus deserving of equal protection. There is no framework that justifies denying them medical care, or balancing their access to care, because of the "state interest" in forcing them to engage in unwanted labor. No other operation of law forces a person to painfully change their body and reconfigure their organs because of a state interest in the results of that transformation.

It is wrong to force a woman to give birth to a baby she doesn't want. And I say that assuming that she consented to have sex in the first place, and that giving birth wouldn't actually kill her. It's barbaric to force a woman who had consensual sex to carry an unwanted pregnancy to term, even if she can carry that fetus to term safely. I don't even have a word for what it is to force a rape victim to carry her assailant's baby to term at the risk of her own life. I don't think there is a word for that.

But you rarely hear even liberals talk about abortion this way. Especially if you listen to liberal white men. The white male liberal talking point on abortion has been that it should be "safe, legal, and rare." Even Tim Kaine, Hillary Clinton's running mate in 2016, has talked about it that way. Liberals consistently fail to articulate an equal protection argument for abortion rights. They cede the "legitimate state interest" ground.

Conservatives talk about abortion like they're on a righteous crusade to stop a baby holocaust, while male liberals talk about it like they're embarrassed and sorry somebody knocked up the cheerleader, but now here we are.

That's why abortion rights are under constant attack. It's not because the attacks are legally any better than what conservatives usually do. Their legal argument against abortion is the same as their legal argument against gay marriage and the same as the legal argument in favor of the death penalty. It's all one monster: they believe in a country that is limited to the best available thoughts of racist, long dead, white men.

No, what makes abortion difficult is not some fancy lawyering from the right, but the near refusal to defend it from the left. The hard sell is almost always left to women and "abortion activists," while men scramble around trying not to piss off a diner in Ohio. I can turn over a rock on Twitter and find some person with no legal training able to passionately explain why segregation is wrong, or why the death penalty is immoral, or how "love is love." But ask people about abortion and it's all, "Well . . . I think the important thing is that women get to choose for themselves! Retweet if you agree!"

Don't get me wrong, "choice" is great. It's a fine frame. It's a language designed to appeal to people who have a genuinely held religious belief about when life begins, and even the word *choice* should remind those adherents that not everybody shares their choice of God either, and yet we co-exist.

But the better legal frame is "Forced birth is some evil shit that can never be compelled by a legitimate government. The end."

Hell, if you don't like my Eighth or Fourteenth Amendment arguments in defense of abortion rights, I could give some *Thirteenth* Amendment arguments. Because the same amendment that prohibited slavery *surely* prohibits the state from renting out women's bodies, for free, for nine months, to further its interests. Forced *labor* is already unconstitutional.

17

YOU KNOW THIS THING
CAN BE AMENDED, RIGHT?

The astute reader will have noticed that a central theme of this book is that conservatives are irredeemable assholes who consistently act in bad faith to uphold white supremacy and patriarchy over the objection of most minorities, women, and decent people.

But perhaps I am wrong about them. Perhaps conservatives simply promote an inert theory of constitutional interpretation because they genuinely believe that legislatures—the "people's" body—is the appropriate place to enshrine "new" fundamental rights. Perhaps conservatives are not desperately committing to *upholding* white male supremacy and patriarchy, they just honestly believe that the only legitimate way to move beyond our white male supremacist roots is through additional amendments recognizing our evolution as a society, as opposed to interpreting old ones with modern sensibilities.

That's certainly what conservatives will tell you they're doing. The ones who can at least be sufficiently shamed into admitting the deep and abiding unfairness and bigotry of their pet interpretational theories always use the amendments process as an out. "Oh, it's not that I think the state should invade a person's home, drag them out of bed, and subject them to humiliation and jail because they engaged in a consensual sex act with a person of the same sex. Goodness, no! It's just that pesky Constitution that doesn't prohibit the state from doing that. It's a shame, really. If only there were some amendment that allowed me to put a stop to it."

But even here, this fallback position of the allegedly reasonable conservative can be shown to be a lie. Because the people who believe in the most shallow and vindictive version of the Constitution are never at the vanguard of amending it.

Here's how the amendment conversation always goes:

Conservative: "Turns out, this machine I'm driving stabs gay people in the face."

Reasonable Person: "Oh my God! Turn it off."

Conservative: "Can't."

Reasonable Person: "What do you mean you can't? You're in the goddamn driver's seat."

Conservative: "Won't."

Reasonable Person: "Why?"

Conservative: "Look, we need this machine to get where we're going."

Reasonable Person: "Who is the we?"

Conservative: "Those of us allowed to drive."

Reasonable Person: "It just stabbed Bob in the face!"

Conservative: "Yeah. Sucks for Bob. If only there was something we could do."

Reasonable Person: "STOP DRIVING IT."

Conservative: "Can't. Oops, sorry, I mean won't. Hey, maybe you could fix it?"

Reasonable Person: "It can be fixed?"

Conservative: "Maybe. Here's the manual."

Reasonable Person: "Okay, it says here that if you and I turn these two keys at the same time, it will stop stabbing gay people. Here's your key."

Conservative: "Thanks." [swallows key]

Reasonable Person: "Oh my God, why did you do that?"

Conservative: "I don't think it needs to be fixed."

Reasonable Person: "It just stabbed Jillian in the face!"

Conservative: "See, it's working as intended."

Reasonable Person: "HELP ME FIX IT!"

Conservative: "Can't. Haha. I mean won't. Whatever. Fuck Jillian."

If they really thought that the organizing document of American self-government didn't, on its face, protect gay people having sex in their own home, or protect Black people from driving without police harassment, or protect women who get a prescription from their doctor, then wouldn't they spend nearly their whole life trying to change such an obviously flawed document? If conservative judges felt they were being forced, for purely doctrinal reasons, to deny fundamental fairness to worthy litigants, wouldn't they spend all their free time begging the people to update the document that binds them to upholding unjust laws?

But we don't see them doing that, do we? We don't see conservative justices demanding a better, more fair Constitution than the one they claim we're stuck with. Instead we see these justices regularly giving talks at fundraising dinners of the Federalist Society, praising the limitations and cruelty of the current Constitution, promising to rule for more of the same, and vowing to defeat the "liberals" who imagine the country as something better than it is. We see the conservative politicians who appoint and confirm conservative judges constantly argue against the amendments that would bring fairness and equality to the document their judges have decided doesn't already include it. And we see conservative jurists, throughout American history, work to limit the scope and effectiveness of what amendments have been passed to make us a more perfect union.

Maybe conservatives don't want the Constitution fixed. Maybe conservatives aren't being entirely intellectually honest when they claim to prefer new amendments to secure rights. Maybe they just don't believe that some people deserve rights at all. Maybe conservatives limit the amendments that should give gay people and Black people and women-people equal rights, because conservatives don't want them to have equal rights.

How many times does the hunter have to shoot Bambi's mom before we stop blaming the deer that got in the way and turn our attention to the person who pulled the trigger?

Nowhere is the intellectual dishonesty of the conservative movement more obvious than in the fight over the Equal Rights Amendment.

Throughout the 1960s and '70s an effort was made to amend the Constitution explicitly to recognize the equality of the sexes. An

Equal Rights Amendment was first proposed back in 1923. The goal was to eliminate legal distinctions between men and women.

By the 1970s, the proposed text of the amendment read:

> Section 1: Equality of rights under the law shall not be denied or abridged by the United States or by any State on account of sex.
>
> Section 2: The Congress shall have the power to enforce, by appropriate legislation, the provisions of this article.
>
> Section 3: This amendment shall take effect two years after the date of ratification.

This is the version of the ERA that finally passed the House of Representatives in 1971. In 1972, the U.S. Senate passed it and submitted it to the states for ratification.

It never made it. The conservative movement, organized under lawyer Phyllis Schlafly, prevented it from being ratified by three-fourths of the states' legislatures, as required to amend the Constitution.

Now, my read of the Constitution tells me that the Equal Rights Amendment is redundant. Remember, I think that the equal protection and due process clauses of the Fourteenth Amendment do *all* the work. Of course women are entitled to equality under the law. Of course that includes employment rights, health and safety protections, and the economic right to equal pay for equal work. Of course women have the substantive right to control their own bodies, including their reproductive system, and to access medical care.

I support the ERA, because sometimes you have to really dumb things down for men to get it. But if you ask me, the Equal Rights

Amendment was ratified in 1868 and the problem is that white guys have spent the last 150 years trying to undo it.

If you don't agree with me—if you *don't* think that the Fourteenth Amendment provided for the full political, civil, and social equality of women—then how in hell are you against the ERA? How can you possibly think that women don't already have equal rights because of your limited, originalist interpretation of the Constitution, but also don't think the Constitution should be changed to right this clear wrong that your interpretation has created?

Unless, at core, you don't think women should have equal rights at all.

The denial of equal rights was what motivated the anti-ERA movement. Schlafly's organization, called STOP, an acronym for "Stop Taking Our Privileges," argued that the ERA would end the gender privileges "enjoyed" by women: like "dependent" wife status for social security benefits, women's restrooms, and exemption from the draft.

Schlafly employed the same two tactics that conservatives always do when attacking equal rights. She reduced equal treatment to "same" treatment and fought most desperately over social equality instead of political or civil equality. This is what conservatives do. This is what they always do. Schlafly had a neat little twist—arguing that social inequality *benefited* women instead of harming them—but even that is not new. Conservatives love arguing that the people they oppress are well taken care of by the oppressors. One prominent conservative once said: "Slaves that worked there were well fed and had decent lodgings provided by the government, which stopped hiring slave labor in 1802."

That quote isn't from a Southerner who was about to beat John Lewis, or former Confederate president Jefferson Davis. That was former Fox cable news host Bill O'Reilly, describing the slaves who built the White House. He said that in 2016. It only sounds like it could have been said by a long-dead conservative, because conservatives have been making the same shitty arguments for all of American history.

In any event, the "privileges" that Schlafly wanted to "stop" the ERA from taking were white women privileges, naturally. Shirley Chisholm, who in 1972 became the first Black woman to run for president, was not the beneficiary of the social privileges Schlafly was so worried about losing. Indeed, her fight to be taken seriously by the political establishment was contemporaneous with Schlafly's fearmongering about what women's "liberation" would mean for America.

Even Schlafly's most effective attack—saying that the ERA would lead to the compulsory draft of women into the armed services—is the kind of thing that is centered in whiteness. Putting aside the issue that an actual draft which fairly called upon all citizens and didn't exempt rich white boys with bone spurs might be the only thing that could arrest this country's habitual global warmongering, the fact is that women and Black women in particular have long broken the infantilizing social mores against women in service. A Pew Research Center report conducted in 2011 found that between 1973 and 2010, the number of active-duty enlisted women grew from 42,000 to 167,000. Over 30 percent of those women are Black. That's despite Black women accounting for only about 13 percent of women in America as a whole.

The world that Phyllis Schlafly despaired for white women already exists for Black women. All that's missing is explicit legal protection for their health and economic rights. Help Black women or get out of their goddamn way.

None of this is to say that conservatives are dead set against *any* amendments to the Constitution. They're generally down for damn near anything that can be used to prevent the government from helping people: a balanced-budget amendment, a line-item veto. If you can show how your amendment will restrict the government's ability to meet modern challenges, the Federalist Society will at least take you out to lunch.

But when it comes to expanding rights, there's really only one amendment that conservatives are interested in: a fetal personhood amendment.

I wouldn't call it mainstream, even given how radicalized mainstream Republicans have become. But there is a movement afoot to amend the federal Constitution, or at least state constitutions, to recognize the unborn as "people" entitled to certain rights. Some of the very same people who would deny a woman equal protection under an Equal Rights Amendment would like to grant those rights to the fetus she carries.

And, like a bizarro image of the ERA fight, there are some hard-core conservatives who will argue that an original interpretation of the Constitution grants personhood rights to fetuses already. Conservative thinker Ramesh Ponnuru has argued that the Fourteenth Amendment should be read to ban "unborn homicide."

Some people may be familiar with modern conservatives invoking the 1857 *Dred Scott* decision as something they're personally against. George W. Bush, during a 2004 debate against Senator John Kerry, mentioned that he thought *Dred Scott* was wrongly decided, in an answer to a question about what kinds of judges he would appoint (Bush would later go on to appoint Justices John Roberts and Samuel Alito). The *Dred Scott* decision famously, and wrongly, held that slavery was legal even as applied to a Black man who had been living free for a number of years. The chief justice at the time, Roger Taney, said that Black people had "no rights that the white man was bound to respect."

I'm happy that conservatives (now) think the *Dred Scott* decision was a bad beat, but given that we now have the Thirteenth Amendment, I'd like to think that the chattel slavery question is no longer a live constitutional issue.

Yet some conservatives argue that *Roe v. Wade* is the intellectual doppelgänger of *Dred Scott*. They argue that the Court in *Roe* found that the unborn had no rights that (actual) people are bound to respect, and they argue that the ruling is every bit as erroneous as the one upholding slavery. They think that the same amendments that functionally overturned the *Dred Scott* decision can and should be used to overturn *Roe v. Wade*, or they're willing to introduce an entirely new amendment to do the work.

To quote TV president Josiah Bartlet: "Your indignation would be a lot more interesting to me if it wasn't quite so covered in crap." How dare the fetal personhood brigade, last seen ripping breastfeeding children away from their mothers at the border, lecture me about the rights of the unborn. How dare they equate the bondage, rape, and torture that was American human chattel slavery to the failure of a clump of cells to implant in a uterus after a woman takes a drug cocktail a few weeks after accidental conception? The supposed rights of the unborn hold no moral suasion in a society that is willing to consign children who are born alive to poverty, malnutrition, and toxic air and water. I am unmoved by the alleged moral clarity of people who throw around the term *anchor babies* and are willing to deport children who have lived in this country for decades because they were brought here "illegally" as babies. These hypocrites want to make rights attach at conception, but not citizenship and representation in the census. These would-be moralists can fuck all the way off.

Their legal arguments are no better than their moral ones. Because fetal personhood amendments aren't really about some kind of theoretical right "to become life." If they were, activists would be busy trying to bring the hundreds of thousands of embryos lying abandoned in frozen stasis at our nation's fertility clinics to life, which they're not. No, what the conservatives want is forced incubation of fetuses by women who are unwilling to perform the work.

There is an amendment that addresses that concern. It's the Thirteenth. It reads:

> Neither slavery nor involuntary servitude, except as a punishment for crime whereof the party shall have been duly convicted, shall exist within the United States, or any place subject to their jurisdiction.

As I've said, the right to an abortion is not even controversial as long as we proceed from the premise that women-people are people. Fetal personhood laws cannot overcome the Thirteenth Amendment's prohibition on involuntary servitude, if we accept that a woman is a person who cannot be forced to labor.

And that's how the law works for actual alive children who do have personhood rights. We do not force a parent to care for their children. If they agree to care, we impose standards of what that care must entail, but if they want to opt out, and both parents agree, we let them. Giving your kid up for adoption is not illegal. If one parent is committed to raising the kid, we ask the other parent to provide some kind of minimal financial assistance. But if both parents are down for adoption, the child becomes the state's problem.

Seeing as the state can't even find enough willing parents to take care of all of its born wards (especially if those wards happen to be Black), I doubt it can find enough willing wombs to make unborn personhood anything more than involuntary servitude, though I suppose it's welcome to try. But forcing a woman to undergo nine months of incubation and labor is a rather obvious violation of her Thirteenth Amendment protections.

I can prove that. After conception, the developing embryo is sustained by the woman's ovum, or egg. This is why an embryo can be (relatively) easy to create and develop in a laboratory; it has something to eat. But embryos can't live on personhood yolk forever, so the woman's body starts building an entirely new organ, the placenta. When fully developed, by about the end of the first trimester, the placenta will leech nutrients from the woman's bloodstream and "feed" it to the developing fetus through the umbilical cord.

Legally, we treat the placenta as the woman's, just like any other organ in her body. She has legal ownership of it, and that's important, because after birth, there are some options for what to do with it. Some women eat it. Others freeze it or donate it to science, because emerging research suggests that placental cells can be useful in the treatment of certain childhood diseases. Most women allow the hospital to discard it.

The placenta is not alive, and never will be. The woman doesn't need it. It seems to me that, if a woman is a person, she has the right to remove an unnecessary organ from her body. Certainly if the placenta malfunctions, as in the case of preeclampsia, which can cause liver or kidney damage, it would seem that the woman should have every right to remove this needless organ that is affecting her health. Nobody makes a constitutional case over an appendectomy.

If I seem flippant about the whole thing, it is because the legal argument that a fetus has a legal status on par with the woman to whom it is literally attached is illogical trash sprinkled with bad faith and misogyny. Fetal personhood amendments are the state writing a check it cannot cash, then forcing women to cover the bill against their will. It cannot be done in a "free" society. The Thirteenth Amendment flatly prohibits forced labor, and it doesn't have an exception for labor that white men won't do themselves but think is really important for others to do for society.

When it comes to amending the Constitution, conservatives still haven't figured out how to grant personhood rights to all of the born people. If you think it's really important for fetuses to become people, then, by all means, make one yourself.

18

THE RIGHT TO VOTE SHALL BE ABRIDGED ALL THE DAMN TIME

The right to vote is nowhere in the original Constitution or its Bill of Rights. That makes perfect sense when you consider what the people who founded America were trying to accomplish. You can't run a great Western slave experiment if you give just anybody the right to participate in the republic. You can't create a male-dominated society if you give women the right both to have an opinion and to voice it. Come on. What the hell kind of country do you think we were created to be? A "free" one? Do you also believe in flying reindeer who are happy to help and a North Pole that recognizes the right of labor to organize? Wake up! The Elf on the Shelf isn't getting time-and-a-half, my friend.

Beyond the obvious and purely evil reasons for denying the right to vote to women, Blacks, and indigenous Americans, the founders had theoretical concerns about extending suffrage even to all white men. Some of those concerns were legitimate and even prescient. The founders were worried about the uneducated masses voting for idiots and con men more interested in the accrual of power than the functioning of government. They were worried about these demagogues inflaming the passions of the majority and using it to trample minority rights.

Anybody want to tell them they were wrong? The founders didn't want poor, uneducated white men to vote, because they pretty much anticipated that poor, uneducated white men would elect a person like Donald Trump. If only they had fully empowered women and minorities, and especially minority women, to counteract their "economically aggrieved" brethren, the country they founded might be less of a mess today.

Of course, the eighteenth-century American revolutionaries, like their seventeenth-century English revolutionary predecessors, and their later eighteenth-century French revolutionary successors, were all basically from the same class of white men: the wealthy bourgeois. From a certain point of view, rich people never have a problem with monarchy; they have a problem with *hereditary* monarchy. Throughout history, regicidal motherfuckers tend to show up when rich people can't buy their way into more power than they were born into. It's all really a *game of thrones*, if you will. And our founders were more Lannister than Stark: just a bunch of rich people rebelling against a "mad king," who weren't really interested in freeing anybody but themselves.

On top of all of that, aside from their political philosophy and moral failures, there was no operational reason for the Constitution to talk about voting at all. From the founders' perspective, voting rights didn't flow from the federal government; citizenship, and the rights and responsibilities thereof, flowed from the states. So a person—well, a white man—wasn't a citizen of the United States of America so much as a citizen of Georgia or Connecticut or whatever. It made sense to the founders that voting rights would be left up to the states, and they saw no inherent problem with those rights being different in every state.

One way to tell the story of America is as a two-and-a-half-century, ongoing struggle to fix their error. The Fifteenth, Nineteenth, Twenty-Fourth, and Twenty-Sixth Amendments all either directly expand the voting franchise or remove restrictions to voting on new classes of people.

- The Fifteenth Amendment says the right to vote shall not be abridged on account of race.
- The Nineteenth Amendment says the right to vote shall not be abridged on account of sex.
- The Twenty-Fourth Amendments says the right to vote shall not be abridged for failure to pay a poll tax or any other tax.
- The Twenty-Sixth Amendment says the right to vote shall not be abridged on account of age, provided that the voter is at least eighteen years old.

That's a lot of work. That's four of the seventeen amendments ratified after the original Bill of Rights. That means nearly 25 percent of our constitutional updates since the founding of the country have been expended on trying to secure and expand the right to vote. And that's not counting the Seventeenth Amendment, which allowed for direct popular election of senators instead of appointments by state legislatures. That's amazing, especially when you consider that without the right to vote there is no way to participate in the passage and ratification of these amendments that expand the franchise. People have had to use *persuasion* to secure their rights, because they were excluded from actually participating in the votes on whether they would be allowed to vote.

On paper, our gradual expansion toward universal suffrage has been a success story of written constitutional government. That's how everybody learns about these amendments in school. "America used to deny voting rights to nonwhites and women, but now everybody can vote. Yay."

Except that schoolhouse story is a lie. The truth is that the expansion of the franchise has been resisted and undercut by the judicial branch and conservative politicians at nearly every turn. I take a dim view of our ability to amend the Constitution into a more perfect document, because I know too well what courts can do to a freaking amendment they don't like. I am too aware that an amendment that the president refuses to enforce, or one that Congress refuses to flesh out with legislation, is not a solution—it's merely a suggestion. Amendments are just as useless in the face of dedicated white supremacy as anything else.

We have not lived one day in this nation, we have not passed through one election, where all four of the voting rights amendments were made real by Congress and enforced by the executive branch to their fullest potential. Conservatives have never accepted the proposition that "everybody gets to vote now" and so they've turned voting rights into a game of constitutional whack-a-mole. There's always somebody, somewhere, whose voting rights conservatives figure out how to suppress.

Nobody even tried to enforce the Fifteenth Amendment from the time Rutherford B. Hayes pulled troops out of the South until the passage of the Voting Rights Act in 1965, and even then white people were still willing to crack the skulls of Black people who tried to vote. Because the Fifteenth Amendment has rarely been enforced, the Nineteenth Amendment has done very little for Black and brown women trying to vote. While the Twenty-Fourth Amendment did a fair job of eliminating a direct poll tax (until Florida reinstituted one for ex-felons who now need to pay legal fees before they can vote again), the "or other tax" part of the amendment has largely been forgotten, clearing the way for all sorts of economic barriers to voting or registering to vote. And the Twenty-

Sixth Amendment? Sure, go ahead and register to vote, young buck. Just tell me where, because depending on where you live and where your parents live, you may or may not meet residency requirements of the county where your college is located. And your dorm might technically be in a different county than the main campus, so check up on that. Also, I hope you have a driver's license because your college ID might not cut it. And you have your birth certificate, right? Every kid keeps a copy of that lying around, don't they?

At least eighteen-year-olds can vote. People who are seventeen cannot, even if they turn eighteen between the election and the end of the year. The Twenty-Sixth Amendment doesn't require it to be that way; it's just an arbitrary cutoff the states have decided to run with.

Oh, and did I mention that 230-odd years after the founders punted this issue to the states, and 150-plus years since the Fourteenth Amendment made citizenship a federal grant, we're still operationally running voting rights through the states? Yes, for reasons that are at this point intentionally stupid, we still don't have one federal election system; we have fifty state electoral systems for federal office holders. When you can register to vote, whether you can vote early, whether you need ID, what kind of ID you need, whether you can vote absentee, whether you can fix or "cure" an absentee vote that has been rejected for a clerical error, whether you have to specify party affiliation to vote in a primary, whether there will be a runoff after the general election, and damn near everything else that has to do with "the right to vote" is determined by each of the individual states.

Our electoral system is madness. And it's madness on a good day. It would be madness when all involved are acting in good faith to try to help people access their rights. But in this country, we have one party—the Republicans—who have decided to act in bad faith and exploit aspects of the madness to suppress and discourage people from voting based on the color of their skin. As I've said elsewhere, conservatives don't take constitutional amendments as a denouncement of their racism; they take them as a challenge to become more creative in their bigotry.

Nowhere have conservatives succeeded in ignoring the Constitution as much as they have with neutering the Fifteenth Amendment. If all the amendments were in high school, the Fifteenth Amendment would be the kid who gets stuffed in a locker every day. Conservatives try to avoid picking fights with the Fourteenth Amendment. Hell, when it comes time to discriminate against women who want access to health care, they'll even try to invite the Fourteenth over to their keg party. But they'll give the Fifteenth Amendment a wedgie while waterboarding it in the toilet just for the entertainment value. They bully it all the time.

The one time the Fifteenth Amendment fought back was in the aforementioned 1965 Voting Rights Act. The Fourteenth Amendment has been supported through all kinds of legislation, notably the Civil Rights Acts of 1866, 1875, and 1964. But the Voting Rights Act was the first time Congress really put its back into making the Fifteenth Amendment a thing. Because of that, to my mind, the Voting Rights Act is the most important piece of legislation in American history.

It does a lot. It bans creating a discriminatory "standard, practice, or procedure" for voting, and it gives victims a right to sue in federal court over any discriminatory restrictions. It specifically bans a "test or device" used to prohibit voter eligibility, which functionally bans things like literacy tests or other inventions white governments would use to deny the vote to Black citizens. It bans voter intimidation. It guarantees that votes have to be *counted* without discriminatory intent, a rule that the Republican Party evidently forgot in the aftermath of the 2020 presidential election.

In 1982, the Voting Rights Act was amended to prohibit not just discriminatory intent, but also discriminatory effect. That means that the old conservative trick of passing facially "race neutral" laws that deny equality under the cover of "sameness" is not something conservatives can do when it comes to voting. And it doesn't just prohibit voter "denial" on the basis of race; it bans voter "dilution." The Voting Rights Act makes it illegal to gerrymander away the voting power of Black communities by submerging their votes within majoritarian white districts.

And that's all just one part—Section 2—of the Act. Section 5 of the Voting Rights Act requires certain jurisdictions that had a history of racially discriminatory voting procedures to ask the federal government's permission before changing their election laws. This scheme is called "preclearance."

Preclearance is dope. It's just a fantastic way to keep states honest. Normally it takes a lot of time to overturn an onerous state law, even one that is unconstitutional on its face. You have to wait for the right "victim" to be harmed by the law, one who has what lawyers call "standing," to sue the government. Then that victim has to suffer some identifiable harm, because courts only engage in actual "cases or controversies." They do not issue advisory opinions; they can't say "That law looks like it's going to be unconstitutional" until the dubious law is applied to someone in violation of their constitutional rights. Even once those structures are in place, the litigation can take years before the law is overturned by the Supreme Court or the relevant regional courts of appeal overseeing that state. And even that assumes courts aren't controlled by conservatives and therefore willing to overturn racist laws in the first place.

Preclearance shortcuts that whole process. Under a preclearance scheme, states have to get permission from the federal government, usually the Department of Justice, to change their laws *before the fact*. While the federal government will allow the states to get away with a lot of racism, especially if the government is controlled by modern Republicans, the president and the Justice Department are accountable to all of the people, not just racists interested in denying the vote to Black people. Preclearance has been one of the most effective schemes in stopping states from enacting discriminatory voter suppression.

Which is why it no longer exists. Conservative judges will find a way to do racism. They literally always have. There is no law, rule, or constitutional freaking amendment that will stop them.

In this case, it took conservatives a while to shove the Fifteenth Amendment back in a locker. Longer than ever before. But they overcame the Fifteenth Amendment again in 2013. To put it in *Clue* form: The deed was done by Chief Justice John Roberts, with a majority opinion, in *Shelby County v. Holder*.

The *Shelby County* case involved a challenge to Sections 4 and 5 of the Voting Rights Act by Shelby County, in central Alabama. Section 4 basically determines which counties are required to get preclearance before changing their voting laws, under Section 5. Republicans argued the "coverage formula" described in Section 4—which was reauthorized by Congress in 2006 and promoted by noted non-carer-about-Black-people George W. Bush—exceeded Congress's authority under the Fourteenth and Fifteenth Amendments.

Writing for a 5–4 majority, Roberts determined that the coverage formula in Section 4 was unconstitutional. His logic, essentially, was that racism had been sufficiently defeated in the South, thus requiring certain counties to submit themselves for preclearance was no longer necessary. From his opinion:

> It was in the South that slavery was upheld by law until uprooted by the Civil War, that the reign of Jim Crow denied African-Americans the most basic freedoms, and that state and local governments worked tirelessly

to disenfranchise citizens on the basis of race. The Court invoked that history—rightly so—in sustaining the disparate coverage of the Voting Rights Act in 1966. . . .

But history did not end in 1965. By the time the Act was reauthorized in 2006, there had been 40 more years of it. In assessing the "current need[]" for a preclearance system that treats States differently from one another today, that history cannot be ignored. During that time, largely because of the Voting Rights Act, voting tests were abolished, disparities in voter registration and turnout due to race were erased, and African-Americans attained political office in record numbers. And yet the coverage formula that Congress reauthorized in 2006 ignores these developments, keeping the focus on decades-old data relevant to decades-old problems, rather than current data reflecting current needs.

There are a few obvious errors with Roberts's logic. The first, and most problematic error, is that racism has not been defeated. Racism in voting has not been defeated. White people have been hanging "Mission Accomplished" banners on every courthouse since Appomattox, declaring victory over their own bigoted filth, and they're always wrong. There are white people in Alabama today who are every bit as racist as white people in Alabama in 1965, who themselves were every bit as racist as white people in Alabama in 1865, or 1787, or 1619.* Roberts is just rewarding racist white people who have learned not to say the n-word aloud when suppressing the votes of Black people.

The second error is that when racism is defeated, Roberts and his

---

* Maybe not 1619 because the Cherokees were busy keeping racist white people out of Alabama back then.

Supreme Court will be the last guys to know. I mean that's how our government is literally supposed to function. It is on Congress—you know, the people we'd be allowed to vote for if not for white guys like John Roberts—to declare victory over racism. All the courts are supposed to do is determine when Congress violates our constitutional protections against racism. In Shelby County, Roberts is limiting Congress's legislative authority under the Fifteenth Amendment to the scope of his own personal opinions about when racism is really "bad." If the Federalist Society were an organization that stood for anything more than white supremacy, they'd hate this Roberts opinion way more than his decision to uphold the Affordable Care Act as a tax. Because this decision takes power directly away from Congress and places it in the sociological musings of unelected justices.

Lastly, to the extent that Alabama is slightly less lynchy of Black people trying to vote now than they were forty years ago, it is because of laws like the Voting Rights Act. Ruth Bader Ginsburg, may her memory be a blessing, in probably her best dissent of her many outstanding ones, put Roberts's willful ignorance on blast. She wrote: "Throwing out preclearance when it has worked and is continuing to work to stop discriminatory changes is like throwing away your umbrella in a rainstorm because you are not getting wet."

Roberts's decision to destroy the coverage formula of Section 4 effectively gutted Section 5 of the Voting Rights Act. Clarence Thomas, in a concurring opinion, argued that the Court should have ruled Section 5 unconstitutional on its face too, because Clarence Thomas doesn't think racism is "over" so much as he thinks the government should be powerless to stop it. But Roberts's opinion does more than enough of the work. It is practically impossible to think of a Section 4 preclearance formula that would satisfy Roberts's *Shelby County* logic enough to revive Section 5.

His opinion purposefully opened the door to all manner of voting rights restrictions, and Republican politicians took full advantage. Voter ID laws went supernova. Polling locations in predominantly Black communities were closed. When you see lines of Black people waiting hours and hours to vote, you can largely thank John Roberts for these scenes of racism.

And he hasn't gotten nearly enough blame for it. Everybody knows that the Supreme Court made George W. Bush president in 2000 with its ruling in *Bush v. Gore*. But most people don't realize the Court made Donald Trump president in 2016 with its ruling in *Shelby County*. The voter suppression unleashed by that decision is what made it possible for Trump to eke out his narrow electoral college victory in that election.

Never forget, Black people are not evenly distributed throughout the country. Most Black people still live in the states where their ancestors were enslaved. The state with the highest population of Black people, per capita, is Mississippi. (It would be the District of Columbia, if DC were a state, but white people, in their infinite self-interest, have declined to extend statehood to a territory that is nearly 50 percent Black. I wonder why.) After that it's Louisiana, followed by Georgia, Maryland, South Carolina, and Alabama.

Do you know how different this country would look if the Black voters in those states enjoyed frictionless access to the ballot? Joe Biden defeated Donald Trump in the 2020 general election in Georgia by 11,779 votes. That's out of nearly 5,000,000 votes cast. That margin is functionally entirely due to people like Stacey Abrams and LaTosha Brown, and organizations like Fair Fight Action and Black Voters Matter.

Black voter suppression is a biological imperative for white supremacy. It is a survival strategy. White supremacists, and the political parties and organizations that support them, have no plan to convince Black voters of their point of view. Oh, white supremacists have tons of plans and arguments to attract a healthy minority of Latinos and Asians or other more recent immigrant groups. But they ain't got nothing for Black people. A few Blacks will always vote for Republicans on the "if you can't beat 'em, join 'em" line. But in the main, the only strategy white supremacists have to deal with Black political concerns is to suppress their votes so that they cannot effectively voice those concerns.

That's why the Fifteenth Amendment continues to walk these halls with a giant "Kick Me" sign on its back. That's why all of the voting rights amendments either are left to wither on the parchment, or are so weakened that they can support only the most literal and reductive version of voter protections imaginable.

Suppressing the vote, no matter what the Constitution says otherwise, is the prime directive for conservative jurists. It's why they get appointed; it's the credential that is even more important than a hostility toward abortion. Voter suppression is what binds a Trump judge to a Bush judge to a Bush 41 judge to a Reagan judge.

They can't win any other way.

19

WHAT IF YOUR VOTE ACTUALLY DIDN'T MATTER?

The first Republican I met in real life was former congressman and one-time Senate candidate Rick Lazio, when I was in my tweens. I mean, I'm sure I had technically met Republicans before then. My family didn't socialize with Republicans (a tradition I have maintained), but I'm sure I had an elementary school teacher or coach or something who was a registered Republican. But Lazio was the first person I interacted with who was an "official" Republican, you know? The first person who made his living off of being Republican whom I met in the flesh.

Unfortunately, a lot of people remember Lazio from his failed Senate campaign against Hillary Clinton in 2000. He was doing okay in that race, until the debate. During his showdown with Clinton, Lazio left his podium and approached hers, haranguing her to sign some kind of campaign finance pledge he pulled out of his pocket.

The stunt backfired badly. It will be hard for people reading this in the post-Trump era to understand, but in the before times, in the long, long ago, a candidate bullying another candidate onstage was considered bad form. Republican voters used to belong to a political party instead of a deranged cult, and, for some of them, the appearance of interpersonal brutishness mattered. Lazio started falling in the polls after that debate, bounced back, but ultimately lost that race.

From where I sit, Lazio got a bad rap. I can't speak to his debate etiquette, but I can vouch that he's great with kids. When I met him in 1991, we were in a literal smoke-filled "room where it happens." My father was the chief legislative aide for a woman named Maxine Postal, who was a Democrat in the Suffolk County (Long Island) legislature. Lazio, who had been a district attorney, was a newly elected Republican in that legislature. A failure of childcare required my father to bring me to work right after he picked me up from football practice, and he let me sit in on his redistricting meeting if I promised to keep my mouth shut.

As most people know, the Constitution requires a census every ten years. Here's Article 1, Section 2:

> Representatives and direct Taxes shall be apportioned among the several States which may be included within this Union, according to their respective Numbers, which shall be determined by adding to the whole Number of free Persons, including those bound to Service for a Term of Years, and excluding Indians not taxed, three fifths of all other Persons. The actual Enumeration shall be made within three Years after the first Meeting of the Congress of the United States, and within every subsequent Term of ten Years, in such Manner as they shall by Law direct.

Sorry, I left in the original constitutional language because that's what those founding assholes wrote. But I'll note the "three fifths" language has been amended.

After that census, the states redistrict to account for the new numbers. Some states lose members in the House of Representatives. Others gain. The number of representatives had been set at one member per 30,000 people, but in 1929 the number of House members was locked at 435 people, where it still sits today. So states trade house seats back and forth now. Redistricting often happens at the local and county level too, after the census.

In 1991, the Suffolk County Legislature was redrawing its lines, and my dad was in the middle of that battle. He had a real feel for this stuff; my childhood house was always cluttered with maps. And push pins. And string. It all came together on one giant map my dad had in his office: a street-level view of all of Suffolk County with pins and string denoting where the lines were, where they should be, and where they would be if Republicans let him have his way.

Ms. Postal was white, as were all the legislators at that time. But my dad was Black, and the reason he was invaluable in the redistricting process was that he knew where all the Black and brown people lived. All of them, I once thought. When I was a kid I thought my dad knew every time a new minority family bought a house anywhere in the county. At the meeting I attended, my dad's instruction to shut up was irrelevant; nobody was getting a word in over my father anyway.

But that was partially because everybody was waiting for Lazio. In the car on the way over, my dad explained he had two main goals: he wanted to move one pocket of Black people into Ms. Postal's district, essentially turning her "winnable" district (centered around Amityville) into a "safe" district for Democrats and putting it on the path to becoming a majority-minority district. And he wanted to move another pocket of Latinos mainly out of Lazio's district (where Republicans were crushing it anyway) and move them into one where Democrats were more competitive. But he couldn't get that without "fucking Lazio's" signoff.

Lazio was late. Probably intentionally, because it sent my dad into some kind of rage. I was sitting by the door and had become bored listening to my dad literally scream at people while pointing to a version of his giant county map, now at the center of the room. I couldn't even really see the middle of the room through all the cigarette and cigar smoke. But I was the first person to notice Lazio quietly come into the room, though I didn't know that this was the man my dad had been screaming about. Lazio sat down next to me and asked, "So, that's your dad?" At first I thought, "How did he know?" before remembering I was the only other Black person in the room. Since my father was in full tilt about something, I deflected and said, "No, my dad is Doc Gooden."

We talked for about five minutes—about the Mets and how I was liking school—before my dad brought us back to reality. He yelled, to no one in particular, something like: "If Rick isn't here in five minutes, I'm taking his Dominicans and his balls."

"You talk like that in front of your son?" Lazio piped up.

Unfazed, my dad says: "I talk like that in front of my fucking daughter, if I fucking feel like it." He was telling the truth.

"Time to go to work, kid," Lazio says to me, before standing up and joining the group at the center of the room.

As I recall, Lazio was amenable to my dad's proposal for his district. I kept waiting for Lazio to turn heel, as I had been taught he would, but he never did. Indeed, the person really getting screwed over was a Republican in the district the Dominicans were going to, and he wasn't even in the room. But Lazio had bigger plans than the Suffolk County Legislature. From what I was told by my father later, the real issue Lazio was fighting over was that he couldn't be seen as obviously screwing over a fellow Republican by dumping a bunch of Democrats into his district.*

My dad and Lazio worked out some kind of deal. On his way out, Lazio gave me a high five and said, "That's our version of the big leagues."

On the car ride home, my dad explained that Lazio had kept as part of his district a section with a current high population of Latinos (a group Lazio did well with) but was willing to give away a bigger section that was just turning into a cognizable Dominican neighborhood. Meanwhile, everybody let my dad cannibalize the lion's share of a Black community (parts of Wyandanch, to those listening to Billy Joel at home) into Ms. Postal's district.

I suppose it was a win-win. Lazio would be elected to Congress just two years later and was the darling of the New York Republican Party for a time. Meanwhile, after one more round of redistricting in 2001, Ms. Postal's district became winnable for a Black representative. When she passed away, my dad ran for her seat, and in 2004, he became the first Black person elected to the Suffolk County Legislature. I could describe my late father's profession in a lot of ways, but "a gerrymanderer" would be among the most accurate.

The term *gerrymandering* conjures images of smoke-tinted rooms filled with power-hungry politicians splitting up or smushing together entire communities to protect their own political interests. And it is certainly that. But, as an indelible mark from my upbringing, I've come to understand that drawing straight lines

---

* I reached out to Lazio about this reapportionment, over the course of writing this book. He mentioned that while he didn't remember this specific meeting, he remembered being amenable to the split to further the legitimate interest in creating a majority-minority legislative district for a Latino candidate. And he mentioned the somewhat obvious point that is often missed by other Republicans: the party should be more interested in investing in and promoting Republicans of color. Lazio didn't think a majority-minority district was an instant Democratic district.

and pleasing geometry on a map isn't fair either. "Sameness" does not equal "fairness." My dad could draw a legislature where all the districts looked "the same," that Republicans could never win control of, despite having a significant advantage in voter registration in his county. Or he could squiggle out a legislature that would make Pythagoras cry, which was nonetheless a fair representation of all the county's voters. He could do both in a night with the right bottle of scotch.

The problem with geometric integrity and keeping "towns" together is that there is a whole bunch of racism, segregation, and classism baked into where people live. Both current and legacy housing discrimination, for instance, leads racial and ethnic minorities generally to live in densely populated clusters in whatever areas allowed them to buy homes or rent property. Sometimes those clusters overlap town lines; sometimes those clusters abruptly stop wherever some bank decided Black people shouldn't own homes.

I currently live in Westchester County, New York. South Westchester is, essentially, the Bronx in terms of racial and economic makeup. Other parts of Westchester look like something out of an F. Scott Fitzgerald novel. I'm one of three Black families on my street, which also includes a white cop, and a couple I assume are gay because the two ladies who live there pull out a rainbow flag every time a different neighbor unfurls his over-large American flag on the Fourth of July. Whether my congressional representative looks more like Alexandria Ocasio-Cortez or Jay Gatsby has little to do with where I live, and more to do with whether I'm districted with people who live five minutes south of my house, or five minutes north.

Unfortunately, the process of drawing districts that lead to a fair representation of the voters in a legislature is the exact same process as the one used for drawing districts that lead to the effective disenfranchisement of voters. Gerrymandering is like fire: it's just a tool that can cook dinner or burn the house down. The real trick is to keep it contained.

Given the awesome power of gerrymandering to illuminate or functionally destroy democratic self-government, you'd think we'd have very clear legal rules on what is allowed, and what is prohibited. But we don't. The Constitution is silent on how districts are to be drawn, in part because the power to shape districts is clearly in the purview of state, not federal, law. Also because the founders didn't think political parties would really be a thing (a founding flaw in the document we've never really gotten over), and because they restricted the vote so much that the question of underrepresented racial or ethnic minorities just wasn't on the table at the Constitutional Convention.

Despite the lack of any constitutional guidance, the Supreme Court has had to weigh in on the constitutionality of various gerrymandered maps again and again. It's not going to come as a galloping shock to anybody that gerrymanders became a constitutional issue because the South, as usual, refused to stop being racist. I'm basically running out of ways to express how thoroughly the South ignored the Fourteenth and Fifteenth Amendments after Rutherford B. Hayes took the Union foot off their necks, but here again, the moment the South had an opportunity to disenfranchise Black people, white Southerners disenfranchised Black people by apportioning districts so that only people living in white areas mattered.

It was only during the civil rights era that racist gerrymanders were successfully challenged in court. This happened in a 1962 case called *Baker v. Carr*. Tennessee apportioned its state legislature in 1901 and then, never again. Suffice it to say that the 1901 map locked in an advantage for white people living in Tennessee. Civil rights activists argued that Tennessee's map was a violation of the equal protection clause of the Fourteenth Amendment.

The Court ruled that the equal protection claim was a "justiciable" constitutional issue—which just means that the claim is something federal courts are allowed to rule on—and agreed to hear the case. That was huge because, up until then, states had argued that gerrymandering was a state concern that triggered no federal constitutional issues (as the founders surely intended) and that gerrymanders were a "political question" inappropriate for the Court to rule upon. It's not like we want courts picking the winners and losers of elections, right? Right, *Bush v. Gore*?

But here, the Supreme Court ruled that it did have the power to rectify issues of state administration when the state was in violation of constitutional principles. Earl Warren himself said that *Baker v. Carr* was the most important case decided after he was appointed to the bench.

A lot of gerrymandering cases have been in front of the Supreme Court since *Baker v. Carr*. Excavating sixty-odd years of gerrymandering jurisprudence to tell a coherent story about where we are and how we got here is beyond my narrative and (probably) cognitive powers. It's like trying to explain the final battle in *Avengers: Endgame* to someone who didn't see all the other Marvel Cinematic Universe movies. ("Captain America can use Thor's hammer that was destroyed by his sister, but Thor recovered when he went back in time to visit his dead mother. Cap made it budge once, so this makes sense.") Matters are further complicated because the Supreme Court slightly changes its mind nearly every time a new justice joins the bench. Take my word for the following:

- **Negative racial gerrymanders:** not okay. Courts will not let state legislatures draw maps to target and disenfranchise racial minorities. These maps are thought to violate the Fourteenth Amendment.
- **Positive racial gerrymanders:** sometimes okay. Maps

drawn to ensure majority-minority districts, in the name of encouraging diverse representation in the legislature, are subjected to strict scrutiny. That means the state needs to show a "compelling" interest for the racially gerrymandered map, and the map must be "narrowly tailored" to achieve that interest. It's a tough standard, but some racially gerrymandered maps can meet it. Functionally, the only "compelling" state interest courts will recognize is the Voting Rights Act of 1965. But if you can sell your map as "necessary to enforce the Voting Rights Act," and the districts drawn are contiguous and not outright bizarre, courts may allow it.

- **Political gerrymanders:** always okay. The Court has a long history of trying to look the other way when maps are drawn purely to benefit one party over the other, even when those maps are demonstrably unfair. A 2019 Supreme Court decision fully unleashed legislatures dominated by one party to do their absolute worst with the maps. In *Rucho v. Common Cause*, Chief Justice John Roberts ruled that "political" gerrymanders were "nonjusticiable," meaning that federal courts had no authority to stop the states from doing what they wanted.

While the rules seem logical on paper, they really make no sense on the ground. Nobody ever writes "This is a negative racial gerrymander" or "This map is necessary to keep uppity Negroes in their place" in the margins on their map. White supremacist mapmakers are not stupid. In fact, a lot of negative racial gerrymanders can be sold as positive racial gerrymanders. Creating one super-majority-minority district is actually a great way to keep minorities out of all the other districts.

In many cases, the difference between a positive and negative racial gerrymander comes down to the good faith of the politicians involved. People like my dad and Rick Lazio were trying to *enhance* representation for underrepresented people.

But what if they had been doing the other thing? Would anybody have even noticed the difference? How could I even prove they were doing the other thing? How do you prove the absence of good faith that animates a negative racial gerrymander?

Unfortunately, as we've seen time and again, conservative justices require their racists to self-identify as such. They require specific, "magic" words or even more explicit actions. Even here, in a field of law where the Fourteenth Amendment's guarantee of equal protection and the Fifteenth Amendment's right to vote are the only constitutional principles that matter, conservatives still act like disenfranchising or diluting the votes of minorities is something that just kind of happens without the "bad" intentions of anybody involved.

That willful ignorance is most shamelessly on display when conservatives try to erect bright-line distinctions between racial gerrymanders and political gerrymanders. As of the *Rucho* decision, the courts aren't even allowed to look at political gerrymanders, but racial ones, even ones designed to enhance diverse representation, may still be struck down by courts.

But the distinction between political gerrymanders and racial gerrymanders doesn't exist when you're inside the map room. When politicians are trying to draw a Republican district or a Democratic district, they're looking at everything: party affiliation, voter registration rolls, housing or rental prices, race, color, creed, church-to-strip-club ratio, all of it. To think that they're looking only at "political" factors and not "racial" factors requires one to be more naive than I was when I was twelve. To think that there is even a meaningful distinction between "political" factors and "racial" factors requires one to be more naive than me, and white.

Looking at all factors is how politicians get to know the difference between a politically "safe" district versus a competitive one in the first place. And these gerrymanders are getting more accurate—thereby locking in one-party domination—all the time. At least human politicians could be wrong. I said that it *felt* like my dad knew whenever a Black person bought a house in Suffolk County. But he didn't actually.

Zillow does. Target knows when you're about to have a baby. Facebook . . . I don't even want to know what Facebook knows about me, but it probably knows when I'm going to die, and which current twenty-five-year-old I will end up voting for in the last election before my death. With modern technology and "big data" at their fingertips, politicians can now gerrymander down to the cul-de-sac.

Left unchecked, Republican state legislatures will use that power to disenfranchise racial minorities. That's not a guess; it's just literally what Republicans already always do whenever given the slightest opportunity. Thanks to John Roberts, they'll say their maps are "political" gerrymanders: it's just a coincidence that Black people happen to overwhelmingly vote for Democrats, because Democrats seem to be the only party that can go four years at a stretch without giving aid and comfort to Klansmen.

Like everything else involving gerrymandering, the same thing causing the problem can in fact be the solution. Computers and big data have thrown gasoline onto the gerrymandered campfire, but they can also douse the flames and take the human inclinations toward racism and power grabs out of the equation. Programs can tell us how representative a legislature is of its constituents, how much it should be, and draw the maps accordingly. I don't understand all the math on this, but I also don't need to understand all the math on how a GPS works to trust it enough to turn left when it tells me to. There is a technocratic solution now to this decennial democratic battle.

But conservatives don't like math either. Conservatives like John Roberts don't want to rely on math, they don't want to rely on the Fifteenth Amendment, and then they don't want to rely on the Voting Rights Act. They just want to let Republicans disenfranchise Black voters, call it "political," and hope history misses their role in the centuries-long oppression of Black people in the New World.

On the car ride home from my first gerrymandering meeting, I couldn't understand how they could just "let" my father and a couple of other guys decide who was going to win the legislature for a decade. And then I remembered that my dad was staff and not an actual elected official. "What happens when they don't invite you to these meetings?" I asked.

"Black people get fucked," he answered. At the time, I thought he was bragging. I was only twelve.

20

ABOLISH THE ELECTORAL COLLEGE

I've spent the last few chapters explaining why even amending the Constitution is generally pointless in the face of arch-conservative Supreme Court justices determined to continue the legacy of bigotry and oppression this country was founded upon. But there is one amendment that would immediately end one of the most obvious structural features of white supremacy in this country: Abolish the Electoral College.

And while we're at it, it would be great to abolish the Senate. I don't mean "abolish the Senate" the way a Roman Emperor would have uttered it. Republican self-government is good, or at least better than strongman despotism. The problem is that the United States Senate is not an exercise in republican government; it's a prophylactic to *prevent* republican self-government.

Every state gets two senators. Every state has the same representation in the Senate. And that is straight-up not fair. Tying representation to the land as opposed to the people living on it is, among other things, fucking stupid. North and South Dakota (combined population of about 1.6 million people) have four senators in total, while New York *City* has 8 million people and gets, like, a large say in the two senators that the 19.4 million people living in New York *State* are allotted. Queens (population 2.2 million) should have four senators if the Dakotas do.

Not that New Yorkers can really complain. Washington, DC, gets zero senators.

As most people know, the structure of the Senate is the result of the "Great Compromise" or "Connecticut Compromise" at the Constitutional Convention in 1787. Smaller states were worried about being controlled by larger, more populous states. The South in particular was worried about losing the privilege to work and rape Black people to death. The compromise provided that one chamber of the legislature, the House of Representatives, would be apportioned based on population, while the other, the Senate, would give equal representation to each state.

To put it another way: white slavers feared "democracy" so much that they wrote it out of the Constitution. Keep in mind that at the founding, the limited group of white male landowners who were allowed to vote weren't even allowed to vote for their senators. State legislatures picked their federal senators, thus further insulating the Senate from any direct democratic accountability. We didn't move to direct popular elections of senators until 1913 with the ratification of the Seventeenth Amendment.

Conservative defenders of the Senate as an institution (and it's almost always conservatives, in either party, who defend this intentionally antidemocratic institution) abandon any pretense of originalist arguments to explain the continued justification for the Senate. They'll say that the Senate gives strength to rural interests that would otherwise be overpowered in a direct democracy. But that argument is a little thin. The Senate functionally ignores rural voters in high-population states with dense city populations. The

Senate doesn't even really empower rural voters in low-population states. It mainly empowers city voters lucky enough to live in low-population rural states. Again, land doesn't vote. If white people in Des Moines and Dubuque voted like white people in Portland, and Salem, and Eugene, Iowa would be every bit as blue as Oregon.

There is a real urban versus rural divide in this country, but the Senate isn't designed to favor rural voters. It's designed to favor white people. As the country rushes toward becoming a majority-minority nation, the Senate acts as the ultimate refuge for white power. That's because people of color are not evenly spread throughout the country, and because the Senate is, by its nature, a "winner take all" system. As long as white people make up a plurality of voters in a state, and as long as white people stick together in that state, white people get to control both of the state's allotted senators.

That basically explains the modern South. I've mentioned before that the states with the most Black people by percentage of the population remain, largely, the states where Black people were enslaved. Here are the ten "Blackest" states (or, in the case of DC, nonstate), by percentage of population, according to a 2018 projection for the 2020 census:

1. Washington, DC (45.99 percent)
2. Mississippi (38.40 percent)
3. Louisiana (33.43 percent)
4. Georgia (31.47 percent)
5. Maryland (31.23 percent)
6. Alabama (27.19 percent)
7. South Carolina (26.91 percent)
8. Delaware (23.08 percent)
9. North Carolina (21.97 percent)
10. Virginia (20.48 percent)

You'll note that Black people make up a majority in none of those states. In the House, Black people still have a chance to be represented by a congressperson from their minority district—at least they do in theory, depending on how bigoted the gerrymandering of those districts is. But in the Senate, you win statewide or you win nothing at all.

Hiram Revels, Blanche K. Bruce, Edward Brooke, Carol Moseley Braun, Barack Obama, Roland W. Burris, Tim Scott, William "Mo" Cowan, Cory A. Booker, Kamala D. Harris, Raphael Warnock: that is the full and complete list of African Americans to serve in the United States Senate in the history of this country. That's eleven people. Revels and Bruce were appointed to the Senate by Reconstruction Southern legislators while the slavers weren't allowed to hold office. Burris, Scott, and Cowan were initially appointed to their seats by governors. Only six Black people in American history just went out and won a U.S. Senate seat via popular vote (though Scott eventually won a reelection campaign). Black people have had more prophets than goddamn senators.

The structure of the Senate is racist. It inherently promotes majoritarian white concerns over those of everybody else. And that structure cannot be changed, even through constitutional amendment. That's because, get this, the people who agreed to structure the Senate in this patently unfair way provided that its structure was the one thing that could never be changed. Article V of the Constitution, which describes the process for amending the document, has this to say about the Senate:

> [A]nd that no state, without its consent, shall be deprived of its equal suffrage in the Senate.

Ain't that something? To amend the structure of the Senate the people who most benefit from its bigotry have to first agree to give up their advantage. Tell me this document wasn't written by slavers and colonists who knew exactly the kind of white supremacist society they were trying to write into existence.

The Senate is a lost cause. There are some things we can do at the margins: admitting DC as a state is not even a Senate reform so much as a moral imperative of representative government, and adding a place with the highest percentage of Black people by population (compared to the current fifty states) would at least be something. But at core, the Senate cannot be fixed. It was erected as a bulwark of white power, and it will stay that way long after white people become a minority in this country. Alien historians will one day try to piece together why the American hegemony was so unable to deliver justice to its own people, and when they uncover the Senate they'll say, "Oh, well that was never going to work."

The best we can do is limit the antidemocratic destructiveness of the Senate, which is how we come to eliminating the Electoral College.* The Electoral College grants power to the states to elect the president (who then is allowed to appoint Supreme Court justices upon advice and consent of the Senate) based on their number of House members, plus their two senators. This system therefore takes the white supremacist structure of the legislature and ports it over to the executive branch and the judicial branch.

But the Electoral College is not protected by Article V shenanigans.

Everybody who realizes that the Electoral College is antithetical to democracy has their favorite numbers to explain why the system

---

* We should also eliminate the filibuster, but since the filibuster—which requires the Senate to cobble together sixty votes instead of fifty-one to pass legislation, further entrenching the antidemocratic nature of the institution—isn't even in the Constitution, it's outside the scope of this book. The filibuster is just the senators themselves getting together and thinking, "How can we make things worse?"

is trash. My current favorite comes from Cardozo School of Law professor Kyron Huigens, who wrote this in the *Observer* in 2019:

> The total number of each state's electors is not the relevant number in this calculation. . . . The reason the popular vote diverges from the Electoral College vote is that *each voter* in Wyoming has more voting power in the *Senate* [emphasis added]—and so in the Electoral College—than *each voter* in California.
>
> Here is the proper calculation. California has 25,002,812 eligible voters and two senators. Wyoming has 434,584 eligible voters and two senators. Carol's voting power in California's Senate delegation is diluted because she shares it with 25,002,811 other voters. Will's voting power in Wyoming's Senate delegation is also diluted because he shares it with 434,583 other voters. Since Will's voting power in the Senate is less diluted, it's greater than Carol's voting power in the Senate. If Carol has one vote in the Senate, how many votes in the Senate does Will have?
>
> Fifty-seven.

That's the right way to think about it. Instead of "one person, one vote," it's actually "white people in Wyoming get fifty-seven votes." I can make an argument that this kind of "vote dilution" violates the Fifteenth Amendment, or the equal protection clause of the Fourteenth Amendment, but both of those are tough cases since Wyoming (and other low-population states) are not required to be mostly white. If there are any liberal billionaires reading: finding half a million Black people willing to take a free townhouse, and building them one in Wyoming, would be a better way to influence democracy than running a useless presidential campaign.

In any event, the best and most intellectually clean argument is not that the Electoral College is already unconstitutional, but that it should be made so by a new amendment.

New York Times journalist Jesse Wegman has written the definitive book on abolishing the Electoral College. His work, *Let the People Pick the President*, explains that lawmakers have tried to amend or abolish the Electoral College seven hundred times. Wegman describes how an attempt to amend the Constitution to allow for a national popular vote failed in 1969–1970. Maybe if Martin Luther King had survived white supremacy, things would be different now.

The prospects of a constitutional amendment abolishing the Electoral College seem dimmer now than ever before. The Democratic candidate for president has won the popular vote in seven of the last eight elections. That trend is likely to continue as the Republican Party continues its descent into a modern-day Afrikaans party incapable of winning the popular vote in a steadily browning country. Amending the Constitution—which requires a two-thirds majority in both the House and the Senate, followed by ratification by three-fourths of states (which would mean thirty-eight states)—to take away an antidemocratic pathway for Republican victory seems unlikely.

The solution that Wegman and many others endorse is the National Popular Vote Interstate Compact. It's a pretty simple idea: states pass legislation promising that their electors will go to the winner of the national popular vote. If states holding at least a combined 270 electoral votes (the current number needed to win a majority in the Electoral College) agree to do it, we have a de facto national popular vote for president.

As of this writing, fifteen states and DC, holding a combined 196 electoral votes, have passed the necessary legislation, so this is closer to happening than some people might think. Another nine states, holding 88 electoral votes, have passed legislation through at least one chamber of their legislatures.

The plan has downsides. If the aftermath of the 2020 election showed one thing, it was that Republicans are willing to use any available means to thwart democracy and overturn the results of an election they lose. Thanks to Donald Trump's post-2020 clown-coup attempt, everybody should now know that a number of state laws about the counting of votes, certification of those votes, and awarding of Electoral College voters could well flummox a compact agreed to by a thin majority of states. States that sign on to the compact might well try to get out of it should Republicans control the statehouse and the Republican presidential candidate doesn't win the popular vote. And it's not like there's even any mechanism for certifying the national popular vote, so if there was a dispute about the winner of the national popular vote, it's not clear who would have the final say on the vote totals.

Any election where the national vote compact conflicted with the state-by-state Electoral College results would end up in front of the Supreme Court. The case would get there, likely, as an equal protection challenge under the Fourteenth Amendment. Republicans made that claim after the 2020 election: Texas sued Pennsylvania arguing that Pennsylvania's voting laws deprived Texas voters of their equal protection rights, because Pennsylvania's laws allowed for easier access to mail-in voting.

That case was thrown out on a rail by the Supreme Court, and rightly so. Under our current system of fifty separate state-run elections, Texas's complaint was one of the dumbest things I've ever seen. The rights of Texans to choose a president were in no way impacted by Pennsylvania's voter rules in their own statewide election.

But under a national popular vote compact, I don't know that I'd be as confident about beating back Republican challenges. It's hard to have a *national* popular vote system if we don't also have nationwide uniformity in terms of election rules, ballot access, and vote counting and recounting rules. I do feel confident saying that, given the Republican control of the Supreme Court, any actually intelligent legal claim about the true winner of a presidential election would be resolved in favor of the Republican candidate.

Trying an untested system to pick the leader of a deeply polarized country, one where Republicans have already shown their willingness to use violence to get their way, is dangerous. The National Popular Vote Interstate Compact feels a little bit like fixing the wing of a plane with duct tape: it might work, but I wouldn't want to fly in somebody's weekend DIY project.

What's broken here is the Constitution. It needs to be fixed, not jerry-rigged together to make it through another election. The unlikely path of abolishing the Electoral College through the amendment process is, sadly, the only one that will actually work. This is where all the "amend the constitution" energy should be on the left, because it's the thing that can't reasonably be fixed any other way.

We almost got rid of this thing during Reconstruction but failed. We almost got rid of it during the Civil Rights Era but came up short. A September 2020 Gallup Poll showed that 61 percent of Americans now favor moving to a national popular vote.

Do you know the state where Trump got the most popular votes in 2020? It was California. Do you know the state where Joe Biden received his third-largest cache of popular votes in 2020? It was Texas. Republicans in California and Democrats in Texas should matter at least as much as every sentient blade of goddamn swamp grass in Florida does now.

It's implausible that we'll ever get Republicans to see it that way, but not impossible. And so we have to try. Otherwise, we should just start the whole experiment over from scratch . . . which probably also requires a two-thirds majority in the hopeless fucking Senate.

21

THE FINAL BATTLE

The final two amendments to the Bill of Rights, the Ninth and Tenth Amendments, are hilarious. Every time I read them, I imagine James Madison dressed up like Kevin Bacon at the end of *Animal House*, screaming "All is well!" while an actual riot breaks out around him.

Remember, Madison and the other authors of *The Federalist Papers* didn't think amendments to their new Constitution were necessary. More than that, they thought a bill of enumerated rights could be dangerous. They worried that if they specified a few rights, some fools in the future would conclude that their list of rights were the *only* rights people had or should have. They worried that the federal government would grow to take power over *everything but* the few special carve-outs they bothered to enumerate.

They had a good point. If you open a restaurant and put up a sign saying "No shirt, no shoes, no service," best believe that somebody is going to show up with no pants. Some people take a list of rules as a challenge. Some jokers just want to see the world burn.

And yet, like Aaron crafting the golden calf, Madison gave in to the politics of the moment and drafted the Bill of Rights. He did something he knew was wrong to appease the crowd. But, he tried to give himself—and, you know, all of us living in the future—a couple of outs.

The Ninth Amendment is one sentence:

> The enumeration in the Constitution, of certain rights, shall not be construed to deny or disparage others retained by the people.

The Tenth Amendment is also just one sentence:

> The powers not delegated to the United States by the Constitution, nor prohibited by it to the states, are reserved to the states respectively, or to the people.

Taken together, these two amendments throw massive shade on the previous eight. If you think of the Bill of Rights like a hostage video, the first eight are Madison saying, "They are treating me well. I am being fed and receiving medical treatment for my injuries." The last two are when he blinks out "They electrocuted my testicles" in Morse code before they cut the feed.

A version of what Madison might have wanted is explored in Columbia law professor Jamal Greene's book *How Rights Went Wrong*. In it, Greene argues that our obsession with individual rights has led us to a zero-sum brawl over which rights get to defeat other rights, far from what the founders intended. Instead of applying individual rights as legal absolutes, we should instead seek to balance competing legitimate state interests with an eye toward justice and fairness instead of rights and prohibitions.

You know me, by this point. If it were up to me, I'd light the entire

Constitution on fire and start over with a document that wasn't so goddamn racist. But as we are currently stuck with this thing that Madison wrought, my inclination is not to abandon a rights-based approach to legal protections, but to capture at last the full protections of the Ninth Amendment—an amendment that Federalist Society originalists like to pretend doesn't exist.

When I say that originalists pretend that the Ninth Amendment doesn't exist, I mean that they literally try to read the amendment out of the rest of the document. In a 2013 interview with Jennifer Senior of *New York Magazine*, none other than Antonin Scalia said this about the Ninth Amendment:

> You know, in the early years, the Bill of Rights referred to the first eight amendments. They didn't even count the ninth. The Court didn't use it for 200 years. If I'd been required to identify the Ninth Amendment when I was in law school or in the early years of my practice, and if my life depended on it, I couldn't tell you what the Ninth Amendment was.

Scalia was simply channeling Robert Bork. In his 1987 (failed) confirmation hearing, Bork pretended that the Ninth Amendment was inscrutable, as if he were Mariah Carey saying, "I don't know her."

> I do not think you can use the Ninth Amendment unless you know something of what it means. For example, if you had an amendment that says "Congress shall make no" and then there is an inkblot and you cannot read the rest of it and that is the only copy you have, I do not think the court can make up what might be under the inkblot if you cannot read it.

Here we have two men who allegedly dedicated their careers in service to the vision of America as articulated by the authors of the Constitution, and yet they regulate an essential provision, made to redeem the document from the parochial political interests of its authors, as an inkblot that they can't even be bothered to think about.

There's a reason that Scalia, Bork, and other conservatives deny the existence of the Ninth Amendment: it's because the Ninth Amendment blows their whole little project apart. A theory of constitutional interpretation that restricts the rights of humans to a finite list agreed to by eighteenth-century slavers cannot survive a provision from one of those slavers that explicitly says their list is not exhaustive of all rights. Madison put the Ninth Amendment in to counteract what he knew small-minded people would do to the rest of the document, and so small-minded conservatives have to pretend it's not even there in order to achieve their goals of retarding progress.

We have more rights than those that are explicitly conferred in the Constitution. The Constitution says so!

The limiting principle on those rights is not the eighteenth-century perception of rights or privileges. It's not informed by Clarence Thomas conducting a séance to talk to his ancestral captors, or Neil Gorsuch unearthing the original Constitutional Convention lunch menu to divine whether "roasting" was a delicious punishment allowed by the founders. The limiting principle on the rights contemplated in the Ninth Amendment is found in the very next amendment.

Rights speak to what the government cannot do, and the Tenth Amendment reminds us that the federal government cannot do most things. The people who didn't think we needed a Bill of Rights in the first place thought that the rights of the people were protected by a government too weak to impinge on any fundamental rights, even if it wanted to.

Here's the conversation I'll be having with James Madison when I die:

Me: Why didn't you at least enumerate the right to do what you want in the privacy of your own bedroom?

Madison: Son, if the federal government is in your bedroom, I've already failed.

Me: Well, you did fail. And don't call me "son."

Madison: Boy, I'm talking to a slave, this is hard for me.

Me: I'll kill you.

Madison: Also not explicitly prohibited by the federal constitution, but bring it on. Brother Malcolm does it every Tuesday just for sport.

Satan: This is why only Buddhists go to heaven.

Unlike their stance on the Ninth Amendment, originalists pay a lot of attention to the Tenth Amendment. The Tenth Amendment is a reaffirmation of limited government, state's rights, and federalism. Originalists use the Tenth Amendment as their ultimate moral absolution from the practical consequences of their actions. They don't want to "ban" abortion, you see; they just want to "leave it up to the states" as the Constitution intended. They don't want to be bigoted toward the LGBTQ community; they just want the states, not the federal government, to determine the appropriate level of gay bashing that's right for them.

I have spared readers of this book a discussion of "incorporation," and you should thank me, because the history of constitutional incorporation is long and technical and so boring it's like watching a football game where they only show the huddles. But suffice it to say here that, for a lot of our history, there was a pitched battle about whether the Bill of Rights even *applied* to the state governments. A world where the federal government couldn't restrict the freedom of the press, but Georgia could, was something that people actually believed for a long time, and is a world that still exists on the margins today.

Even though most rights have now been "incorporated" against the states, our federalist system still locates most power to do most things with state governments, not the federal government.

As a Black man, I struggle with federalism. I find it difficult to develop an intellectually consistent view on the thing. As I've mentioned, my mother was born in 1950 in Mississippi. I have family currently living in states often controlled by Republican legislatures like Indiana and North Carolina. I am constantly aware that *federalism* usually means Black people living in red states get screwed. I'm always inclined to support aggressive use of federal power to save my people.

Until Republicans are in control of the federal government. When that happens, I'm quick to remember I live in New York State. I get real federalist, real quick, when national Republicans try to apply their "Christianity, but just the mean bits" theory of law to my blue state. It wouldn't take much to turn me into a guy outfitted in army fatigues (supplied by Pyer Moss, I imagine) standing on the George Washington Bridge talking about "state's rights."

I'd feel bad about my indecisiveness on the issue, but I'm generally saved from pangs of shame by remembering the blatant conservative hypocrisy around Tenth Amendment jurisprudence.

Conservatives are happy to ignore the Tenth Amendment when they want to obliterate state laws that serve goals they don't think are important. Conservatives never talk about the Tenth Amendment when they're striking down state regulations on the sale and purchase of firearms. It never stays their hand when it comes time to strike down state environmental regulations. In 2020, we saw the federal Supreme Court telling states that they couldn't mandate certain public health and safety restrictions to combat the deadly coronavirus. Where was the Tenth Amendment when conservative justices were telling the governor of New York that he couldn't take certain measures to protect the most densely packed island in the nation from disease?

Originalists will always point to an enumerated right when they want the federal government to do something in violation of the Tenth Amendment and the principle of federalism. But that is why they work so hard to deny the existence of unenumerated rights. There's no objective reason that the Ninth Amendment should be applied to the states any less robustly than the Second Amendment. The only difference is that the rights and privileges that the Ninth Amendment protects weren't on the original white supremacist, noninclusive list.

I might decide how much gas I put into the Tenth Amendment depending on who won the last election. Conservatives choose how much gas they put into constitutional rights based on the color and status of the people the states are trying to hurt. My way is better; at least I'm trying to protect vulnerable people from harm, not the ancient right of state legislatures to screw over up to 49 percent of their populations.

The structure of our Constitution pits the Ninth and Tenth Amendments against each other, locking them in an existential battle for our nation's soul. The Ninth contemplates robust protection of individual rights that defends minority interests against the excesses of the majority. The Tenth contemplates a society where the states are free to do what they want against minority populations in their state, but are themselves protected from the majority views of the nation.

This is the conflict at the core of our Constitution. Conservatives almost always resolve this conflict for the benefit of white people. White minorities want to hold slaves? Cool. White minorities want to impose segregation? Cool. White minorities want extra representation in the Electoral College? Cool. But white *majorities* want to take Black land to build a park? Also cool. White majorities want the cops to get away with the murder of Black people? Cool. White majorities want to suppress voting rights of Black and brown people? Cool.

Conservatives could not win these constitutional arguments if they put it up for a vote. In a free and fair election, there are just enough white people who reject their white supremacist arguments. When those white people can be linked up with the emerging majority of nonwhite people in this steadily browning country, conservatives lose.

And so, conservatives do not put it up for a vote. They do not allow a free and fair election on their actual platform. They use the judiciary, the least transparent and least responsive branch of government, to push through their antebellum values, and rely on ignorance to mask their true agenda.

Redeeming our failed Constitution from its bigoted and sexist sins does not require new amendments. It does not require a few new ornaments hung upon its crooked boughs. It requires the emerging majority in this country to reject the conservative interpretation of what the Constitution says, and adopt a morally defensible view of what our country means.

I'm here to tell you that the Constitution is trash. Conservatives are the ones who say it always has to be.

EPILOGUE

There is no law or piece of legislation that conservatives on the Supreme Court cannot limit, frustrate, or outright overturn. There is no constitutional amendment that conservatives cannot functionally ignore. There is no principle that conservatives cannot ruin. Without commanding a single troop or passing a single bill, a conservative Supreme Court is not a check on the other branches of government, but a check on progress itself. We can move only as far and as fast as the nine unelected and unaccountable justices on the Court allow us to.

What can we do about that?

One obvious solution would be to strip the federal courts of their power of judicial review. Remember, the power to render acts of Congress unconstitutional was not conferred in the original Constitution or any amendment since. The Court just took that power for itself in *Marbury v. Madison*, and nobody ever stopped them. Indeed, ever since the Reconstruction Amendments, the text of each amendment has included phrases like "Congress shall have the power to enforce this article," the clear implication being that it is up to Congress, not the Supreme Court, to determine what *equal protection* or *due process* or *voting rights* are supposed to look like. But the Supreme Court has regularly ignored this limitation and decided on its own which laws are allowed under the provisions of those amendments.

The power, enjoyed by our Supreme Court, unilaterally to revoke laws passed by the democratic branches of government, is uncommon on the global stage. Other advanced democracies, from Canada to South Africa, do not have high courts that are nearly as powerful as ours. In most other countries, high courts resolve disputes between laws, not whether laws are valid. Maybe we need to do the work the founders never did and amend Article III to define and limit what the Supreme Court can, and cannot, do.

Nerfing the power of the Supreme Court comes with downsides, however. Much as I hate the constitutional interpretations of conservative jurists, I fear the legislative machinations of conservative politicians even more. Most of the ones I've met aren't as decent as Rick Lazio, a man I could easily fill a book disagreeing with. As I've shown, the democratic branches of government are already tilted toward everlasting white supremacist domination. Through gerrymandering, equal state representation in the Senate, and the Electoral College, white people already have the tools to overrepresent themselves in the House, Senate, and Executive Office of the President. Historically speaking, those committed to decency have held all of those levers of power for only the briefest of times. Then they either lose to a conservative counterreaction or lose the will to keep fighting their racist siblings and cousins.

Absent throwing out the Constitution and starting over with a document written by an inclusive body that represents the interests of people of color and women this time (which I'd be in favor of but doubt will happen absent some kind of disaster-movie apocalypse where the seas rise but only bad faith white people get wet), it feels to me like some institution is necessary to counteract the white power of the so-called "democratically" elected branches of government. I wouldn't be wild about unelected judges putting up guardrails around our democracy, if we had a democracy. But since we have a republic infected with slavers' rights and representation, I am reluctant to throw away any tool whatsoever that can be won and used to force white people to chew with their mouths closed and behave more reasonably, even if that tool is used in furtherance of evil more often than not. A broken clock will at least be right twice a day; white conservatives never seem to know what time it is.

My preferred solutions focus on restructuring and reforming the Supreme Court, not eliminating it or its power. The unelected, unaccountable branch of government could be made less of a horror show if it were just a little more representative, and if the judges were just a little more responsive to the realities of our times.

Luckily, for me, we have a lot of options here. Article III mostly leaves the structure of the Supreme Court and the federal judiciary up to Congress.

One of the most popular reforms is to impose term limits on federal judges. Modern medicine has, among other things, totally overpowered judges who hold their positions for life. Coupled with the Federalist Society's push to appoint ever younger judges, lifetime appointments mean that judges can now wield power in our system across multiple generations of humans. Some of the judges appointed by Donald Trump may hold power for fifty years. It's hard to imagine, but it's entirely possible that some person not yet conceived will be fighting for postapocalyptic climate regulation in the 2070s, only to have their law declared unconstitutional through the vestigial power of a judge appointed by a twice-impeached con man. Those are the stakes when we talk about lifetime appointments.

But getting rid of lifetime tenure, absent a constitutional

amendment, is tricky. That's because Article III, while generally silent about the structure of the courts, does specify that federal judges serve while in "good behavior."

There are creative ways around this problem. The leading plan, endorsed by scholars such as Aaron Belkin of Take Back the Court Action Fund and Harvard law professor Laurence Tribe, involves forcing Supreme Court judges to take "senior status" after eighteen years on the bench. Senior status is something that we do for lower federal courts, and it has been deemed perfectly constitutional. It's a semiretirement option offered to judges who still take cases and draw a full salary but don't occupy a "seat" on their federal benches. Judges who take senior status can be replaced by new judges, appointed by the president and confirmed by the Senate. Currently, over 40 percent of the federal circuit court judges are on senior status; it's a nice way to ease older jurists out of their lifetime positions of power, without requiring them to move "to a farm, upstate."

The Constitution says Supreme Court justices have to serve for life; it doesn't say they have to serve "on the Supreme Court" for life. This version of the term limit plan would see justices take senior status and rotate down to a lower federal court for the remainder of their lives. These judges could be called back up to the Supreme Court in the event sitting justices needed to recuse themselves.

Meanwhile, rotating through nine justices on eighteen-year term limits would create an opening on the Supreme Court every two years. Obviously, creating an opening does not ensure that the Supreme Court would become more liberal over time; the Federalist Society would still exist and would still be pushing for arch-conservative justices willing to turn the clock back to 1787. But term limits would ensure that the federal judiciary was more responsive to the winners and losers of elections. As of this writing, the last three Republican presidents (George H.W. Bush, George W. Bush, Donald Trump) served for a combined sixteen years and are responsible for six of the justices on the Supreme Court (alleged sexual harasser Clarence Thomas, John Roberts, Samuel Alito, illegitimately appointed Neil Gorsuch, alleged attempted rapist Brett Kavanaugh, and hypocritically speedily appointed Amy Coney Barrett). Meanwhile the last two Democratic presidents (Bill Clinton and Barack Obama) also served for a combined sixteen years, yet are represented by only three justices (Stephen Breyer, Sonia Sotomayor, and Elena Kagan). President Joe Biden will be able to fill a seat on the Supreme Court only if Breyer retires, or an actual unforeseen tragedy befalls one of the conservatives (whose average age is now sixty-one).

Our system of justice should not be like this. Whether some people have rights or not should not depend on when the random wheel of death strikes down an octogenarian justice. Nor should it depend on the kind of strategic retirement gamesmanship employed by Republican-appointed justices.

Democratic appointees don't tend to play "strategic retirement" particularly well. Take for instance the tragedy of Thurgood Marshall. He was appointed in 1967 and hung on valiantly all the way through the Ronald Reagan years in the 1980s. But by the time Reagan was succeeded by yet another Republican, George H.W. Bush, Marshall's health was failing. He hung on for as long as he could do the job credibly, but in 1991 he finally decided to retire. Bush replaced him with Clarence Thomas, and Thomas has worked tirelessly to undo Marshall's great legacy. But Marshall didn't *die* until January 24, 1993, mere days after Bill Clinton was inaugurated as president. If Marshall had been willing essentially to compromise his duties and health and wait to be carried out of the Court in a coffin, the last twenty-five years of American jurisprudence would be significantly different.

By contrast, Sandra Day O'Connor strategically retired in 2006, both because her husband was sick and she wanted to care for him, and because she wanted to retire under a Republican. Her seat was then filled by Bush 43, who replaced O'Connor's brand of moderation with the arch-conservative Alito.

Likewise, in a move designed to preserve his conservative legacy, Anthony Kennedy was perfectly healthy but relinquished his seat to his protégé, Kavanaugh, in 2018.

Meanwhile, Ruth Bader Ginsburg could have retired in 2014 under the Obama administration, but she felt she could still do the job and didn't want to be pushed out by men telling her what to do. She hung on but didn't it make it, dying in September 2020, just weeks before Trump lost the presidential election to Biden. In a wildly hypocritical move, given that they had blocked the appointment of Merrick Garland during Obama's final year as president, Republicans rushed to replace Ginsburg in Trump's final weeks, putting in her stead the conservative zealot Amy Barrett.

Two moderates who left strategically, and two liberals who didn't, has resulted in four hard-right extremists who will define the limits of human rights for a generation of Americans. This is not the way.

Term limits would fix that, at least. But the Supreme Court, stacked as it is with conservatives justices, is unlikely to accept term limits as constitutional. Conservatives would cling to the language of Article III the way a person adrift would cling to a life raft and reject any term limits bill passed by Congress. Again, legislation cannot survive conservative justices if conservative justices don't like the law.

The way to get term limits (which I support) is not to offer up legislation that will be ruled unconstitutional by the conservative Court before breakfast; it's to pack the Court with liberal justices who believe the term limits plan is constitutional and have them there to defend whatever term limits legislation Congress passes.

The number of Supreme Court justices is not set by Article III or anything else in the Constitution. The Supreme Court opened with six justices. John Adams, as a lame-duck president who had lost to Thomas Jefferson in 1800, issued the "Midnight Judges Act," which reduced the number of justices to five "upon the next vacancy" on the Court. That's an important distinction. You can't remove a federal judge, including a Supreme Court justice, absent the constitutional provision for impeachment. So you can't take away members already on the Court, but you can, upon their death or retirement, reduce the number of seats on the Supreme Court.

Jefferson, however, restored the number of Supreme Court justices to six upon taking office.

Then, in 1807, as Jefferson was nearing the end of his second term, he enlarged the Supreme Court to seven justices, and appointed another one himself.

A seven-member Court was in place when Andrew Jackson set his sights on it in 1837. Jackson added two more seats to the Supreme Court and filled them. It was the first time the Supreme Court reached nine justices, which represents a 50 percent increase from the number of justices on the court at the founding, less than fifty years earlier.

During the Civil War years, the number of justices on the Supreme Court ballooned to ten. That was in part because Chief Justice Roger Taney—he of the infamous *Dred Scott* decision in 1857—continued in his role on the Court and was a constant thorn in Lincoln's side.

After the war, Congress reduced the number of justices back down to seven, mainly to spite the reviled Andrew Johnson. Finally, the Judiciary Act of 1869 set the number of justices as nine, and we've been there ever since.

The Supreme Court is not baseball; nine is not a magic number. Our history shows that changing the number of justices on the Supreme Court is the actual normal political response to a Court that is out of step with the times. It is, if anything, the way the Constitution wants us to handle the Supreme Court: treat each individual justice as an independent arbiter who cannot be fired by an angry president and is protected from the political fray by a lifetime appointment, but treat the Supreme Court as a subservient branch that can be "corrected" by Congress and the president through various means.

I therefore favor adding additional justices to the Supreme Court, often derisively called "court packing," as the appropriate constitutional solution to the problem of generational overrepresentation of conservatives on the Court. Conservatives enjoy overrepresentation in the Senate and the White House because of structural flaws in our Constitution. But they enjoy overrepresentation on the Court because liberals have not been willing to do whatever it takes to stop them.

Court expansion is the way to overcome the power conservatives have locked in for themselves, likely until the 2070s. A judiciary act increasing the number of justices on the Supreme Court can be passed by a Democratic Congress, signed by a Democratic president, and then new justices can be nominated by that president and confirmed by a Democratic Senate. It's simple. It will work. All it takes is political will.

But if a Democratic president can expand the Court, can't a Republican president do the same if that party controls all of government again? And won't that lead to an endless tit for tat, where the Supreme Court is an endlessly increasing body that turns into a "super legislature" that changes control based on the party in power?

Yes. And I don't care. I don't care because the Supreme Court is already a super legislature that works to frustrate and disrupt law passed by democratically elected representatives. I don't care because, absent a couple of decades in the middle of the twentieth century, that super legislature almost always works against the

interests of minorities and women. I don't care because telling people that we have to wait until Neil Gorsuch (appointed after Mitch
McConnell refused to even hold a hearing on Barack Obama's nom-
inee, Merrick Garland) and Brett Kavanaugh (appointed despite
credible accusations of attempted rape) and Amy Coney Barrett
(appointed after an election had already started to replace the
twice-impeached man who nominated her) literally have to drop
dead before we can advance urgent legislation needed to combat
climate change, is unacceptable. The country cannot be held hostage by four years' worth of Trump judges for the next fifty years.
I don't care about what Republicans will do if they ever control all
of government again, because a Supreme Court willing to protect
voting rights and take the Fifteenth Amendment out of cryostasis
makes it unlikely that an openly white nationalist party *will* control
all of government again.

Beyond the stark political realities, there are wonderful reform
reasons for Court expansion. We can probably never return the
Supreme Court to the "least dangerous" status imagined by Alexander Hamilton, but we can diminish the power of each individual
Supreme Court justice.

That would be an unqualified good. Understand that while
Republicans have politicized and manipulated the nomination and
confirmation process to ensure that only justices committed to the
Republican political agenda end up on the Supreme Court, they're
not wrong to do so. Each justice represents a vector of power that
far outlasts any presidential administration and most legislation.
One justice committed to bigotry and oppression, or liberty and
plurality, can change the course of history, much less three or four
or five. Republicans are right to go to the mattresses every time one
of these openings come up, and Democrats have been fools not to
adopt the same tactics.

Adding more justices is a way to *de*politicize the entire

nomination process. It lowers the stakes for each confirmation battle. Fighting for one of nine is just a different political calculus than fighting for one of nineteen, or one of twenty-nine. That's just math. It's like the way parents of only one child will monitor that kid on the playground from a helicopter, while parents of five children send them out to play in traffic and only do a head count at bedtime to see if they all made it back alive (note: I may be a bad parent).

I would like to see the Democrats add twenty justices to the Supreme Court, to bring the number of justices up to twenty-nine. Partially, that's to diminish the Republican appetite for counter-expansion, but I also objectively think that twenty-nine is about the right number. The Ninth Circuit Court of Appeals (which is responsible for California, and a number of western states) currently seats twenty-nine judges; they seem to function just fine.

A key benefit of court expansion is moving the Supreme Court to the kind of "panel" system employed throughout the rest of the federal judiciary. Appeals to any circuit court of appeal are first heard by a three-judge panel. The panels are chosen by random lot from among the available judges (including senior status judges). That panel issues a ruling. If the rest of the bench doesn't like it, a majority of the judges on the circuit vote to rehear the case as a full body (called en banc review).

I cannot emphasize how much better that system is for the appearance of impartiality than the current Supreme Court system of hearing all cases as a full body. Even a Court "stacked" with justices from one party or the other might wind up with a panel dominated by justices appointed from the minority party. Even courts with a few extremists on either side of the law will find that those extremists are not involved in most of the cases that court hears. And even when extremists end up on the same panel, their opinions have to be tempered enough not to be struck by en banc review.

When it gets to en banc review, the chances that a twenty-nine-member Court is going to break 15–14 along strict party lines is just rare. The law is complicated. Judges, who remain independent, unaccountable arbiters, are quirky. Even judges who share an ideological framework don't always agree on how that ideology should be applied in every case. Even originalists don't always agree: some will use Strunk and White to limit the rights of men and women, others will pull an eighteenth-century farmer's almanac out of their asses, and I swear to God that Neil Gorsuch will one day quote the Wife of Bath from *The Canterbury Tales* in a judicial opinion: "The wife, an authority on the common law perception of marriage, may have had many husbands, but they were all of the opposite sex-at-birth to her own."

I can't guarantee that a super-expanded court would produce "better" opinions, but I am confident that it would produce more moderate and mainstream opinions. Herding fifteen people together to form a majority opinion is just a different beast than keeping five Federalist Society members on board.

Moreover, an expanded Court opens the possibility for more diversity on the bench, so that the Court looks more like the country it lords over. Exactly three people of color (Marshall, Thomas, and Sotomayor) have served on the Supreme Court in American history. There've been a total of five women (O'Connor, Ginsburg, Sotomayor, Kagan, and Barrett).

That's fucking embarrassing.

Always remember, the arch-conservative view of the law trumpeted by the Federalist Society is a *minority* opinion. It's a minority opinion in law school, in academia, and within the legal profession writ large. Anything that can be done to drown out conservative voices on the Court should be done, and the quickest and easiest way to do that is simply to add more voices. Conservatives never win when everybody gets to play. In the words of Kermit the Frog in *The Muppets Take Manhattan*, "That's what we need! More frogs and dogs and bears and chickens and . . . and whatever! You're not gonna watch the show, you're gonna be in the show!"

The legitimate knock on adding additional justices is not "Twenty-nine sounds like a lot" or "But what will Republicans do?"; it is "Doesn't twenty-nine justices make the court even less responsive to the will of the people?" Conservatives have shown that you can diminish the rights of entire groups of people just by changing a couple of justices on the Supreme Court, but liberals showed during the civil rights era that you can grant rights to entire groups of people with just a couple of appointments. Arguably, a twenty-nine-member Court would be even more resistant to democratic-inspired change than our current one, because to change the opinion of the Court you have to swap out as many as fifteen justices instead of just four or five.

It's a real concern, but that's why I started this discussion with term limits. Expand the Court, pass term limits, have the expanded Court rule that term limits are constitutional, then start rotating one of the current justices off the bench about once a year. The Supreme Court as an institution would remain a powerful check on the constitutional excesses of the elected branches. But the institution would be responsive to the winners of democratic elections over time. The individual justices would remain independent and unremovable during their terms in office. But the confirmation process would be depoliticized to the point of becoming almost rote, and each individual justice could not hold sway over our polity for as long as Pfizer can keep them alive.

An expanded Supreme Court is a path toward a better future, but one that cannot be realized unless liberals and progressives get in the game and demand that the Democratic Party take the courts seriously. This book is a guide, not for how we win, but why we must. I believe that if more people knew what was at stake, they wouldn't cede an entire branch of government to conservatives dedicated to holding back the rest of society.

Never accept the conservative interpretation of the Constitution. Never accept the conservative limitations placed on our political, civil, and social rights. They have literally always been wrong, and they are wrong now. Justice is not one constitutional option among many—it is a requirement of a free and equal society. Demand nothing less.

NOTES

With gratitude to Jessica Suriano for her research support.

2 *Lock, Stock, And Two Smoking Barrels*: *Lock, Stock, And Two Smoking Barrels*, directed by Guy Ritchie, PolyGram Filmed Entertainment, 1998.

12 **"heckler's veto"**: Patrick Schmidt, "Heckler's Veto," *The First Amendment Encyclopedia*, The Free Speech Center at Middle Tennessee State University.

14 **Gawker published a story "outing" him in 2007**: Derek Thompson, "The Most Expensive Comment in Internet History?" *The Atlantic*, February 23, 2018.

14 **He told the *New York Times***: Andrew Ross Sorkin, "Peter Thiel, Tech Billionaire, Reveals Secret War with Gawker," *The New York Times*, May 25, 2016.

17 **"intimidate" him**: Allyson Chiu, "'This Was an Orchestrated Effort': Devin Nunes Sues Twitter, 'Devin Nunes' Cow' for Defamation," *The Washington Post*, March 20, 2019.

19 **Religious Freedom Restoration Act (RFRA)**: H.R.1308, 103rd Congress (1993–1994), "Religious Freedom Restoration Act," November 16, 1993.

19 *Employment Division v. Smith*: *Employment Division, Department of Human Resources of Oregon v. Smith*, 494 U.S. 872 (1990).

20 *Sherbert v. Verner*: *Sherbert v. Verner*, 374 U.S. 398 (1963).

20 **"strict scrutiny"**: "Free Exercise of Religion," Cornell Law School, Legal Information Institute.

21 **"distinguishing"**: "Distinguish," Cornell Law School, Legal Information Institute.

22 *Burwell v. Hobby Lobby Stores*: Burwell v. Hobby Lobby Stores, 573 U.S. 682 (2014).

25 **Colorado's Anti-Discrimination Act (CADA)**: Colorado Revised Statutes (C.R.S.) Title 24, Article 34, Parts 3–8, 1957.

26 *Lawrence v. Texas*: Lawrence v. Texas, 539 U.S. 558 (2003).

26 *U.S. v. Windsor*: United States v. Windsor, 570 U.S. 744 (2013).

26 *Obergefell v. Hodges*: Obergefell v. Hodges, 576 U.S. __ (2015).

26 *Citizens United*: Citizens United v. Federal Election Commission, 558 U.S. 310 (2010).

26 *Masterpiece Cakeshop*: Masterpiece Cakeshop, Ltd. v. Colorado Civil Rights Commission, 584 U.S. __ (2018).

28 **"Christian beliefs"**: Isabella Grullón Paz, "Colorado Baker Fined for Refusing to Make Cake for Transgender Woman," *The New York Times*, June 18, 2021.

29 **"anti-LGBTQ hate group"**: "Extremist Files: Alliance Defending Freedom," *Southern Poverty Law Center*.

29 **Blackstone Legal Fellowship**: Sharona Coutts and Sofia Resnick, "Not the 'Illuminati': How Fundamentalist Christians Are Infiltrating State and Federal Government," *Rewire News Group*, May 13, 2014.

32 **Tomahawk missile**: "Tomahawk," Missile Defense Project; "Missile Threat," Center for Strategic and International Studies, September 19, 2016, last modified November 4, 2019.

33 *USS Ticonderoga*: Guy Joseph Nasuti, "USS Ticonderoga (CG-47)," Naval History and Heritage Command, Dictionary of American Naval Fighting Ships, published November 22, 2019.

33 **events of January 6, 2021**: Luke Mogelson, "Among the Insurrectionists," *The New Yorker*, January 15, 2021; "Inside the Capitol Riot: An Exclusive Video Investigation," *The New York Times*, June 30, 2021.

34 **"copwatching"**: Torin Monahan, *Surveillance and Security: Technological Politics and Power in Everyday Life*, Taylor & Francis, August 4, 2006.

34 **Mulford Act**: Adam Winkler, "The Secret History of Guns," *The Atlantic*, Sept. 2011.

34 **Gun Control Act of 1968**: "Gun Control Act of 1968," Bureau of Alcohol, Tobacco, Firearms and Explosives, last reviewed January 23, 2020.

34 ***U.S. v. Miller***: *United States v. Miller*, 307 U.S. 174 (1939).

34 **National Firearms Act of 1934**: "National Firearms Act," Bureau of Alcohol, Tobacco, Firearms and Explosives, last reviewed April 7, 2020.

36 **Revolt at Cincinnati**: Joel Achenbach, Scott Higham, and Sari Horwitz, "How NRA's True Believers Converted a Marksmanship Group into a Mighty Gun Lobby," *The Washington Post*, January 12, 2013.

36 **Firearm Owners Protection Act of 1986**: S. 49, 99th Congress (1985–1986), "Firearms Owners' Protection Act," May 19, 1986.

36 **Patrick Henry and George Mason**: Dave Davies, "Historian Uncovers The Racist Roots of the 2nd Amendment," NPR, June 2, 2021.

37 **Professor Carl Bogus**: Carl T. Bogus, "Was Slavery a Factor in the Second Amendment?" *The New York Times*, May 24, 2018.

37 **"If they neglect or refuse"**: "Document: Patrick Henry Speech Before Virginia Ratifying Convention (June 5, 1788)," *Teaching American History*.

38 ***D.C. v. Heller***: *District of Columbia v. Heller*, 554 U.S. 570 (2008).

39 **Reagan and company**: Thad Morgan, "The NRA Supported Gun Control When the Black Panthers Had the Weapons," *History.com*, published March 22, 2018, updated August 30, 2018.

45 ***Terry v. Ohio***: *Terry v. Ohio*, 392 U.S. 1 (1968).

45 ***Carroll v. U.S.***: *Carroll v. United States*, 354 U.S. 394 (1957).

45 ***Miranda v. Arizona***: *Miranda v. Arizona*, 384 U.S. 436 (1966).

45 **served Burger King**: Staff Reports, "Charleston Shooting Suspect's Burger King Meal Gets National Attention," *The Charlotte Observer*, June 24, 2015.

46 **"casing the joint"**: *Terry v. Ohio* Oral Arguments Transcripts, December 12, 1967, Courtesy of the University of Minnesota.

47 **New York State's stop and frisk law**: New York State Legislature, C.P.L. § 140.50, "Temporary questioning of persons in public places; search for weapons," September 1, 1971.

48 **"broken windows policing"**: Chris Benderev, Tara Boyle, Renee Klahr, Maggie Penman, Jennifer Schmidt, and Shankar Vedantam, "How a Theory of Crime and Policing Was Born, and Went Terribly Wrong," NPR, November 1, 2016.

49 *Floyd v. City of New York*: *Floyd, et al. v. City of New York, et al.*, 959 F. Supp. 2d 540 (S.D.N.Y. 2013).

50 **"In all honesty, I just didn't like them."**: Christina Bucciere, "Ambassador Stokes Discusses Diversity, Stop-and-Frisk Laws," *KentWired.com*, September 18, 2014.

52 **"When I grabbed him"**: CNN Newsroom Transcripts, "No Indictment in Ferguson; Grand Jury Evidence Released in Brown Case," November 25, 2014.

53 *Graham v. Connor*: *Graham v. Connor*, 490 U.S. 386 (1989).

57 **"pattern and practice"**: The United States Department of Justice, "How Department of Justice Civil Rights Division Conducts Pattern-or-Practice Investigations," May 8, 2015.

61 *Leviathan*: Thomas Hobbes, *Leviathan: Or the Matter, Forme and Power of a Commonwealth Ecclesiasticall and Civil*, published 1651.

63 **"affirmative defense"**: "Affirmative Defense," Cornell Law School, Legal Information Institute.

63 **"Stand Your Ground" laws**: "Guns in Public: Stand Your Ground," Giffords Law Center.

63 **One well-respected study**: John K. Roman, "Race, Justifiable Homicide, and Stand Your Ground Laws: Analysis of FBI Supplementary Homicide Report Data," Urban Institute Justice Policy Center, Published July 2013.

64 **It found**: Nicole Ackermann, Melody S. Goodman, Keon Gilbert, Cassandra Arroyo-Johnson Marcello Pagano, "Race, Law, and Health: Examination of 'Stand Your Ground' and Defendant Convictions in Florida," *Social Science & Medicine*, volume 142, pages 194–201, 2015.

65 **"provocation" rule**: "As a Matter of Law and Policy, the Ninth Circuit's 'Provocation Rule' Must Stand," Harvard Civil Rights, Civil Liberties Law Review, February 9, 2017.

65 *County of Los Angeles v. Mendez*: *County of Los Angeles v. Mendez*, 581 U.S. __ (2017).

65 **The facts in *Mendez***: Elie Mystal, "The Supreme Court Makes It Even Easier for Cops to Shoot You," *Above the Law*, May 30, 2017.

66 **"qualified immunity"**: "Qualified immunity," Cornell Law School, Legal Information Institute.

67 *Bivens v. Six Unknown Named Agents of Federal Bureau of Narcotics*: *Bivens v. Six Unknown Named Agents of Federal Bureau of Narcotics*, 403 U.S. 388 (1971).

68 *Harlow v. Fitzgerald*: *Harlow v. Fitzgerald*, 457 U.S. 800 (1982).

69 **Kafkaesque loop**: Nathaniel Sobel, "What Is Qualified Immunity, and What Does It Have to Do with Police Reform?" *Lawfare*, June 6, 2020.

69 *Pearson v. Callahan*: *Pearson v. Callahan*, 555 U.S. 223 (2009).

69 **introduced legislation**: H.R. 1470, 117th Congress (2021-2022), Rep. Ayanna Pressley, "Ending Qualified Immunity Act," March 1, 2020.

74 **Amy Cooper**: Matt Stieb, "Amy Cooper Didn't Learn Much from Her Time as 'Central Park Karen,'" *New York Magazine*, May 26, 2021.

77 **Yale Law Journal article**: Jed Rubenfeld, "The Paradigm-Case Method," *The Yale Law Journal*, 2006.

80 *Roe v. Wade*: *Roe v. Wade*, 410 U.S. 113 (1973).

80 *Planned Parenthood v. Casey*: *Planned Parenthood of Southeastern Pennsylvania v. Casey*, 505 U.S. 833 (1992).

81 *Dickerson v. United States*: *Dickerson v. United States*, 530 U.S. 428 (2000).

82 **At that new trial**: History.com Editors, "Miranda Rights," *History.com*, Published November 9, 2009, updated June 12, 2019.

83 **full page ad**: Jan Ransom, "Trump Will Not Apologize for Calling for Death Penalty Over Central Park Five," *The New York Times*, June 18, 2019.

84 **exoneration report**: Nancy E. Ryan, "Affirmation in Response to Motion to Vacate Judgement of Conviction," *Supreme Court of the State of New York, County of New York, Part 58*, December 5, 2002.

88 **were bought for $125**: The Central Park Conservancy, "The Story of Seneca Village," January 18, 2018; Sam Neubauer, "Seneca Village: A Forgotten Settlement Buried Under Central Park," *I Love the Upper West Side*, July 23, 2020.

88 **New York African Society for Mutual Relief**: James Sullivan, "The New York African Society for Mutual Relief (1808–1860)," *BlackPast.org*, January 22, 2011.

88 **bought 12 lots for $578**: The Central Park Conservancy, "The Story of Seneca Village," January 18, 2018.

89 **male landowners in possession of $250 worth of property**: The Central Park Conservancy, "The Story of Seneca Village," January 18, 2018.

89 **ten lived in Seneca Village**: Douglas Martin, "Before Park, Black Village; Students Look Into a Community's History," *The New York Times*, April 7, 1995.

91 **In 1626**: Janos Marton, "Today in NYC History: How the Dutch Actually Bought Manhattan (the Long Version)," *Untapped Cities*, May 6, 2015.

91 **Robert Miller makes clear**: Robert J. Miller, "Economic Development in Indian Country: Will Capitalism or Socialism Succeed?" *Oregon Law Review*, Vol. 80, No. 3, 2001.

91 ***Law in American History***: G. Edward White, *Law in American History: Volume 1: From the Colonial Years Through the Civil War*, Oxford University Press, January 3, 2012.

91 ***On The Law of War and Peace***: Hugo Grotius, *De Jure Belli ac Pacis: On the Law of War and Peace*, 1625.

92 **"Wall Street"**: "Wall Street and the Stock Exchanges: Historical Resources," *Library of Congress*.

93 ***Kelo v. City of New London***: *Kelo v. New London*, 545 U.S. 469 (2005).

93 **"rededicated"**: "The Kelo House (1890)," *Historic Buildings of Connecticut*, March 20, 2009.

94 ***The Power Broker: Robert Moses and the Fall of New York***: Robert A. Caro, *The Power Broker: Robert Moses and the Fall of New York*, Knopf Doubleday Publishing Group, 1974.

95 **Article 15 of New York Consolidated Laws, Section 500**: Consolidated Laws of New York: General Municipal, "Article 15: Urban Renewal," Section 500–525, The New York State Senate.

97 **Jones's Wood**: "What Was Jones' Wood?" New York Historical Society Museum and Library.

98 **"swamp . . . squatters"**: "Seneca Village, New York City," National Park Service.

98 **was paid $2,335 for his three lots and house**: "Andrew Williams' Affidavit of Petition," *New York City Municipal Archives*, Bureau of Old Records; Douglas Martin, "A Village Dies, a Park Is Born," *The New York Times*, January 31, 1997.

100 ***Commentaries on the Laws of England***: William Blackstone, *Commentaries on the Laws of England*, Oxford: Printed at the Clarendon Press, 1765–1769.

102 ***Strauder v. West Virginia***: *Strauder v. West Virginia*, 100 U.S. 303 (1880).

103 **"law French"**: "Law French," Cornell Law School, Legal Information Institute.

104 ***Swain v. Alabama***: *Swain v. Alabama*, 380 U.S. 202 (1965).

105 ***Batson v. Kentucky***: *Batson v. Kentucky*, 476 U.S. 79 (1986).

105 **"object anyway"**: Sean Rameswaram, "Object Anyway," *More Perfect*, WNYC Studios, July 16, 2016.

106 ***J.E.B. v. Alabama ex rel T.B.***: *J.E.B. v. Alabama ex rel T.B.*, 511 U.S. 127 (1994).

107 ***University of Michigan Journal of Law Reform* article**: Michael J. Raphael and Edward J. Ungvarsky, "Excuses, Excuses: Neutral Explanations Under Batson v. Kentucky," *University of Michigan Journal of Law Reform*, Volume 27, 1993.

109 ***Holland v. Illinois***: *Holland v. Illinois*, 493 U.S. 474 (1990).

114 **twenty-five different crimes that were punishable by death**: "Early History of the Death Penalty," *Death Penalty Information Center.*

114 **condemn innocent people**: "Description of Innocence Cases," *Death Penalty Information Center*, last updated 2021.

114 **against Black and Brown defendants**: "Race and the Death Penalty," *ACLU*; "Race and the Death Penalty," *Prison Policy Initiative.*

117 ***Furman v. Georgia***: *Furman v. Georgia*, 408 U.S. 238 (1972).

118 ***Gregg v. Georgia***: *Gregg v. Georgia*, 428 U.S. 153 (1976).

119 ***Bucklew v. Precythe***: *Bucklew v. Precythe*, 587 U.S. __ (2019).

128 ***The Second Founding***: Eric Foner, *The Second Founding: How the Civil*

War and Reconstruction Remade the Constitution, W. W. Norton & Company, 2019.

134 **without Grant**: Ron Chernow, *Grant*, Penguin Books, September 25, 2018.

137 *Slaughter-House Cases*: *Slaughter-House Cases*, 83 U.S. 36 (1873).

138 **The Civil Rights Act of 1875**: André Munro and Melvin I. Urofsky, "Civil Rights Act of 1875," *Britannica*, March 31, 2014.

139 **The *Civil Rights Cases*: *Civil Rights Cases*, 109 U.S. 3 (1883).**

139 **"within two blocks"**: "Jim Crow Laws," National Park Service, Last updated April 17, 2018.

142 *Plessy v. Ferguson*: *Plessy v. Ferguson*, 163 U.S. 537 (1896).

142 *Brown v. Board of Education of Topeka*: *Brown v. Board of Education of Topeka (1)*, 347 U.S. 483 (1954).

144 **The Civil Rights Act of 1866**: "Civil Rights Act of 1866," *Federal Judicial Center*, April 9, 1866.

145 *UCLA Law Review* **article**: Ronald Turner, "A Critique of Justice Antonin Scalia's Originalist Defense of Brown v. Board of Education," *UCLA Law Review*, Discourse 170, 2014.

145 *Reading Law: The Interpretation of Legal Texts*: Bryan A. Garner and Antonin Scalia, *Reading Law: The Interpretation of Legal Texts*, Thomson West Publishing, 2012.

147 *Loving v. Virginia*: *Loving v. Virginia*, 388 U.S. 1 (1967).

147 **When he was seventeen**: Brynn Holland, "Mildred and Richard: The Love Story That Changed America," *History.com*, Published February 17, 2017, Updated October 18, 2018.

148 **"Act To Preserve Racial Integrity"**: "Racial Integrity Act of 1924," The Virginia Center for Digital History at the University of Virginia.

148 *Pace v. Alabama*: *Pace v. Alabama*, 106 U.S. 583 (1883).

148 **Mildred Loving later told an interviewer**: Phyl Newbeck, "Loving v. Virginia (1967)," *Encyclopedia Virginia*, December 7, 2020.

151 **2012 law review article**: Steven G. Calabresi and Andrea Matthews, "Originalism and Loving v. Virginia," *Faculty Working Papers*, *Northwestern University School of Law*, Paper 206, 2012.

152 **"anti-sodomy" law**: Texas Penal Code § 21.06, Title 5, "Offenses Against the Person, Chapter 21 Sexual Offenses," Section 21.06, "Homosexual Conduct," effective January 1, 1974.

158 **"strict scrutiny"**: "Strict scrutiny," Cornell Law School, Legal Information Institute.

158 *Marbury v. Madison*: *Marbury v. Madison*, 5 U.S. 137 (1803).

160 *Craig v. Boren*: *Craig v. Boren*, 429 U.S. 190 (1976).

161 *Korematsu v. U.S.*: *Korematsu v. United States*, 323 U.S. 214 (1944).

161 **Executive Order 9066**: "Executive Order 9066," General Records of the United States Government; Record Group 11, National Archives, February 19, 1942.

162 *Trump v. Hawaii*: *Trump v. Hawaii*, 585 U.S. __ (2018).

163 *The New Republic*: Brian Beutler, "Anthony Kennedy's Same-Sex Marriage Opinion Was a Logical Disaster," *The New Republic*, July 1, 2015.

170 *Lochner v. New York*: *Lochner v. New York*, 198 U.S. 45 (1905).

171 *Lochner* era: "Lochner Era," Cornell Law School, Legal Information Institute.

172 **In his article**: Mark Joseph Stern, "A New Lochner Era," *Slate*, June 29, 2018.

172 *Janus v. American Federation of State, County, and Municipal Employees*: *Janus v. American Federation of State, County, and Municipal Employees, Council 31*, 585 U.S. __ (2018).

172 *Adair v. United States*: *Adair v. United States*, 208 U.S. 161 (1908).

173 *Perry v. New Hampshire*: *Perry v. New Hampshire*, 565 U.S. 228 (2012).

177 *Griswold v. Connecticut*: *Griswold v. Connecticut*, 381 U.S. 479 (1965).

178 **Comstock law**: "Anthony Comstock's 'Chastity' Laws," *PBS: American Experience*.

179 **Margaret Sanger**: Nikita Stewart, "Planned Parenthood in N.Y. Disavows Margaret Sanger Over Eugenics," *The New York Times*, July 21, 2020.

188 **"safe, legal, and rare"**: Emily Crockett, "Tim Kaine's Evolving Views on Abortion, Explained," *Vox*, October 3, 2016.

194 **"Equal Rights Amendment"**: Daniel Read Anthony, Jr., H.J. Res. 75, 68th Congress (1923–1925), Committee on the Judiciary, December 13, 1923.

195 **"Stop Taking Our Privileges (STOP)"**: "Phyllis Schlafly (1924–2016)," *Biography.com*, April 1, 2020.

195 **"Slaves that worked there"**: Daniel Victor, "Bill O'Reilly Defends Comments About 'Well Fed' Slaves," *The New York Times*, July 27, 2016.

196 **Pew Research Center report**: Eileen Patten and Kim Parker, "Women in the U.S. Military: Growing Share, Distinctive Profile," Pew Research Center, Social & Demographic Trends, 2011.

196 **13 percent**: Maria Guerra, "Fact Sheet: The State of African American Women in the United States," Center for American Progress, November 7, 2013.

197 **"unborn homicide"**: Ramesh Ponnuru, "What If a Fetus Has Constitutional Rights?" *Bloomberg Opinion*, March 31, 2021.

197 *Dred Scott*: *Dred Scott v. Sandford*, 60 U.S. 393 (1857).

207 **"standard, practice, or procedure"**: Section 2 of The Voting Rights Act of 1965, *The United States Department of Justice*.

209 *Shelby County v. Holder*: *Shelby County v. Holder*, 570 U.S. 529 (2013).

212 *Bush v. Gore*: *Bush v. Gore*, 531 U.S. 98 (2000).

212 **Joe Biden defeated Donald Trump**: "Georgia Election Results," *The New York Times* and National Election Pool/Edison Research, Last updated March 6, 2021.

220 **Baker v. Carr**: *Baker v. Carr*, 369 U.S. 186 (1962).

222 *Rucho v. Common Cause*: *Rucho v. Common Cause*, 588 U.S. __ (2019).

227 **"Great Compromise" or "Connecticut Compromise"**: "A Great Compromise," established July 16, 1787, *United States Senate*.

228 **Here are the ten "Blackest" states**: "Black Population By State," *World Population Review*; "2018 National and State Population Estimates," United States Census Bureau, December 19, 2018.

228 **Washington D.C.**: "Washington, District of Columbia Population," *World Population Review*; "QuickFacts: District of Columbia," United States Census Bureau.

228 **Mississippi**: "Mississippi Population," *World Population Review*; "QuickFacts: Mississippi," United States Census Bureau.

228 **Louisiana**: "Louisiana Population," *World Population Review*; "QuickFacts: Louisiana," United States Census Bureau.

228 **Georgia**: "Georgia Population," *World Population Review*; "QuickFacts: Georgia," United States Census Bureau.

228 **Maryland**: "Maryland Population," *World Population Review*; "QuickFacts: Maryland," United States Census Bureau.

228 **Alabama**: "Alabama Population," *World Population Review*; "QuickFacts: Alabama," United States Census Bureau.

228 **South Carolina**: "South Carolina Population," *World Population Review*; "QuickFacts: South Carolina," United States Census Bureau.

228 **Delaware**: "Delaware Population," *World Population Review*; "QuickFacts: Delaware," United States Census Bureau.

228 **North Carolina**: "North Carolina Population," *World Population Review*; "QuickFacts: North Carolina," United States Census Bureau.

228 **Virginia**: "Virginia Population," *World Population Review*; "QuickFacts: Virginia," United States Census Bureau.

231 **who wrote this in the *Observer***: Kyron Huigens, "The Electoral College Is Actually Worse Than You Think—Here's Why," *Observer*, February 27, 2019.

232 ***Let The People Pick The President***: Jesse Wegman, *Let the People Pick the President: The Case for Abolishing the Electoral College*, St. Martin's Press, March 17, 2020.

232 **As of this writing**: "Agreement Among the States to Elect the President by National Popular Vote," *National Popular Vote Inc.* and The National Popular Vote Interstate Compact Bill (NPVIC).

234 **September 2020 Gallup Poll**: Megan Brenan, "61% of Americans Support Abolishing Electoral College," *Gallup*, September 24, 2020.

237 ***How Rights Went Wrong***: Jamal Greene, *How Rights Went Wrong: Why Our Obsession with Rights Is Tearing America Apart*, Houghton Mifflin Harcourt, March 16, 2021.

238 ***New York Magazine***: Jennifer Senior, "In Conversation: Antonin Scalia," *New York Magazine*, October 4, 2013.

238 **Bork pretended**: Kurt T. Lash, "Inkblot: The Ninth Amendment as Textual Justification for Judicial Enforcement of the Right to Privacy," *University of Richmond Law Faculty Publications*, 2013.

248 **endorsed by scholars**: Richard Wolf, "Liberal Groups Seek to Make Supreme Court an Issue in 2020 Presidential Race, and Conservatives Exult," *USA Today*, July 28, 2019; "Term Limits," *Fix the Court*.

251 **"Midnight Judges Act"**: Winston Bowman, "The Midnight Judges: The Judiciary Act of 1801," *The Federal Judicial Center*.

255 **Strunk and White**: William Strunk Jr. and E. B. White, *The Elements of Style*, Harcourt, Brace & Howe, 1920.

255 *The Canterbury Tales*: Geoffrey Chaucer, *The Canterbury Tales*, Written 1387–1400, First Printed by William Caxton in 1476 in London, England.

255 *Muppets Take Manhattan*: *The Muppets Take Manhattan*, Directed by Frank Oz, Henson Associates and Tri-Star Pictures, 1984.

ABOUT THE AUTHOR

Elie Mystal is *The Nation*'s justice correspondent, an Alfred Knobler Fellow at the Type Media Center, and the legal editor of the *More Perfect* podcast on the Supreme Court for Radiolab. He is a graduate of Harvard College and Harvard Law School, the former executive editor of *Above the Law*, a former associate at Debevoise & Plimpton, and a frequent guest on MSNBC and Sirius XM. He lives in New York.

OTHER TITLES OF INTEREST FROM THE NEW PRESS

Captured: The Corporate Infiltration of American Democracy
Senator Sheldon Whitehouse with Melanie Wachtell Stinnett

The Democracy Fix: How to Win the Fight for Fair Rules, Fair Courts, and Fair Elections
Caroline Fredrickson

Democracy, If We Can Keep It: The ACLU's 100-Year Fight for Rights in America
Ellis Cose

Democracy Unchained: How to Rebuild Government for the People
Edited by David W. Orr, Andrew Gumbel, Bakari Kitwana, and William S. Becker

Disrupt, Discredit, and Divide: How the New FBI Damages Democracy
Mike German

Empire of Resentment: Populism's Toxic Embrace of Nationalism
Lawrence Rosenthal

People Like Us: The New Wave of Candidates Knocking at Democracy's Door
Sayu Bhojwani

Strangers in Their Own Land: Anger and Mourning on the American Right
Arlie Russell Hochschild

Tax the Rich! How Lies, Loopholes, and Lobbyists Make the Rich Even Richer
Morris Pearl, Erica Payne, and The Patriotic Millionaires

Use the Power You Have: A Brown Woman's Guide to Politics and Political Change
Pramila Jayapal

Usual Cruelty: The Complicity of Lawyers in the Criminal Injustice System
Alec Karakatsanis

PUBLISHING IN THE PUBLIC INTEREST

Thank you for reading this book published by The New Press. The New Press is a nonprofit, public interest publisher. New Press books and authors play a crucial role in sparking conversations about the key political and social issues of our day.

We hope you enjoyed this book and that you will stay in touch with The New Press. Here are a few ways to stay up to date with our books, events, and the issues we cover:

- Sign up at www.thenewpress.com/subscribe to receive updates on New Press authors and issues and to be notified about local events
- Like us on Facebook: www.facebook.com/newpressbooks
- Follow us on Twitter: www.twitter.com/thenewpress
- Follow us on Instagram: www.instagram.com/thenewpress

Please consider buying New Press books for yourself; for friends and family; or to donate to schools, libraries, community centers, prison libraries, and other organizations involved with the issues our authors write about.

The New Press is a 501(c)(3) nonprofit organization. You can also support our work with a tax-deductible gift by visiting www.thenewpress.com/donate.